OTHER MAGE TITLES BY WILLEM FLOOR

THE PERSIAN GULF SERIES

A Political and Economic History of 5 Port Cities, 1500–1750
The Rise of the Gulf Arabs, The Politics of Trade on the Persian Littoral, 1747–1792
The Rise and Fall of Bandar-e Lengeh, The Distribution Center for the Arabian Coast, 1750–1930
Bandar Abbas: The Natural Trade Gateway of Southeast Iran
Links with the Hinterland: Bushehr, Borazjan, Kazerun, Banu Ka'b, & Bandar Abbas

IRANIAN HISTORY

Agriculture in Qajar Iran
Public Health in Qajar Iran
The History of Theater in Iran
A Social History of Sexual Relations in Iran
Guilds, Merchants, and Ulama in Nineteenth-Century Iran
Labor & Industry in Iran 1850-1941
The Rise and Fall of Nader Shah: Dutch East India Company Reports 1730-1747
Games Persians Play: A History of Games and Pastimes in Iran from Hide-and-Seek to Hunting

ANNOTATED TRANSLATIONS

A Man of Two Worlds: Pedros Bedik in Iran, 1670–1675
Pedros Bedik
translated with Colette Ouahes from the Latin

Astrakhan Anno 1770
Samuel Gottlieb Gmelin

Travels Through Northern Persia 1770–1774
Samuel Gottlieb Gmelin

Titles and Emoluments in Safavid Iran: A Third Manual of Safavid Administration
Mirza Naqi Nasiri

IN COLLABORATION WITH HASAN JAVADI

The Heavenly Rose-Garden: A History of Shirvan & Daghestan
Abbas Qoli Aqa Bakikhanov

Travels in Iran and the Caucasus, 1652 and 1655
Evliya Chelebi

The Bay of Taheri

THE PERSIAN GULF

THE HULA ARABS
OF THE
SHIBKUH COAST
OF
IRAN

WILLEM FLOOR

COPYRIGHT © 2014 WILLEM FLOOR

All rights reserved.
No part of this book may be reproduced
or retransmitted in any manner whatsoever,
except in the form of a review, without the
written permission of the publisher.

Library of Congress Cataloging-in-Publication Data
Available in detail at the Library of Congress

ISBN
1-933823-66-6
978-1-933823-66-9

Printed and Manufactured in the United States

MAGE PUBLISHERS
Washington DC
202-342-1642 • as@mage.com
Visit Mage Publishers online at
www.mage.com

CONTENTS

INTRODUCTION xi
   Where and what is the Shibkuh coast? xii

CHAPTER ONE

WHO WERE THE NIQUELUS? 1
   Origin of the Niquelus 1
   Name of the Niquelus. 5
   Trouble with the Niquelus.. 5
   Disaster and the Niquelus Strike. 6
   Continued negative impact of the Niquelus.. . . . 8
   Niquelus, a political weapon. 8
   The 1614 Murder of Niquelus: a casus belli. . . . 9
   Nakhilu: a port of call. 11
   The Niquelus after 1622 12
   Were the Niquelus pirates?. 13
   Discussion 15

CHAPTER TWO.

THE BANI HULA IN THE EIGHTEENTH CENTURY 19
   Where did the Hulas live? 21
   The Hulas, most known for their maritime violence. . 23
   The Al Nasur of Kangan 25
   Who were the Al Nasur? 27
   Business as usual in the eighteenth century? 29
   Hulas and the Zands. 34
   The Al Ali cause trouble 35
   Battle for Bahrain 37
   Strife in the Bandar Abbas area. 39
   Final confrontation at Bandar Abbas. 42
   Kangan – Taheri in trouble 44

CHAPTER THREE

THE AL NASUR IN THE NINETEENTH CENTURY 49
   Where were the Hulas located? 49
   The Al Nasur 54
   The Family Tree.. 57
   The Decline of Kangan and of the Al Nasur . . . 62
   First sack of Kangan – 1844. 64
   Conflict with Asalu 65
   Conflict with Charak 68

    Second sack of Kangan – 1858. 71
    Third Sack of Kangan – 1862. 74
    The Fourth Sack of Kangan – 1867 77
    Problems at Charak 78
    Downfall of Sheikh Mazkur 80
    Did the Fall of Sheikh Mazkur Meant
        the End of Arab Authority? 84
    Was the Situation in the other Shibkuh Ports Different? 87
    The Local Authority of the Hula Sheikhs. . . . 90
    Feuding About Nakhl-e Taqi. 92
    Continued Feuding and Defying
    the Central Government 95
    The Final Chapter of the Arab Shibkuh Sheikhs. . . 102

CHAPTER FOUR

THE EXTENT OF AL NASUR TERRITORY 107
    The Kangan-Taheri District 108
    Kangan 108
        Population 109
        Economic activity 112
        Taxation 116
    Taheri 119
    The Gavbandi District 127
    Gavbandi. 127
    Shivu or Shiyu. 132
    Bostaneh 134

AFTERWORD 135

BIBLIOGRAPHY 139

GLOSSARY 145

Appendix 1. 147
    A TALE ABOUT THE ORIGIN OF THE HULA OR HUWALA . 147
Appendix 2. 148
Appendix 3. 150
Appendix 4. 152
Appendix 5. 154
Appendix 6. 156
Appendix 7. 158
Appendix 8. 160
Appendix 9. 162

INDEX. 163

TABLES

TABLE 3.2: Distribution and size of Arab tribes of the Shibkuh Coast	85
TABLE 3.3: Administrative districts of Shibkuh	88
TABLE 3.4: Official tax burden of various Arab coastal Sheikhs	91
TABLE 4.1: Estimated population size of Kangan	110
TABLE 4.2: Ships owned by inhabitants of Kangan	114
TABLE 4.3: Exports from Bushehr to Kangan	115
TABLE 4.4: Route between Kangan and Firuzabad	115
TABLE 4.5: Ships owned by inhabitants of Akhtar	117
TABLE 4.6: Ships owned by inhabitants of Banak	118
TABLE 4.7: Ships owned by inhabitants of Mianlu	118
TABLE 4.8: Ships owned by inhabitants of Nakhl-e Taqi	119
TABLE 4.9: Export from Bushehr to Taheri	124
TABLE 4.10: Ships owned by inhabitants of Taheri	125
TABLE 4.11: Ships owned by inhabitants of Tombak	127
TABLE 4.12: List of the villages of Gavbandi District	128
TABLE 4.13: Population distribution in Gavbandi	129
TABLE 4.14: Ships owned by inhabitants of Shivu	133

IMAGES

The Bay of Taheri	II
Ports of the Shibkuh Coast	VIII
Hula ports and their tribal groups	IX
Jazayer Arabs	X
The People of Hormuz	XV
Nautaques pirates	3
Arab Coastal Dwellers	15
Inner court, with wind catcher, of the Taheri residence	18
Dehu Fort Ruins	48
Kangan Fort	60
Qalat-e Sorkh	79
Wall decoration and column plinth of the Taheri residence	105
Kangan Fort	112
Parak Fort	117
Mural decoration of scene from the Shahnameh, and doorway of the Sheikh's Taheri residence	121
Mural decorations of the Sheikh's Taheri residence	122
Tombak Fort	125
Gallery of the Gavbandi fort	130
Calligraphed lintel headpiece from gate of Taheri Residence	164

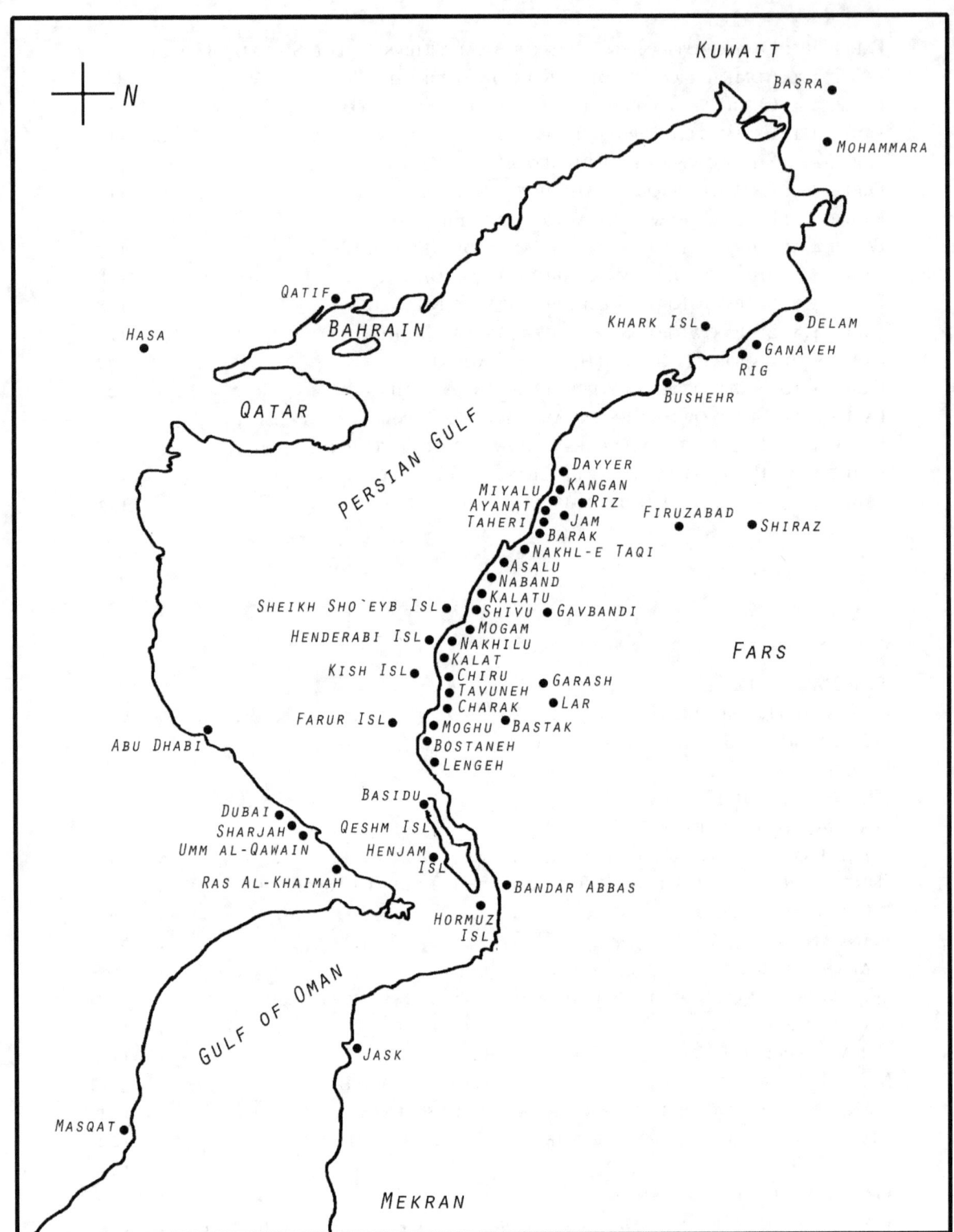

Ports of the Shibkuh Coast

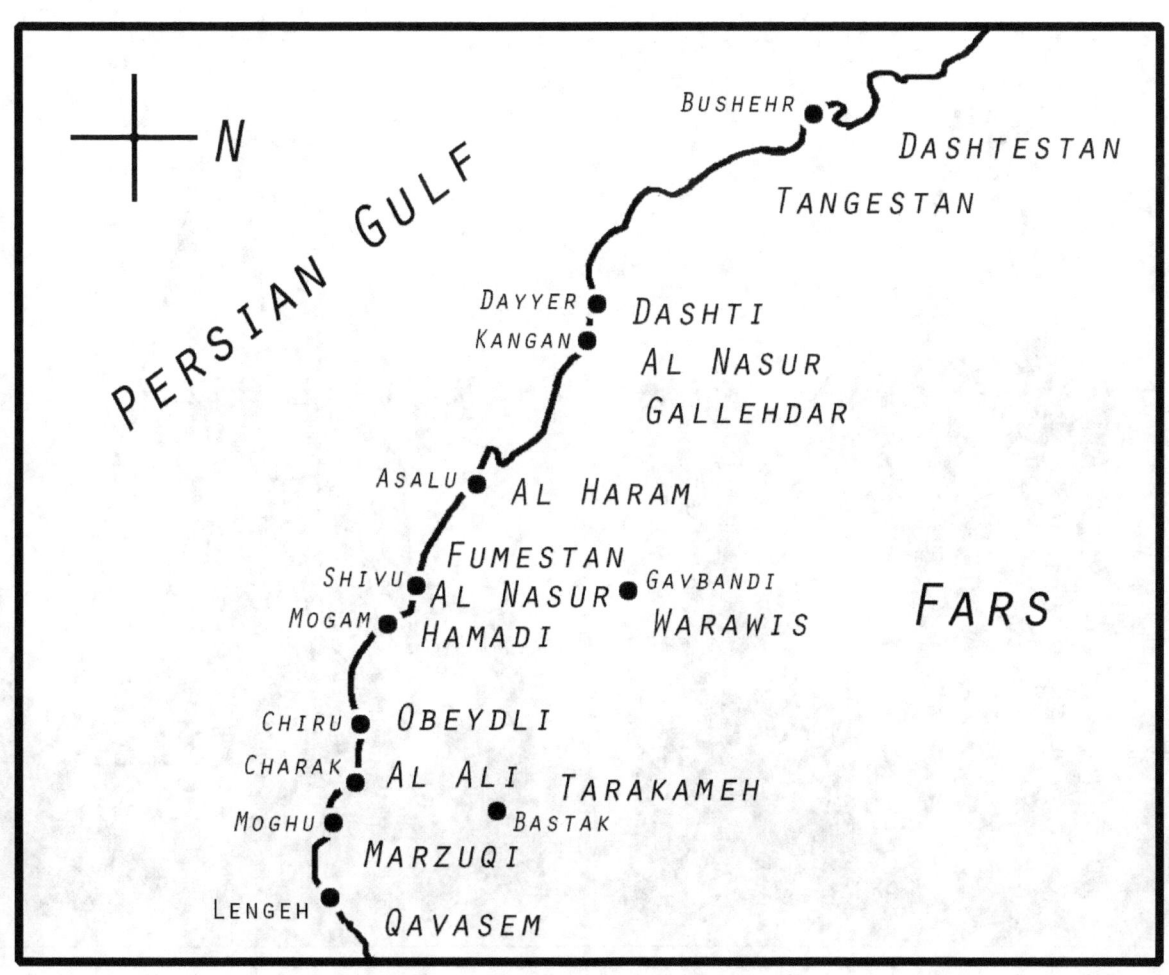

Hula ports and their tribal groups

Jazayer Arabs

INTRODUCTION

The Iranian littoral of the Persian Gulf is dotted with small ports whose people for centuries have been engaged in fishing, pearl diving, trade, agriculture, and occasionally in maritime violence to complement their generally poor revenues. This held in particular for the small ports of the so-called Shibkuh Coast. The rivalry between some of these Shibkuh ports could be fierce, often leading to murderous feuds. Their chiefs often provided naval services to the central government or some powerful local force on either the Arabian or Iranian littoral, if required or forced. Its population consisted mostly of Arab migrants, who differed in language, customs and religion (they were Sunnis) from the population on the Iranian mainland. Although these small ports were of lesser importance than Bandar Abbas, Bushehr, Kong or Lengeh, they nevertheless played an important role in local Persian Gulf distribution trade for certain products as well as a marginal one in long-distance trade to India and the Red Sea. Sometimes, these ports played an important local military role, even conquering other territory.

Despite their centuries long presence, the Arab groups living in these small Iranian ports are almost invariably ignored in historical texts and studies. In this study I, therefore, discuss the history of these Arab migrant groups of the Shibkuh Coast, who from the late sixteenth century onwards acquired a reputation of being 'pirates.' In and after the 1570s there was a wave of Arab migratory movement towards the Iranian coast, which led to the settlement of small heterogeneous group of Arabs, belonging to different small groups. Already soon one group, called Niquelus, acquired a reputation for maritime violence, which is the subject of chapter one. As of the late seventeenth century this group of Arabs was generally referred to a Hulas or Huwalas. They still had a reputation for committing acts of maritime violence, but in particular in the eighteenth century, they tried to play a more important political-military role in local Persian Gulf affairs. Although for some time they dominated the 'news', their resource base was too weak to sustain their bid for regional power (see chapter two). In the nineteenth century, the Hulas were still engaged in violence, both maritime and land-based, and more in particular intra-Hula feuding resulting in bloody encounters. The focus is mostly on the Al Nasur of Kangan, whose history is emblematic for the behavior and fate of the other Arab chiefs on the Shibkuh coast. Although the government of Iran tried to bring the Arab groups under more direct control, it failed to achieve this objective, because (i) it was too costly, and (ii) central government authority and power proved to be too weak. In fact, rather than submissive Sheikhs, we see Arab chiefs who challenge the government's hold over them and play the political game to enhance their own position. It was only with the establishment of a new, powerful and centralizing state after 1925 that the Arab Sheikhs were muzzled, although some still continued to play a role within the new central administrative system, because of their continued local influence (chapter three). In the last chapter, the extent of the jurisdiction of the Al Nasur Sheikhs is discussed, and details are provided about the demographic and socio-economic characteristics of each of the ports and villages that formed part of this jurisdiction.

Finally, I thank Keith Openshaw for editing and polishing my effort to write in English. Also, many thanks to Guus Floor for making the maps.

WHERE AND WHAT IS THE SHIBKUH COAST?

Iran's Arab population is mostly concentrated on the littoral of the Persian Gulf. Those Arab groups that live in Iran's interior are remnant pockets of Arab groups that entered Iran from Iraq as part of the conquering Moslem armies between the seventh and tenth centuries. In the Persian Gulf region, the Arabs came from Basra and Oman, many of whom settled on the Iranian coast. It is quite likely that some or many of these early Arab settlements are the same as those that were inhabited by the Hulas, because Arab migration from the Arab littoral to the Iranian littoral continued well into the nineteenth and even some in the twentieth century. There was also continued immigration of Arab groups via S. Iraq into Khuzestan.[1] As a result, there were two areas in Iran that were characterized by having a majority Arab population. The first area was that of S. Khuzestan that for centuries and until the 1920s, therefore, was aptly called Arabistan.[2] The second area was that of the Shibkuh coast.

Shibkuh means 'below the hills' and this name refers to the 280 km long area stretched along the Iranian littoral between Banak in the North and Lengeh in the South, although some argue that Shivu or even Mogam is its northern end. On one side the area is bounded by the Persian Gulf and inland by a range of hills that at Kangan are 10 km inland and at Moghu 50 km. This narrow coast is dotted with various ports, indented by several bays, while the islands of Sheikh Sho`eyb (now Lavan Island), Shatvar, Henderabi, Kish, and Farur administratively were part of the Shibkuh ports.[3]

What now is called the Shibkuh was once the littoral of an area broadly known as Irahestan, from Middle Persian *irah*, meaning 'beach' and *-stan*, meaning 'area, region.' This area was part of the Ardashir Khurrah district, and its coastal area was known as *sif* (shore, beach) of which there were three along the littoral of the Persian Gulf. There was Sif `Umarah east of Kish, Sif Zuhayr south of Irahistan and near Siraf (later Taheri), and Sif Muzaffar north of Najiram. Early Arab geographers name several coastal towns or villages such as Sif Bani Saffaq, Sif Bani Zuhayr, and Sif Banu `Umarah. Zuhayr and

---

1 Elton Daniel, "`Arab, (iii) Arab settlements in Iran," *Encyclopedia Iranica* (iranica.com); B. Spuler, "al-`Arab, (iii) the expansion of the Arabs: Iran in early Islamic times," *Encyclopedia of Islam*2.
2 For a discussion of the history of one of these Arab groups, the Banu Ka`b, see Willem Floor, "The rise and fall of the Banu Ka`b. A borderer state in southern Khuzestan," *IRAN* XLIV (2006), pp. 277-315; John R. Perry, "The Banu Ka'b an amphibious state in Khuzistan," *Le Monde iranien et l'Islam* 1 (1971), pp. 131-52.
3 For a detailed description of physical geography of the Shibkuh coast, see Lorimer, J. G. *Gazetteer of the Persian Gulf* (Calcutta, 1915 [1970]), vol. 2, pp. 1780-82; Ludwig A. Adamec, *Historical Gzetteer of Iran*, 4 vol. Graz: Akademische Druck, 1989, vol. 3, pp. 673-85.

Mozaffar are the names of Arab tribes that had crossed the Persian Gulf and settled in what is now known as the Shibkuh, which perhaps is the modern version of the medieval Sif Zuhayr. According to Istakhri, the Saffaq family, after whom Sif Bani Saffaq was named, belonged to the Gulanda, which was part of the south Arabian tribe of Azd. "They are longer in Iran than the other Moslem emirs and have the best protection against all attacks." Another place that had very good defenses was Sif 'Umarah, which was known for its impregnable castle known as Dikdan or Dikbayeh, where 20 vessels could find safe shelter. To the west of it was Kish island. Huzu was the coastal port of Kish, and near to it was Saviyeh or Tanah, Tabah. West of Sif 'Umarah was the Zuhayr coast of which Siraf and Naband were its famous ports.[4]

In the twelfth century CE, it appears that the so-called Sif districts (*a'mal-e sif*) situated along the southern part of the Shibkuh coast had a mostly Arab population, while its northern section, such as in Siraf, did not have any Arabs.[5] The climate, then as later, was extremely unhealthy due to the high temperatures. The names of the best known of these coast districts still were the two called respectively the Sif of the People of Abu Zuhayr [near Siraf] and the 'Umarah Sif [opposite Kish island]. "In neither district is there any town with a Friday mosque, and nothing is grown here but dates."[6] Like in later centuries it was a very unsafe area "for all the people are footpads and everyone carries arms seeing that each man robs his neighbor and to shed his blood." ... "Further, the people here are always in revolt against the Government, since no army can stay in these parts for more than the three months of the springtime, for they cannot hold out the winter here by reason of the rains, with the consequent lack of fodder [for their beasts], nor during the summer by reason of the heat." They only paid taxes when forced by arms.[7] The fourteenth century text, Mustawfi's *Nuzhat al-Qolub* does not create the impression that the Shibkuh coast was important or heavily populated as he mentions, like his main source Ibn Balkhi's *Farsnameh*, only Siraf, Irahestan, Kaharjan, Huzu (=Chiru?), Saviyah (=Tavuneh?) and no other locations.[8]

Under the Arabo-Persian kingdom of Hormuz that came into being about 1300 and whose territory straddled the Arab and Iranian coast the population on the northern Shibkuh seems generally to have been Persian. Many of its bureaucrats and some of its leading political families came from Fal or Khonj, i.e. from the Shibkuh hinterland. Around 1520, the Portuguese author, Barbosa mentions the various islands in the Gulf, as does Ibn Majid, but neither mentions any of the small ports on the Shibkuh coast. Barbosa mentions that there were many little places along the coast, without naming any apart from Naband near Bandar Abbas, which like the others were all near Hormuz.[9]

---

4 I have kept the orthography of the place and tribal names as given in the following references. Schwarz, Paul 1993. *Iran im Mittelalter nach den Arabischen Geographen*. 9 parts in 4 vols. Frankfurt am Main: Institute for the History of Arabic-Islamic Science (reprint of the 1896-1936 edition), vol. 2, pp. 75-78; Le Strange, Guy. *The Lands of the Eastern Caliphate* (London 1905 [1966]), pp. 256-58.

5 Ibn Balkhi, *Description of the Province of Fars in Persia, in the beginning of the fourteenth century*, London: RAS, 1912, pp. 41-42.

6 Ibn Balkhi, *Description*, pp. 47-48.

7 Ibn Balkhi, *Description*, p. 49.

8 Mustawfi, *Geographical Part*, pp. 116, 118; Ibn Balkhi, *Description*, pp. 49-50.

9 Duarte Barbosa, *The Book of Duarte Barbosa* translated by M. Longworth Dames, 2 vols. (London, 1918-21), vol. 1, p. 75; Ibn Majid, *Arab Navigation in the Indian Ocean before the coming of the Portuguese*. Translated by G.R. Tibbets. London, 1972.

The Portuguese chronicler, Barros mentions the islands, and of the small ports only Bedicne (Bidkhun), Chilau (Shilaw) and Cabo Vedeitao (Bardestan).[10] The traveler Pedro Teixeira also mentions the islands, and further only Nakhilu, Chilao (Shilaw), Verdostam (Bardestan) and Point Vedicam, which is Ras Naband, suggesting that other small ports were totally insignificant and not noteworthy, and perhaps even non-existent.[11]

It appears that only in the late sixteenth century Arab groups who later became known under the generic label of Bani Hula, Huwala or Hulas migrated from Oman and Trucial Oman (now UAE) to the Iranian coast. In the next chapter I discuss the group that settled in Nakhilu, and that as far as we know was the first group of Hulas to migrate to the Shibkuh coast. In the sixteenth and early seventeenth centuries the Portuguese referred to them as Niquelus, i.e. those from Nakhilu, which was one, and probably the first Iranian port in the Safavid period, settled by this disparate group of Arabs. As of the mid-seventeenth century these groups of Sunni Arabs were referred to as Hula (Arabic: هولة) or Huwala (Arabic: حولة). The first term means ‹monster, terror› (see Appendix One), presumably this interpretation of the term was chosen, because the Hulas inspired fear and terror. The other term, *huwala* means 'migrant, i.e. those who move from one location (the Arabian peninsula) to another (Iran), which undoubtedly was the correct meaning of the appellation. The terms are also used for Persian speakers who moved from Iran to Bahrain, the Emirates and other locations on the Arabian peninsula. However, this study is not concerned with that group of migrants. In the eighteenth century, the Bani Hula played an increasingly important role in the Persian Gulf in the start and settlement of local political conflicts due to the weak central government of Iran. In the nineteenth century these Arab groups tried to maintain their quasi-independence, a dynamic situation that I analyze based on the up-and-downs of the ruling Al Nasur family of the port of Kangan-Taheri, whose role and position stands as an example of its many sister Shibkuh ports.

We have no information about the pattern of migration of these migrant Arab groups, but it would seem that they continued to receive fresh settlers from the Arabian coast. It would seem, however, that this influx of Arab newcomers diminished in the nineteenth century. Some groups, such as the Bu Sumeyt, in fact were engaged in location hopping, going from one place to the other, and finally, some even returning to their point of origin.[12]

---

10 João de Barros, *Da Ásia. de João de Barros e de Diogo de Couto.* Nova ed. 24 vols. Lisboa, Na Regia Officina Typografica, 1777-1788 [reprint: Livraria S. Carlos, 1973-1975], III/4-6, p. 316.

11 Pedro Teixera, *The Travels*. tr. William F. Sinclair. London 1902 [1991], pp. 20-22; C. Federici and G. Balbi, *Viaggi di C. Frederici e G. Balbi alle Indie Orientali* ed. Olga Pinto. Rome, 1962, p. 113 (Silau); Ibn Battuttta probably visited Shilu, Ibn Battutta, *The Travels of Ibn Battuta*, translated by H.A.R. Gibb, 4 vols. Cambridge, Cambridge UP, 1962, vol. 2, pp. 407-08

12 Willem Floor, *The Rise and Fall of Bandar-e Lengeh. The Distribution Center for the Arabian Coast, 1750-1930.* Washington DC: MAGE, 2010, pp. 161-62.

The People of Hormuz

CHAPTER ONE

WHO WERE THE NIQUELUS?

Despite the fact that the Niquelus caused major problems for the Portuguese in the Persian Gulf at times, it is amazing that so little is known about them. This is partly due to the fact that there is no mention of them in Persian sources at all, while even in Portuguese sources they are infrequently mentioned and not before 1570. It is thus no wonder that we have only a superficial idea about who they were and about their activities in the Persian Gulf. In this chapter, therefore, I want to present what is known about this group of Arab coast dwellers and assess their role in the Persian Gulf, in particular in relation to the Portuguese.

Origin of the Niquelus

The Niquelus belonged to an unknown tribal group from Oman, who, like all other similar coastal dwellers, were engaged in fishing, pearl fishing, agricultural activities, some trade and probably some piracy, which latter activity was not uncommon among coastal populations at that time throughout the world. It was not piracy, but pearl fishing that first got them into trouble and ironically launched their 'career' as pirates. The Niquelus cannot be blamed for the predicament they and other coastal Arabs found themselves in, for theirs was a case of *force majeure*. In the beginning of the sixteenth century the Persian Gulf lost one of its two great pearl fisheries, probably due to over fishing, and the Niquelus had to compete for the remaining fisheries with other Arab pearl diving groups. According to Silveira, the Niquelus were ousted from Oman after they had lost the battle for control over the pearl grounds against their main rivals the Alimoeiros.[1] The Niquelus then moved their entire tribe (men, women and children) into their *terrada*s and requested the Portuguese captain of Hormuz to be allowed to take up residence on the uninhabited island of Larek. In return, as compensation for this permission, the Niquelus

---

1 The Alimoeiros most likely are the Al Bu Moheyr, who are currently mainly residing in the United Arab Emirates, previously known as Trucial Oman, in particular in Dubai, Ras Al-Khaimah, Sharjah, Ajman and Umm al-Quwain. They also migrated to the Persian side of the Gulf in the 17th century, if not earlier, and the principal family of Bushehr between 1750 and 1850, the Al Mazkur, were members of this tribe, for example.

offered to patrol the Straits of Hormuz against attacks by the feared Nautaques, pirates of the Mekran coast, at no cost to the *Estado da India*.[2]

When did this migration and contact with Hormuz take place? Silveira, who is the source of the above information, does not give an indication. He probably wrote the part concerning the Niquelus in his treatise in the first decade of the seventeenth century, when he had spent some 20 years in Asia. His information undoubtedly is based on material that he had collected locally in Hormuz as it is clear from his text that he had been there and had discussed these matters with those who were 'in the know.' This does not give us a clear idea, however, when the events he referred to have happened, whether before or after the year 1585 when he came to Goa for the first time. An indication that these events must have taken place in the 1570s is given by Couto, who in his *Década* X states that the Niquelus were to take up residence on Larek "as had been agreed to by captain Ruy Consalves da Camara in *Década* IX."[3] As Ruy Consalves da Camara was captain of Hormuz from 1577 to 1580 the events referred to must have taken place during or before this time period. There is, however, a problem with this time frame. First, nowhere in Couto's *Década* IX is there any mention of this agreement or of the Niquelus for that matter, but since he mentions it in *Década* X we may assume that this information is correct. There is another reason why these events probably have taken place in the 1570s. In that decade, pirates, most likely the Niquelus, also started to attract the attention of the Ottoman authorities. To contain their activities the Porte had given instructions to guard the coast of Hasa (Lahsa), one of the targets of the pirates. In October 1574, the fleet commander at Basra (*donama-i humayun ketkhudasi*) was appointed as commander of the vessels stationed at Hasa (*Lahsa kapudani*) with the task to watch the infidel Arab pirates or *Kefere Arablari*. In October 1577 these had attacked Qatif and had caused so much damage that the merchants moved to Bahrain.[4] These events, presumably followed by some Ottoman punitive action, may have made the Niquelus more amenable to reach an agreement with the Portuguese and this would chronologically tie in with the time frame given by Couto.

However, to complicate matters, Silveira states explicitly that the proposal of the Niquelus was discussed at Hormuz by the captain and his council and was rejected. This implies that the migration must have taken place before 1578 and that the agreement reached by da Camara must have happened after a few years of marauding by the Niquelus. This then would suggest a date for their migration of about 1570 or earlier. Whatever the truth of the matter, Silveira found the decision not to allow the Niquelus to settle on Larek incomprehensible, because the Niquelus as pearl fishers could easily have taken care of the Nautaques, who were less strong. This is highly questionable given the fact that the Nautaques even attacked armed Portuguese vessels, because they themselves

---

2 Francisco Rodrigues Silveira, *Reformação da milícia e governo do Estado da Índia Oriental*, transcripted, annotated and indexed by Benjamin N. Teensma, and with a historical introduction by Luís Filipe Barreto, George D. Winius and Benjamin N. Teensma. Lisbon, Fundação Oriente, 1996, pp. 45-46.

3 Diogo de Couto. *Da Ásia de João de Barros e de Diogo de Couto*. Nova ed. 24 vols. Lisboa, Na Regia Officina Typografica, 1777-1788 [reprint: Livraria S. Carlos, 1973-1975], *Década* 10ª, II-x, pp. 215-219 (cited as Couto, *Década*).

4 Salih Özbaran, *The Ottoman Response to European Expansion. Studies on Ottoman-Portuguese Relations in the Indian Ocean and Ottoman Administration in the Arab Lands During the Sixteenth Century*. Istanbul, 1994, p. 139; Ahmet Tabakoğlu, "The Economic Importance of the Gulf in the Ottoman Era," *Studies of Turkish-Arab Relations* 3 (1988), p. 161.

Nautaques pirates

also carried cannon and guns.[5] However, the real reason for the rejection of the proposal, according to Silveira, was that the captain of Hormuz in league with some five of his rich cronies made much money in supplying and sending out ships to protect Hormuz. Accepting the proposal by the Niquelus would have meant that they would lose part of their income and, therefore, it was of no interest to them. Thus, so opined Silveira, they were putting their private gain before that of the common weal and the king's interests.[6]

It would seem that Silveira's version of the early contacts between the Captain of Hormuz and the Niquelus is the more correct one as he would not have provided this example for his arguments for reform when it could have been easily refuted by reference to hard facts that would contradict his statement. In any event, whether the Niquelus

---

5 For the activities by the Nautaques, who were Baluchis of the Nodhaki tribe in Mekran. Barbosa *The Book*, vol. I, p. 87, note (the Nodhaki or Notakani tribe); "Estado da Índia e aonde tem o seu princípio", in *Documentação Ultramarina Portuguesa*, vol. I, p. 209 (noutaques); Teixera, *The Travels*, p. 162 (Moutaqui)] see Brás Afonso de Albuquerque, *Comentários do grande Afonso de Albuquerque, capitão geral que foi das Indias orientais em tempo do muito poderoso Rey D. Manuel, o primeiro deste nome* 4 vols., translated into English by Walter de Gray Birch as *The Commentaries of the Great Afonso DAlboquerque, second viceroy of India*. 4 vols. London, 1875, vol. IV/30, p. 136, IV/33, p. 148, IV/38, p. 168; Tomé Pires, *The Suma Oriental of Tomé Pires, an account of the East, from the Red Sea to Japan, written in Malacca and India in 1511-1515* translated and edited by Armando Cortesão 2 vols. London, 1944, vol. 1, p. 31; Barros, *Ásia*, 2ª-X-ii , p. 411; Ibid., 2ª, X-iv, pp. 427-28; Francisco Paulo Mendes da Luz, *Livro das cidades e fortalezas que a coroa de Portugal tem nas partes da India e das capitanias e mais cargos que nelas e da importancia delles*[1581] in *Studia* 6 (1960) and as separate off-print, f. 37; J. de Coutre, *Aziatische omzwervingen. Het leven van Jacques de Coutre, een Brugs diamant handelaar 1591-1627*. Berchem, 1988, p. 222; Ronald Bishop Smith, *The First Age of the Portuguese embassies, navigations and peregrinations to the ancient kingdoms of Cambay and Bengal (1500-1521)*. Bethesda, 1969, pp. 65-66. As to their tactics to capture ships, using towing ropes with iron chains, see Gaspar Correia, *Lendas da India* ed. Rodrigo José de Lima Felner 4. vols. in 8 parts. Coimbra, 1860-66, vol. I, p. 793. For a picture of these pirates, who by then were armed with muskets and cannon, made around 1550 see Luís de Matos ed., *Imagens do Oriente no século XVI. Reprodução do códice português da Biblioteca Casanatense*. Lisbon, Imprensa Nacional Casa da Moeda, 1985, plate XXI.

6 Silveira, *Reformação*, pp. 45-46.

were or were not allowed to take up residence on Larek, they, after the rejection of their proposal, "in desperation" then contacted the governor of Lar and asked his permission to settle on an abandoned beach on the Iranian coast. The Niquelus then moved to Nakhilu after having received permission from the governor of Lar to settle there.[7] Outwardly, they had no trouble to blend with the people on the other side of Persian Gulf, for the women in Nakhilu were dressed similarly to those living elsewhere along the Iranian coast. According to Newberie, they "weare long Mantles, which they draw after them like a traine: and farther in the Countrey they weare their Garments with three slits, one before, and one on either side; and their sleeves are like the sleeves of Morris-dancers. And they have round about their eares pack-threed sewed. And they weare great Rings in their Noses; and about their Legs, Armes, and Necks, Iron hoops."[8]

Thus, it would seem that the Portuguese had not gone about dealing with the Naquilus in the most effective manner. First they denied them access to the island of Larek, which drove the Naquilus into the hands of the governor of Lar. Then, when they had become troublesome, the Portuguese assumed that they could make them vassals of the king of Hormuz and thus have them obey the kingdom's rules. But at the same time the Portuguese were undermining the king of Hormuz's authority, thus weakening his hold over his subjects and neighboring chiefs. This was in particular the case with the payment of the so-called *moqarrariyeh*, a transit fee for its caravans, which the kings of Hormuz had paid to the ruler of Lar and other chiefs having control over coastal areas to be free from interference with its trade for decades before the arrival of the Portuguese. The latter at first refused to pay this fee, because they mistakenly believed it to be a payment of tribute. Later they allowed the payment to take place, but this was done by the king of Hormuz and not by the Captain of Hormuz, the representative of the king of Portugal. However, as part of the total takeover of the customs administration of Hormuz in 1568 the Portuguese also reduced the revenues that were allocated to the king and vizier of Hormuz. This translated into a lower payment of *moqarrariyeh* to those to whom it had traditionally been paid, which led to a less friendly and less collaborative attitude of the coastal chiefs such as those of Makran. This in turn had an impact on the restraint that these chiefs could or were willing to exercise over the activities of their subjects. Over time, this contributed to more piratical activities by the Nautaques and Niquelus, thus increasing maritime insecurity in the Persian Gulf and the Gulf of Oman on which the wealth of the kingdom was based. The weaker position of the king, both in terms of political and economic power, also resulted in the weakening of his control over the vassal chiefs of the kingdom. At the same time, payment of *moqarrariyeh* was also reduced or even temporarily stopped to the governor of Lar, who then stopped all caravan traffic to and fro Hormuz. Moreover, the newly arrived Niquelus (around 1570) paid the governor of Lar 'protection money' and thus could count on his support in case of Portuguese attacks. The situation might not have become so tense and volatile if the Portuguese had dealt with the Niquelus in a more rational and traditional manner. Certainly, piracy raised transaction cost of trade, but so did military intervention. Payment of *moqarrariyeh*

---

7 Silveira, *Reformação*, pp. 45-46
8 John Newberie, "Two Voyages of Master J.N., One into the Holy Land; The other to Balsara, Ormus, Persia, and backe thorow Turkie," in Purchas, Samuel. *Hakluytus Posthumus or Purchas His Pilgrimes*. 8 vols. Glasgow 1905, vol. VIII, p. 458.

might have prevented a conflict. Thus, the Niquelus in a certain sense were a creation of the Portuguese.

Name of the Niquelus

Having settled at Nakhilu this Arab group at the same time acquired their Portuguese name, for Niquelus means, 'those of Nakhilu.' Portuguese authors, of course, wrote this name in various ways such as Naquilus, Nihhelus, Nuqueluzes and Niquelus. The name that this Arab group gave to themselves has not been reported. It is my contention that they were part of a larger migratory movement of Arabs coming from Oman to the Iranian littoral. In the 17th century this same group of Arabs was known as Hula or Hawala Arabs, meaning 'migrant Arabs'. The reason for this supposition is that in one case the Niquelus are referred to in official correspondence as "the Nequeluz [and those of] Asalu." As Asalu is a minor port on the Iranian littoral and is not synonymous with Nakhilu it means that "those of Asalu" were clearly identified with the Niquelus. A similar situation existed in the 17th and 18th century when the Arabs of Asalu, were identified as Hulas and considered to be part of those of Nakhilu.[9]

Trouble with the Niquelus

Although now living on the other side of the Persian Gulf the Niquelus continued with their traditional way of life, i.e. with fishing and pearl fishing as well as looking after their date groves. Pearl fishing took place near Bahrain (July-August) and Oman's coast (September). Some of them also were involved with piracy, since they had ships and were poor. The location of Nakhilu was ideally situated between Hormuz and Basra and thus all unprotected vessels, which had to pass there, might be imposed upon.[10] It was these piratical activities that drew the attention of the Portuguese at Hormuz, who did not like any activity that might have a negative impact on the customs revenues of the island.

In 1581, the presence of a Portuguese fleet under D. Jeronimo Mascarenhas in Hormuz coincided with military activities by the ruler of Lar, who interfered with caravans coming and going to and from Hormuz, because the *moqarrariyeh* or transit fee had not been paid. It was decided that action would be taken against Lar. D. Gonsalvo de Menezes, the captain of Hormuz (1580-1583) also asked D. Jeronimo, *Capitão Mor*, to take action against the Niquelus and to force them to take up residence on Larek as had been agreed upon with his predecessor, captain Ruy Consalves da Camara. Moreover, he had to put an end to their piracy through which they had acquired many prizes. The fleet of 11 *galeotas* and one galley sailed away, but before attacking Nakhilu, the *Capitão Mor* sent an Arab in a small vessel to talk to the Sheikh of the Niquelus and induce him to adhere to the agreement with the previous captain and become vassals of the king of Hormuz and friends of the Portuguese. The Sheikh of the Niquelus, whose name was Musa, asked free passage to come to talk to the *Capitão Mor* in his galley. When this was given Sheikh Musa with some of his counselors came aboard. After discussion they agreed

---

9 R.A. Bulhão Pata and A. da Silva Rego eds., *Documentos Remetidos da India ou Livros das Monções* 12 vols. Lisbon, 1880-1972, cited as *DRI* VII-81 (n.d.), p. 85.
10 Teixeira, *Travels*, pp. 175-177; Silveira, *Reformação*, pp. 45-46.

that the Niquelus would move to Larek and that they would not sail their *terradas* or other vessels, with which they had been committing acts of piracy. They signed documents to that effect and promised to move to Lareka within a given time period and received a document making them vassals of the king of Hormuz. The *Capitão Mor* then returned to Hormuz.[11]

Disaster and the Niquelus Strike

There is no report in what manner and to what extent the Niquelus implemented the 1581 agreement. Although they refrained from piracy it is not known whether they all moved to Lareka or only part of them. For some time at least the agreement was respected until 1583, when the Niquelus broke the peace agreement. Once again they were reported to commit acts of piracy to vessels coming from Basra to Hormuz, near the island of Lara, which caused damage to the customs revenues. Since Couto calls the island Lara and not Lareca, which he also mentions in the same chapter and thus Lara is unlikely to be an error, he probably is referring to Laz, the main village on Sheikh Sho'eyb, another inhabited island in the Persian Gulf opposite Nakhilu. The captain decided to capture some of their *terradas*. One galliot was appointed for that task. It was commanded by Galvao and he had 20 soldiers with him. They had to attack the vessels of the "island of Laz (Lazao)", capture some of the vessels of the Niquelus and use these to protect vessels coming from Basra. On arrival at Laz (Lara), the galliot bombarded a settlement of the Niquelus during the day and at night it returned to its post offshore. The Niquelus having received intelligence from the people of Laz silently attacked the galliot with some vessels during that night; its crew was sleeping and all were killed. The galliot with its guns and equipment was taken to Nakhilu. The captain of Hormuz on learning this news sent another galliot under command of the chief of the naval yard (*patrão da ribeira*) with soldiers and orders to try and capture some Niquelus. However, the ship foundered due to a storm and the chief with five sailors were the only ones who survived this ordeal. Because the population of Laz, although vassals of the king of Hormuz, had made common cause with the Niquelus, while they also had been the cause of the capture of the galliot, it was decided to punish them. Mathias d'Albuquerque, the new captain of Hormuz (1584-1587), armed four vessels under *Capitão Mor* Lucas de Almeida with orders to go to the island, to do as much damage as possible and to try and capture some of the *terrada*s of the Niquelus. Later he sent two other vessels under Alvaro de Avelar to Bahrain with orders to assist de Almeida and kill everybody on Lara. Once again a storm occurred, which led to the loss of the Portuguese vessels and only 11 persons survived. The Niquelus were quite pleased with these developments and in its aftermath seized many *terrada*s, some of which carried each one 40,000 *cruzados* as well as merchants from Baghdad and elsewhere, who they presumably ransomed. Mathias d'Albuquerque was furious about this setback and asked Goa to send him 300 men to punish the Niquelus, because they might stop all traffic with Basra.[12]

In 1586 the requested fleet of 15 vessels with 500 of the *Estado da India*'s best soldiers arrived, commanded by Ruy Consalves da Camara, the former captain of Hormuz. His

---

11 Couto, *Década* 10ª, II-x, pp. 215-19.
12 Couto, *Década* 10ª-VI-x, pp. 68-71.

orders were to attack and destroy the Niquelus. The commander, "by reason of his fatnes and corpulent bodie stayed in Ormus, appointing [a] Lieutenant in his place, one called Pedro Homem Pereira (who although he was but a meane gentleman, yet was hee a very good soldier, and of great experience) commanding them to obey him in all things, as if he were there in person."[13] Pedro Homem Pereira took another five vessels with 150 men from Hormuz with him. The fleet soon learnt that the Niquelus had abandoned their settlements on Laz (Lara), so that there was nothing to destroy and burn. They all had gone aboard their *terrada*s and had sought refuge on the coast. Pereira asked orders from Mathias d'Albuquerque, who replied that he had to attack Nakhilu, which was situated on the Leitão coast [?], adjacent to the island of Kish (Caes). Pedro Homem Pereira decided to disembark his troops to take Nakhilu. He gathered his captains and showed them the letter he had received with his new instructions. All captains said it was too risky to carry out the attack, but they finally went along with Pedro Homem Pereira's insistence to do so. Two companies of 60 men each were to land, one of which (commanded by the *Capitão Mor*) had to provide protective cover to the other (commanded by da Gama).

> They ran their fustes on shore, so that they lay halfe dry upon the sand: every man in generall leaped on land, without any order of bataille, as in all their actions they used to doe: which the Lieutenant perceiving, would have used his authoritie, and have placed them in order, as in warlike affaires is requisite to be done: by they [to the contrarie] would no obay him, saying he was but a Bore [peasant], & that they were better Gentelmen & soldiers then he: and with these and such like presumptuous speeches, they went on their course scattering here & there in all disorders like sheepe without a shepheard, thinking all the world not sufficient to containe them, and every Portingall to bee a Hercules and so strong, they could beare the whole world on their shoulders.[14]

The Niquelus, who had sent for help from the governor of Lar, watched the landings take place, saw the disorder among the soldiers and that their vessels had been hauled onto the beach so that it would be difficult to put them back to sea again. The Portuguese force had barely landed when 500 Niquelus on horse and foot attacked the Portuguese force in half moon formation. The Niquelus overran the Portuguese soldiers and forced them back to the waterline, killing many of them. The confusion among the Portuguese was total; soldiers were drowning or were being killed, while others tried to get aboard small vessels. According to Couto and van Linschoten, this was the worst defeat in the *Estado da Ìndia*'s history, because in less than one hour a mighty fleet had been defeated, which had as many men as the force that had conquered India with all its powerful cities, a force that had defeated the Turks and other enemies. In total 250 men (Couto), or even more than 800 (van Linschoten), the flower of the *Estado da Ìndia*'s armed forces, including many "young and lustie Gentlemen," had perished.[15]

---

13 J.H. van Linschoten, *The voyage of Jan Huygen van Linschoten to the East Indies* ed. and translated into English by A.C. Burnell and P.A. Tiele, 2 vols. London, 1885, vol. 2, p. 184.
14 Linschoten, *Travels*, vol. 2, p. 185. He must have had really good information about this event, because one of those killed at Nakhilu was the brother of the Archbishop of Goa, van Linschoten's employer.
15 Couto, *Década* 10ª-VII-xviii, pp. 247-259; van Linschoten, *Travels*, vol. 2, pp. 184-186.

Continued negative impact of the Niquelus

In the years after the 1586 disaster at Nakhilu published Portuguese sources are silent about the activities of the Niquelus. They must have continued their normal activities, including piracy, as may be inferred from the observations later made about them. In 1604, when making a trip in the area between Hormuz and Nakhilu, Pedro Teixeira observes: "We had sight of several pirates' *terradas*, never absent from those seas; wherefore merchant ships sailing from Harmuz use commonly the convoy of Portuguese fustas."[16] Teixeira further describes how two *terrada*s of the Niquelus attacked "a Moorish terrada laden with cotton." They had approached by stealth and attacked during the morning watch, but resistance was fierce and the people on Teixeira's boat who watched from a distance fired guns to scare them off.[17] In fact, from other remarks made by Pedro Teixeira the marauding of the Niquelus must have gone beyond that of simple acts of piracy, for they also had begun to attack neighboring settlements on shore and on the islands of the Persian Gulf. He noted, for example, that the island of Qeshm was said to have produced a large variety of all kinds of agricultural products when it had been better peopled, but now "there is little produce, by reason of the raids of the Nihhelus Arabs, that lay it waste, through the negligence of the Captains of Harmuz, only three leagues' sail distant, who could easily and cheaply amend the same."[18] The same held for other islands in the Gulf that were "ill inhabited, by reason of the raids of the Noutaues and Nihhelus, Arabs who dwell on the Persian shore so called, and take their name from it."[19] Kish that once had been was once a staple of trade, "but now desolate since the loss of its trade, for fear of the Noutaqui and Nichelu robbers, two breeds of pirates that ever infest that sea."[20] In fact, the entire coastal area near Nakhilu had become unsafe and the Portuguese did not even dare to go ashore, because "Some Nihhelus, [are] looking out for Portuguese shore parties, to kill them." This is an indication of the hatred that those of Nakhilu and other coastal dwellers felt for the Portuguese. Even when the Portuguese or other travelers were strong enough to risk a landing when provisions began to fail, they could not renew them there, "for all that shore is disturbed by the wanton ravages of the Portuguese fustas, which commonly cruize there."[21]

Niquelus, a political weapon

Meanwhile piracy, allegedly supported by Abbas I the king of Persia, increased in the Persian Gulf. This was the result of a desire of the Safavid Iranian king to incorporate all territories, which he considered to be part of his kingdom, which included the kingdom of Hormuz. His forces slowly, but surely, were encroaching upon Hormuz territory (Bahrain 1602, Qeshm 1608). If official Safavid support was given to the Niquelus it may have been due to the non-payment by Hormuz of *moqarrariyeh*, a transit fee to allow caravans to pass unhindered, as of 1608. The number of Safavid vessels that allegedly were

---

16 Teixeira, *Travels*, p. 23.
17 Teixeira, *Travels*, p. 22.
18 Teixeira, *Travels*, pp. 19-20.
19 Teixeira, *Travels*, p. 21.
20 Teixeira, *Travels*, p. 162.
21 Teixeira, *Travels*, p. 22.

involved in harassing shipping in the Persian Gulf was estimated at 1,200, of which 800 were the shah's and his allies, and this naval force was growing in number in 1610. Of these vessels 100 were permanently based in Rishahr to attack shipping going to Basra. A great many of the other vessels belonged to the Niquelus, whom the Portuguese considered to be the major threat. The perception of this threat was such that in 1609 the council of Hormuz discussed a plan to fortify the beach of Lard-e Amir (Lardemira) on the island, because it was afraid of an attack by the Niquelus and Noutaques. Although no decision was taken, the same discussion continued into 1610.[22] To combat this piracy the function of *capitão-mor do mar* was revived at Filipe II's instructions in 1609, who had the command of one galleon as well as of the *fustas* at Hormuz. In 1610, the king of Portugal urged the destruction of the vessels of the Niquelus, an order that was repeated 1612. In that same year king Felipe II wrote that the fort of Hormuz had to be made impregnable and that all vessels in the Gulf that were without passes, in particular those of the Niquelus, had to be burnt. In this way the latter would be forced, or so he believed and desired, to transfer to one of the deserted islands in the Gulf that were part of the kingdom of Hormuz and thus become subjects to its king. In that way they also would be much easier to control, or so it was believed. To that end ships and troops would be sent.[23] The viceroy suggested using vessels more appropriate for the Persian Gulf and, as of 1612, the proposals were approved and the naval commander had to patrol the Nakhilu area and to pursue pepper smugglers. The proceeds of the sale of the prizes were to be shared with the crews, who, prior to this new rule had not received anything, and had been paid-off by the smugglers. This measure apparently was effective, for the Niquelus asked for a truce and permission to establish themselves on an island at the border of Hormuz. This truce lasted until mid-1614.[24]

The 1614 Murder of Niquelus: a casus belli

Meanwhile, tensions between Persia and Portugal had risen again. Antonio Gouvea, at whom the Abbas I was very angry about the result of the embassy from which he had just returned, had left Isfahan without the shah's permission. Moreover, a Nestorian Christian and interpreter of the shah also had fled to Hormuz, because he feared that he was going to be forced to become a Moslem. D. Luís da Gama, the new captain of Hormuz (1614-1619) detonated this explosive situation in 1614. His brother, Don Rodrigo, had been killed a number of years earlier by Arabs of Nakhilu (niqueluzes). To revenge his brother D. Luís had given orders to massacre the crews of a number of Nakhilu *terradas* that had come to sell wheat at Hormuz. The result was that 70 men were killed. The murders

---

22 *DRI* II-205, p. 100, 103-105 (15/03/1611); *DRI* II-224, p. 142 (26/02/1612); *APO* 6-1083, pp. 911-913 (09/02/1613); William Foster, *Letters received by the East India Company from its servants in the East* 6 vols. London, 1896-1902, vol. 2, p. 146. During its history Hormuz had been invaded four times and each time the invaders had landed at the Lard-e Amir beach. The last time had been in 1552 by Piri Reis. See Willem Floor, *The Persian Gulf. A Political and Economic History of Five Port Cities 1500-1730*. Washington DC, 2006, p. 213.

23 *DRI* 3-226 (31/01/1612), pp. 146-47.

24 João Manuel de Almeida Teles y Cunha, *Economia de um império. Economia política do Estado da Índia em torno do mar Arábico e golfo Pérsico. Elementos conjuncturais: 1595-1635*. Universidade Nova de Lisboa, 1995, p. 29 quoting TT-Graça ex3-6oD, f. 75-81 (09/08/1617); *DRI* II-226, pp. 146-147 (31/01/1612); *Boletim da Filmoteca Ultramarina Portuguesa* 50 vols. (Lisbon, Centro de Estudos Históricos Ultramarinos, 1955-1990), vol. 4, p. 730 (n. d.; 1614?).

shocked everybody, Christian and non-Christian alike, although Antonio Gouvea, the bishop of Cyrene, felt obliged to approve of the captain's action in a public sermon and castigate those who had condemned him. This upset so many that a few days later the Spanish Fr. Luís da Castilla spoke out "against what the bishop of Cyrene had approved." The families of the murdered Arabs asked Allahverdi Khan, governor of Shiraz for justice. Luís da Gama then was so stupid to arrest the messenger that Allahverdi Khan had sent to ask for blood-money in June 1614, which he also refused to pay. Because of these murders and the refusal to pay blood-money, Allahverdi Khan had to take action, for doing nothing was no option. The result was first a blockade of Bandel de Camorão (later Bandar Abbas) starting in August 1614, followed by a siege and fall of its garrison in December 1614.[25]

Although Abbas I welcomed Portuguese diplomatic overtures, his forces continued to put pressure on the Portuguese. To threaten Portuguese vessels in the Persian Gulf and the Gulf of Oman Safavid forces attacked them with 300 *terradas* as of 1615 using the Niquelus and Nautaques.[26] However, not all Niquelus accepted to collaborate with the Safavid government, an attitude in conformity with their strong feelings to remain independent, which they continued to display throughout the 17th and 18th centuries. Around 1617, a certain Ali Kamal (Ali Cumal), "being a valiant man, who had done courageous deeds in war, could not suffer the pride and insolence of the Persians; he lived in continuous defiance of the Khan of Shiraz and the king of Persia, who planned to capture him, because with these qualities he could have started a rebellion with the people of his country who would have gladly followed him and would have obeyed his orders." He therefore left Nakhilu and settled near Jolfar on the other side of the Persian Gulf. Ali Kamal then offered his services to the captain of Hormuz against the Safavids, who declined the offer, "because the governors of Hormuz look too much after their own interest ... that they did nothing." Because he had defied Safavid authority Shah Abbas I sent troops to the coast of Oman and destroyed the small Niquelu settlement and killed more than 60 Niquelus,[27] which put an end to Niquelu rebelliousness for the time being.

Despite these alleged naval attacks the Hormuz merchants continued to do business with Safavid Persia and therefore the piratical attacks cannot have been that effective and/or numerous as Portuguese sources want us to believe.[28] There was, of course, a good reason to sent alarming reports, because that meant more money could be kept locally purportedly to be spent for defensive purposes, but in reality to line the pockets of the captain of Hormuz and his cronies. And indeed, uncertain about the outcome of the negotiations with Abbas I, Lisbon ordered the strengthening of Hormuz and the reconquest and reinforcement of Qeshm in 1619. Rui Freire was sent to the Persian Gulf with a large fleet to maintain Portuguese control of the Straits, eliminate the Niquelus as well as coastal settlements on either side of the Persian Gulf and expel the English from

---

25 António Bocarro, *Década 13 da Historia da India*, ed. Rodrigo José de Lima Felner, 2 vols. Lisbon, Academia Real das Ciências, 1876, p. 373; Anonymous. *A Chronicle of the Carmelites in Persia and the Papal mission of the seventeenth and eighteenth centuries*, 2 vols. London, 1939, vol. 1, p. 212.

26 *DRI* VII-81, p. 85 (Memorial sobre Ormuz; n.d. 1615-20).

27 Don Garcia De Silva y Figueroa. *Comentarios de la embajada que de parte del rey de España Don Felipe III hizo al rey Xa Abas de Persia*. António Baião ed., 2 vols. Madrid, 1903, vol. 2, pp. 465-66. Ali Kamal's migration to Jolfar and the Safavid attack may also have been in relation to unrest in the Jolfar area in 1614-15. Bocarro, *Década 13*, p. 347.

28 Bocarro, *Década 13*, p. 671.

Jask, who had established a trading station there since 1617.[29] The reign of terror in the Persian Gulf initiated by Rui Freire, both before and after his escape from English captivity in 1622 led to great fear and hatred for the Portuguese among the population on the Iranian littoral. Although his orders mention the Niquelus explicitly, there is no mention of the Niquelus at all in Rui Freire's *Commentaries*. He certainly did not eradicate them as had been ordered to do, and the Niquelus therefore were able to participate in the siege and conquest of Qeshm and Hormuz in 1622. Della Valle noticed the presence of the Arabs from Nakhilu and their vessels, who also assisted the Safavid army to take Hormuz.[30]

Nakhilu: a port of call

So far I have only mentioned once the port of Nakhilu, whence its residents acquired their Portuguese appellation. It is necessary to take a closer look at the role of this port, because it shows another, more peaceful side of the Niquelus. Nakhilu is situated on the Iranian littoral opposite the island of Shitvar. The approach to the town had to be done by sounding, for depths were under 15 fathoms at 1,600 meters offshore and 5 to 6 fathoms near the beach. Its anchorage was exposed to N.W. winds. Nearby also was the island of Abu Sho`eyb, which was subject to the Sheikh of Nakhilu, its nearest eastern point was only 1,200 meters away from Shitvar.[31] When sailing from Bandar Abbas towards Basra, while hugging to the coastline, the next port you reached was Nakhilu. This is not just a geographical observation made for completeness' sake, for merchants actually called on the port to do business. Newberie landed at Necchel [Nakhilu] during his voyage in the Persian Gulf in 1584. He "paid for carrying of my things on shaore at Necchel two Larins, and for landing them five Larins."[32] This suggests that Nakhilu was a normal typical Persian Gulf fishing port where regular merchants as well as smugglers came to trade or who used it as a port to forward their goods to the markets in central Persia. Among these merchants was the Portuguese pepper trader Mateo de Britto, for whom in 1621 Nakhilu was his home base. This shows that the hatred of the Arabs for the Portuguese was a selective one, mainly aimed at its officialdom, but not at Portuguese whom they did business with.[33] Niquelu traders also visited Hormuz for commercial purposes and thus it would appear that relations between Portuguese and Niquelus were not always hostile and only when one or the other party found it useful to raise the threat of Niquelus. That does not mean that there were not real violent clashes between them, for there were, but that was only one side of the relationship.

---

29 *DRI* V-1139 – orders for Rui Freire de Andrade, pp. 255-260 (15/01/1619); *DRI* VI-40, p. 77 (27/03/1620); *DRI* VI-204-205, pp. 240-244 (15/03/1620 + 07/02/1620); *DRI* VII-140, p. 210 (14/12/1620).

30 Pietro Della Valle, *Les Fameux Voyages* 4 vols. Paris: Gervais Clouzier, 1664, vol. 3, pp. 578, 643. The Nakhilu Arabs also had assisted with their vessels in the capture of Qeshm. Luciano Cordeiro, *Questões Histórico-Colonais* 3 vols. Lisbon, 1936, vol. 3, p. 346. They also continued to harass the Portuguese in the years thereafter. The *Nautaques*, which had been a major problem for the Portuguese in the past, had been decimated by Rui Freire's punitive expeditions. C. R. Boxer, "Anglo-Portuguese rivalry in the Persian Gulf," in E. Prestage ed. *Chapters in Anglo-Portuguese Relations*. Watford, 1935, p. 128.

31 James Horsburgh, *India Directory or Directions for Sailing to and from the East Indies* 4th ed. London, 1836, vol. 1, p. 343.

32 Newberie, "Two Voyages," pp. 458-459.

33 Coutre, *Aziatische omzwervingen*, pp. 138, 228.

The Niquelus after 1622

After the fall of Hormuz in April 1622 some Armenian and Moslem traders continued to use Nakhilu as their main point of transshipment on the Iranian littoral rather than the larger ports on their return from Masqat.[34] The Portuguese still were fearful of the Niquelus, also because of the hatred among the coastal population for the Portuguese due to Rui Freire's killing and destructive raids. In 1625, the chief of Nakhilu offered safety to the inmates of a Portuguese vessel on which Della Valle sailed from Masqat to Basra and invited them to come and trade at Nakhilu. He had great need of merchandise. However, the crew of the Portuguese vessel, although they were Indian Moslems, did not entirely trust his word.[35] This is understandable, because the pirates of Nakhilu regularly attacked mercantile vessels.[36] Only the heavily armed Portuguese galliots outgunned Persian Gulf pirates from Nakhilu, who still provided convoys to ships sailing from Masqat-Kong to Basra.[37] Other Europeans were not attacked by the Niquelus. In 1643, those of Nakhilu captured a vessel with a Dutchman with money to buy pearls for the VOC at Bahrain. However, on learning that he was Dutch they released him and returned the money. Moreover, the Dutch reported that the chief of Nakhilu was "the sworn enemy of the Portuguese and kills every Portuguese in the ships he captures. The Portuguese do the like; although affairs are not going so hotly as that at present, since the Muslims (Arabs) are eating humble pie and ask permission of the Portuguese to sail (the Straits) and the latter readily grant it them as also to others."[38]

Nevertheless, the decline in Portuguese trade and power also slowly led to a different kind of characterization, although feelings were still hostile towards one another. This new situation is clear from Bocarro's remarks ca. 1634, who described the Niquelus, vassals of Shah Abbas, as "valiant Arabs, great mariners, and fierce enemies of the Portuguese."[39] This is quite a change from the vituperative remarks to describe the Niquelus in an earlier period. Even after the Portuguese role in the Persian Gulf had ceased to be of any importance, the Arabs from Nakhilu continued to have a bad reputation, in particular with the Safavid authorities. In 1672, the *shahbandar* of Bandar Abbas did not want to do anything against the Nakhilu Arabs after a complaint about them by the French traveler Carré: "He said he could do nothing against these people, as they were rebellious and would never recognize any authority. Nor had they submitted to two or three governors sent against them to collect some dues from that part of the country."[40]

---

34 H. Dunlop, *Bronnen tot de geschiedenis der Oostindische Compagnie in Perzië*. The Hague, 1930, p. 234.

35 Della Valle, *Les Fameux Voyages*, vol. 3, pp. 426-427.

36 *Nationaal Archief* (The Hague, the Netherlands) Collectie Sweers/Manis 9, f. 122; VOC 1106, Schriftelijcke Relatie," unfoliated (frigates and small vessels), Ibid., VOC 1135, Geleynsz to Batavia (24/03/1641), f. 647-668 (mentions 6-10 armed frigates); P. S .S. Pissurlencar ed., *Assentos do Conselho do Estado 1618-1750*, 5 vols. Goa, 1953-57, vol. II-53, p. 180 (06/08/1637); Arquivo Histórico Ultramarino, Lisbon, India, Cx 19, 5; Linhares, *Diario*, vol. 2, p. 180; Arquivo Nacional da Torre do Tombo, Lisbon (*ANTT*), DRI, 32, f. 35 and *ANTT*, DRI 33 (03/02/1635), f. 35; António Bocarro, *Livro das plantas de todas as fortalezas, cidades e povoações do estado da India Oriental*. 3 vols, Lisbon, 1992, vol. 1, p. 62.

37 Boxer, "Anglo-Portuguese Rivalry," p. 125.

38 Anonymous. *A Chronicle*, vol. 2, pp. 1116-1117; Willem Floor, "Pearl fishing in the Persian Gulf in the 18th century," *Persica* 10 (1982)," p. 211.

39 Bocarro, *Livro das plantas*, p. 61.

40 Abbé Carré, *The travels of Abbé Carré in India and the Near East (1672-74)*, 3 vols. London: Hakluyt, 1947, vol. 1, p. 111.

Were the Niquelus pirates?

Were the Niquelus pirates or just defending their rights, and if the latter, which ones? To answer the question was easy for the Portuguese, for they simply maintained that they were pirates. Van Linschoten summed it up nicely when he wrote: "Certain pirates that held in a place called Nicola, and spoiled such as passed to and fro upon the seas, and did great hurt to the ships and marchants of Bassora, that traffiqued in Ormus, whereby the trafique [to the saide towne of Ormus] was much hindered, to the great loss and undoing of many a merchant."[41] However, was it really that simple, or was more at stake? The literature concerning piracy draws attention to the fact that the discussion on this issue invariably leaves unresolved the question "of what law is invoked against the pirate, and behind the law, of what power is involved in this maritime confrontation over matters of trade."[42] Pérotin-Dumon argues that most important in the question of piracy is the political factor, for piracy mainly came into existence "from change in the political realm–either the will of a state to establish commercial hegemony over an area where it previously had been weak or non-existent, or from the conflict between two political entities, one an established trading power and the other a newcomer. The prize of piracy is economical, but as a historical phenomenon, the dynamic that creates it is political."[43]

Assuming that this characterization of piracy is correct what does it mean for the Niquelus? There had been political change in the Persian Gulf, in that the Portuguese had established a protectorate over the kingdom of Hormuz. However, it were mainly the latter's institutions that still carried out the mainly Hormuz policies. The kingdom had established since centuries a kind of commercial hegemony, i.e. all those entering the Straits of Hormuz had to pay customs duties. However, the Niquelus did not challenge this hegemony; they were not interested in trade per se, and they only preyed on ships passing their place of residence to supplement their income, not to challenge Portuguese trading power. The Niquelus were not really newcomers either. True, they had only taken up residence at Nakhilu in 1570 or thereabouts, but before that date they had been based on the other side of the Gulf and apparently had not been seriously engaged in attacking maritime traffic, at least there are no reports to that effect. Also, the Niquelus did not even want to challenge Portuguese or Hormuzi power. This situation was changed when from about 1608 onwards the real political newcomer into the Gulf, the Safavid state, urged the Niquelus and other Arab coast dwellers to attack vessels going to Hormuz to challenge Portuguese control over that area. These politically inspired raids were intermittent in nature only as one would expect. However, once the Portuguese had lost Hormuz and their trade was dwindling, while Safavid political pressure on the Portuguese had disappeared, due to a loss of interest in exercising influence over the Gulf, the Niquelus continued their piratical activities. They even continued to do so, when none of the characteristics adduced by Pérotin-Dumon applied anymore, when piracy should have ceased to exist. For she argues that "to eliminate piracy as a phenomenon, however, trade monopoly had to be given up altogether,"[44] which was exactly the case after 1622. For

---

41 Van Linschoten, *Travels*, vol. 2, p. 185.
42 Anne Pérotin-Dumon, "The pirate and the emperor; power and the law on the seas, 1450-1850," in James D. Tracy ed. *The Political Economy of Merchant Empires*. Cambridge, 1997, p. 196.
43 Pérotin-Dumon, "The pirate and the emperor," pp. 197-98.
44 Pérotin-Dumon, "The pirate and the emperor," p. 226.

after the fall of Hormuz the Portuguese exercised increasingly less control over trade passing through the Straits of Hormuz, in particular after 1632, and none of the so-called newcomers (Dutch, English, or Safavids) were interested in imposing a trade monopoly. In fact, trade in the Gulf was free. Thus, according to Pérotin-Dumon, piracy should have stopped, but it did not.

If the Niquelus were not pirates in the meaning suggested above, or at least not most of the time, what then were they? It would seem that the Niquelus were just brigands of the high seas, who aimed to supplement their meager revenues with the spoils taken from passing vessels. They were not interested in the nationality or religion of the crew or passengers, for they were equal opportunity brigands; the only thing that was important whether you had goods and/or money or could be ransomed. They made an exception, however, for Portuguese officials, which was due to the severe and cruel punitive actions taken against them, for Portuguese traders were welcome at Nakhilu as were all other traders. The Niquelus behaved in the same manner as highwaymen did on the mainland, such as the Bedouins who intermittently attacked caravans between Basra and Baghdad or Aleppo, which had not made prior arrangements to obtain protection against such attacks.

There is no doubt about the fact that the Niquelus were a thorn in the side of the Hormuz-Basra trade, but how much of a thorn? According to Silveira, much damage was done to trade between Basra and Hormuz and he is joined in this chorus by other sources, including official Portuguese ones. Unfortunately, there is no estimate about the extent of that damage. That it was sometimes of some importance and that the Portuguese authorities took this threat seriously seems to be indicated by the three maritime actions undertaken by the Portuguese in 1581, 1583 and 1586. Silveira, however, scoffs at this notion. He in fact argues that the activities by the Niquelus were advantageous for the captains of Hormuz. The existence of the Niquelus justified their demands for funds to mount punitive and expensive expeditions against these pirates. That there seems to be some truth to this observation may be indicated by the fact that although Hormuz was the best revenue-producing Portuguese factory in Asia it generally sent very little money to Goa. Moreover, Silveira argues that despite the funds made available to the captains of Hormuz they never really tried to effectively eliminate the Niquelus. This, Silveira argues optimistically, might easily have been done by, for example, attacking their vessels when they went pearl fishing and went harvesting the dates in various parts in the Gulf during four months of the year. Then they were at their most vulnerable and could most easily taken care of.[45] Silveira does not refer to the heavy losses the Portuguese incurred in 1583 and 1586 when even he might have agreed that the captain of Hormuz had made a real effort to confront the Niquelus. He is right that after 1586 there seem to have been no more actions undertaken by the Portuguese against the Niquelus. The latter, as is clear from the discussion above, continued with their piratical activities. Moreover, they also became involved in handling contraband trade and operated as a free port where regular traders and smugglers were welcome.[46]

However, these continuing incidents of piracy did not constrain the flow of trade to and fro Hormuz, which since 1560 had been growing increasingly and continued to do

---

45 Silveira, *Reformação*, p. 42.
46 Anthony Disney, "Smugglers and Smuggling in the Western Half of the *Estado da Índia* in the late Sixteenth Century and early Seventeenth Centuries," *Indica*, 26 (Mar-Sept., 1989), pp. 57-75.

so, suggesting that the damage done to trade by the Niquelus may not have as serious as Portuguese sources state. In fact, when discussing the ups and downs in revenues many causes are adduced by Portuguese writers, but not the activities by the Niquelus. Thus, the dreaded major loss of revenues due to piracy did not really happen nor was trade with Basra stopped by it. If anything trade with Basra only increased after the Niquelus had become active as pirates, although there is no correlation between these two phenomena. Apart from the normal development of trade due to market forces, the Niquelus also sold their stolen goods in the market of Hormuz, either directly or indirectly. Thus the customs revenues of Hormuz did not lose a dime.[47]

Discussion

To sum up. In 1570 or thereabouts, the Niquelus came from Oman and wanted to settle on the island of Larek. In return they offered to control the incidence of piracy in the

Arab Coastal Dwellers

Straits of Hormuz. Rejected by the captain of Hormuz they were given refuge by the

---

47 For a discussion of the development of the trade and revenues of Hormuz, see Floor, *Persian Gulf*, pp. 74-88.

governor of Lar at Nakhilu. To supplement their income the Niquelus committed some acts of piracy. The captain of Hormuz then belatedly offered them Larek in 1578-79, which they seem to have turned down. Faced with a Portuguese fleet on their doorstep in 1581 they now accepted to move there and abstain from piracy. However, need drove them once again to piracy and in 1583 the captain of Hormuz sent twice a ship against them. The first one was taken by the Niquelus, the second shipwrecked. To eradicate the Niquelus Goa then sent a large fleet with 500 men, which, reinforced by those of Hormuz, attacked Nakhilu in 1586. The Portuguese force was defeated in the most disastrous defeat ever suffered by the *Estado da India* up till then. In the years thereafter there are no reports about Portuguese actions against the Niquelus, although, according to Teixeira, they were active in attacking ships and raiding settlements, reason why the Portuguese provided armed convoys to those vessels that carried passes and joined the convoy. When the political situation between Portugal and Iran became less friendly after 1607 Shah Abbas used the Niquelus to attacks vessels going to Hormuz. The Portuguese even feared an attack of Hormuz itself and measures were taken to stem the rise in piracy. These seem to have been effective, or due to political reasons, for the Niquelus agreed to a truce and even started to trade with Hormuz. This truce fell apart because of the murder of 70 Niquelus who had come to trade in Hormuz in early 1614. As a result the Portuguese lost Bandel, while the Niquelus assisted the Persian forces in retaking Qeshm and Hormuz in 1622. They continued with their piratical activities thereafter, but these were much reduced due to Portuguese actions.

It is difficult to maintain that the Niquelus were pirates, created by the Portuguese trade monopoly and one may even question that they were a real problem. The Niquelus did not challenge Portuguese rule, they only wanted to complement their income, in this case acquired through piracy. They also continued to do this when there was total free trade after 1622. They also maintained a free port at Nakhilu, which some Portuguese traders called their home base. Despite the occasional alarming letters about the Niquelus they do not seem to have formed a threat either to the Basra-Hormuz trade or to Hormuz revenues. In fact, Hormuz revenues and Basra trade only increased, while any downs in the Hormuz revenues were not ascribed to piracy by the Niquelus. In short, the Niquelus were pirates, who had no political, but only their own financial interest at heart, and who only became a problem because the Portuguese made them so. Left alone, they would have been a nuisance, be it a minor one, as the situation in the post-Portuguese period shows.

The Hula Arabs of Nakhilu remained feared pirates in the seventeenth century. The Portuguese had relentlessly tried to extirpate them, but had failed to do so. After the fall of Hormuz in 1622, the Portuguese continued to escort their vessels on their annual voyage from Masqat to Basra usually with only one warship. More was not needed, because the English and the Dutch did not sail to Basra respectively prior to 1636 and 1645, while the heavily armed Portuguese galliots outgunned Persian Gulf pirates such as the Hulas from Nakhilu.[48] Their reputation in the seventeenth century once Safavid rule had been more firmly established over the littoral was not much better. Having arrived at Kailo (Nakhilu) Carré was told by a renegade Portuguese in 1672 that the Arabs there was all bandits, "who recognized no authority, for they lived on this tongue of land as if they were an island, and paid no taxes or tribute except to two sheikhs who commanded them,

---

48 Boxer, "Anglo-Portuguese Rivalry," p. 125.

called Zayde [Zaid] and Biouzhayde [Abu Zaid] respectively."[49] Nevertheless, there seems also to have been trade, for a Hindu and Jew also were living there.[50] Although nominally Safavid subjects the Hulas seem to have been an independent lot. Sheikh Zaid of Nakhilu was one of the most powerful Arabs on the coast.[51]

The Arabs in the place [of Nakhilu] are so fierce and wild that they have never wanted to be subjects or to allow any Iranian to command them or to exact dues. Formerly a powerful Iranian king undertook to conquer them and built a fortress in the middle of their houses and tents, keeping a governor and a garrison of fifty men there for several years. The Kailo [Nakhilu] Arabs were not accustomed to be thus curbed or subjected to any one. They resolved to throw off such a servitude and regain their liberty. They kept this plot secret and arranged it so well that one night they surrounded the fortress with machines which sheltered them from the Iranian muskets. They attacked the place, mastered it, and beheaded everyone there without exception. They demolished the fortress of which only two round towers, two walls, and a big door of cut stone, remain on the side facing the sea. They then retired to the islands and neighbouring places on the coast. The king did not deign to punish such an injury, as he did not know where to find the said Arabs, who after several years, returned gradually to the place. Now they are 3,000 strong with some 400 vessels [Ms. *barques*], of which each family owns two or three. They use them for war, pearl-fishing, and to go to Basra for dates, rice, corn, and nearly everything else necessary for life. Kailo is infertile: it produces nothing but some wild dates, as it is all sand and surrounded with salt water, almost like an island.[52]

However, when the Safavid push came to the Nakhilu shove, the latter toed the official line and followed government orders, as is clear from the 1674 summons to attend the meeting in Bushehr.

---

49 Carré, *The Travels*, vol. 1, p. 96.
50 Carré, *The Travels*, vol. 1, pp. 97, 101.
51 Carré, *The Travels*, vol. 3, p. 827.
52 Carré, *The Travels*, vol. 1, pp. 102-03. Later, the Arabs of Nakhilu had over 200 *taranquins*. Carré, *The Travels*, vol. 3, p. 829.

Inner court, with wind catcher, of the Taheri residence

CHAPTER TWO

THE BANI HULA IN THE EIGHTEENTH CENTURY

The Hulas only settled on the Shibkuh coast, which, as described in the Introduction, covers an area stretching from its most north-western point at Banak to its most south-eastern point of Lengeh.[1] This part of the Iranian littoral was targeted by the Arab migrants probably because it was sparsely inhabited by the end of the sixteenth century. This is also implied by the *Tarikh-e Jahangiriyeh*, a local history of the Abbasi dynasty of governors of Bastak, where it is stated that each of the various Hula groups asked and was assigned ports and districts where they were allowed to settle on the understanding that they would not exceed the borders of their allotted area. Unlike for those of Nakhilu we have no precise dates for the settlement of the various Hula groups, but I believe that they also started migrating at the end of the sixteenth and the beginning of the seventeenth century, due to the major upheavals in Oman and Trucial Oman. That this is more than conjecture is suggested by the presence of clearly long settled Hulas who were visited and described by Abbé Carré in 1672.

Whatever the truth of the matter, according to the *Tarikh-e Jahangiriyeh*, Sheikh Mohammad Khan Bastaki went to Bostaneh and Moghuyeh, when the Arab arrivals asked for his permission to settle on the coast. He was welcomed by Sheikh Soleyman Marzuqi Al Ajman who asked Sheikh Mohammad Khan that he and his people would be given the ports of Bostaneh, Moghuyeh, and Hoseyniyeh and the island of Farur to live. This was granted and thereafter this district was known as Dehestan-e Marzuqi. Bandar Charak and its dependencies including the islands of Kish were allotted to the Al Ali. Bandar Tahuneh, Nakhl-e Mir and some other villages were held by the Bashiri Sheikhs. Morbagh, Kalat and some other villages, a district known in the nineteenth century as Hamadi, was granted to the Madani Sheikhs, viz. Sheikh Rashed b. Mostafa, Sheikh Mohammad and Sheikh Ahmad Madani. Khalafani, Golshan, Bandar Chiruyeh and the island of Henderabi were granted to the Obeydli sheikhs (Sheikh Abdol-Rasul b. Soltan Obeydli). Sheikh Sho`eyb was given to Sheikh `Allaq and Sheikh Abdol-Rahman, who also were confirmed in their possession of Nakhilu and Maqam (Dehestan-e Badawi), while the administration of Pumestan or Fumestan was delegated to Ra'is Mohammad Saleh and the other chiefs of Fumestan. Dehestan-e Harami was granted to the Sheikhs

---

1 Lorimer, *Gazetteer*, vol. 2, pp. 1780–82; Hoseyn Ali Razmara, *Farhang-e Joghrafiya-ye Iran*, 10 vols., Tehran: Az entesharat-e da'ereh-ye joghrafiya-ye setad-e artesh, 1329-33/1949-54, vol. 7, p. 145.

of the Bani Tamim, to the Maleki Sheikhs and the Al Haram.[2] A careful reader will have noticed that the Hulas of Kangan and Taheri are not listed in this distribution. This is no omission, but because these districts were not part of the jurisdiction of the governor of Bastak, he, of course, could not arrange for their allocation.

The Arab migrants who settled on the Shibkuh Coast were disparate small tribal groups of sailors, traders, fishermen, divers, and cultivators. Although they were all referred to as Hulas, they were not a uniform group with a common objective. In fact, as is clear from what follows, they were each other's fierce competitors for access to the pearl banks, and therefore, even each other's enemy. This led to sometimes bloody and murderous engagements and feuds (see below).

Although the Hulas were often feuding with each other, they, occasionally, also banded together against a perceived common enemy. For example, all Hulas were united in their enmity towards the Iranian and Arab coastal dwellers between Bardestan and Liravi (see below). However, if there was one common denominator then it was their Arab ethnicity, their adherence to Sunni Islam, and hence their deadly hatred for the Iranians, who were Shiites. According to the Dutch, writing in 1756, therefore, "they never mix with the Persians by marriage, but always marry within their caste, they always keep their own religion and customs. The most important thing to do to win their friendship is to treat them friendly and amiably. A sullen and proud face causes respect and awe among the Persians, but hatred and dislike among the Arabs."[3]

By the mid-eighteenth century the Hulas had the following strength, according to the Dutch. In total they had 400 big and small vessels at their disposal, which each were manned by 10 to 50 men. They were able to muster up to 6,000 sea-going men, of which about 3,000 were armed with match-locks. The largest of their vessels carried 2 to 4 cannons of 2- to 3-pounds; the smaller ones cannons of 1- to ½-pound of iron. "They are fairly courageous and an enterprising people and would not yield to an equal number of Europeans with the broad-sword. However, with a gun they cannot do anything against us, [because] they can handle them very slowly."

Despite this strength, bravery, weaponry, and the will to make their mark in the power vacuum that had arisen in the Persian Gulf, the Hulas were unable to become more than a temporary and occasional military and political force that the rulers on the mainland had to reckon with. For they had neither a common objective, which bound them into a permanent interest group, nor did they have a sufficiently large resource base (financial, manpower, organization) that would have sustained their bid for power over the longer term. This weakness was formulated by the Dutch in 1756 as follows:

> This caste would be very powerful in the Gulf if two defects did not weaken them in particular. The first one is the disagreement about who governs them, and the second is the poverty of their chiefs or sjeeks,[4] who are never able to provide their people with food and ammunition for a long time. They also hardly ever are able to induce them to sea and if they have been able to do so they cannot keep them together. For as soon as something is

---

2 Mohammad A`zam Bani Abbasi-ye Bastaki. *Tarikh-e Jahangiriyeh va Bani Abbasiyan-e Bastak*, Tehran, 1339/1920, pp. 130-31.
3 Willem Floor *The Persian Gulf. The Rise of the Gulf Arabs. The Politics of trade on the northern Persian littoral 1730-1792*. Washington DC: MAGE, 2007, p. 30.
4 Sheikhs are meant.

lacking, which frequently happens, each of them leaves their sjeek to seek his livelihood with fishing, diving, or with the freight-trade.

In addition, there was the problem of the internal organization of each Hula group, which was rather weak. Although in many cases each group consisted in majority of people from the same tribe or lineage, competition within the group, and in particular among members of the lead lineage, was fierce, each candidate jockeying for position with a view to oust his uncle, cousin, or some other relative from his leading position. Also, the powers of the Sheikhs were determined by their personal skills and abilities, and political and military success, than by institutional rights and rules. In 1756, the Dutch characterized this situation as follows:

> The various chiefs of the Houlas are not only, as has been said above, independent from and always in disagreement with one another, but each chief is not at all [an] absolute and despotic [ruler] in his settlement and among his caste. They may not undertake anything without the cooperation and consent of the eldest and most prominent [men]. For the rest he does not collect any [tax] quota or contribution from his people, but lives from the profits of his vessels. The chief may even not demand toll on imports and exports in his settlement with the exception from foreigners. As soon as the caste is not satisfied with him, the chieftainship is conferred on another one of that family and he remains without any respect or authority.[5]

Nevertheless, quite a few Sheikhs, in particular among the Al Nasur, were able to ensure continued and unchallenged rule over their subjects.

Where did the Hulas live?

According to the *Tarikh-e Jahangiriyeh*, the allocation of many of the Hula groups over much of the Shibkuh Coast was brought about by the hereditary governor of Bastak, because that coast was part of his official jurisdiction (see above). He allegedly did so in a manner that he fixed the borders of each district, ensuring that each group would not exceed their boundaries and bother their neighbors. These borders were, of course, not respected in actual practice, and the pious hope that allegedly moved Sheikh Mohammad Khan Bastaki to do so, may have been as imaginary as his alleged pro-active role in the allotment of these various districts. The distribution of the localities as given below does agree with the mid-eighteenth century Dutch description and other later data, but it is unlikely that the governor of Bastak imposed his will unilaterally on these groups when agreeing to their distribution over the various districts. In fact, it is quite unlikely that this distribution of land happened in an organized manner and at the same time. It is more likely that the Arab migrants settled at a certain location, which existing situation later was formalized and endorsed by the governor of Bastak after negotiations concerning quid pro quos, i.e. payments and service duties. This is clear, for example, from his relations with the Qavasem and their settlement of Lengeh, where they took over from the Marzuqis, a reality that was later agreed to by the governor of Bastak. However, the family historian had to play up the role of his ancestors in this and other activities that they were involved in.

---

5 Floor, *The Rise of the Gulf Arabs*, p. 30.

The first place inhabited by Hulas was Lengeh.[6] Initially the Marzuqis held sway there, but by the mid-eighteenth century they were replaced by the Qavasem.[7] In 1756, the Dutch reported: "They are 50 large and small vessels and 700 men strong, of which 350 are armed with match-locks. They are poor and live from [the sale of] firewood and charcoal, which is plentiful near them and which they transport throughout the Gulf. Their present chief is called Sjeek Saijd[8]; the islands of Troer,[9] Tombo[10] and Nabiau,[11] which are not inhabited belong to these Mersoekis and serve them as a refuge during bad times."

The next place of a Hula settlement was Charak,[12] which was inhabited by the Al Ali.[13] Apart from Charak they also controlled the island of Kish. In the mid-eighteenth century they were considered to be the most courageous among the Hulas. They also were almost always at war with one of the other Hula groups (see below). The Dutch reported: "There are 60 vessels, both big and small, and they are 8 to 900 men strong, half of whom are at least armed with match-locks and broad-swords. Their chief is Sjeek Samra.[14] They live with us in very good friendship and they provide us throughout the year with firewood, which is to be found in plenty in Tjarek. Its transportation is almost their only livelihood."

The inhabitants of Moghu and the island of Henderabi were under the control of the Sheikh of Charak. They had been much weakened because of wars." They are not more than 20 vessels and about 150 men strong. They live next to Tjarek in Mogo[15] on the island of Endrabo[16] and are governed by a certain Sjeek Achmet.[17]"

The next Hula settlement was at Nakhilu, as has been discussed above. They also controlled the island of Abu Sho`eyb and Shatvar, which were situated right opposite the town. "Its inhabitants number more than 1,000 able-bodied men of whom more than half are armed and they are 60 vessels strong. They are governed by two sjeks at the same time, [to wit] Mahometh Ebben Sent[18] and Racchma Eben Schain.[19] They live mostly from pearl diving"

---

6 Lengeh, a port about 100 km west of Bandar Abbas. For a description of this port and its history see Willem Floor, *The Rise and Fall of Bandar-e Lengeh. The Distribution Center for the Arabian Coast, 1750-1930*. Washington DC: MAGE, 2010.

7 The Marzuqi Arabs, a branch of the Hula Arabs. According to Fasa'i, the Marzuqi group came from Oman and settled around Moghu. Mirza Hasan Hoseyni Fasa'i, *Farsnameh-ye Naseri*. 2 vols. ed. Mansur Rastgar Fasa'i. Tehran: Amir Kabir, 1378/1999, vol. 2, p. 1618.

8 Sheikh Sa'id.

9 The island of Farur, situated at 32 km south of Moghu.

10 Tonb Island, 20 km south-east of Qeshm Island.

11 Nabiyu or Nabi Island or Little Tonb, 13 km west of Tonb Island.

12 Charak, a small port situated at the bottom of the Bay of Charak.

13 Mohammad Ali Khan Sadid al-Saltaneh, *Bandar Abbas va Khalij-e Fars* ed. Ahmad Eqtedari. Tehran, 1342/1963, p. 617; Andrew S. Cook, *Survey of the Shores and islands of the Persian Gulf 1820-1829* 5 vols. Gerrards Cross: Archive Editions, 1990, vol. 1, p. 190.

14 Sheikh Shamra is probably meant here.

15 Moghu, a town 35 km west of Lengeh. It is not situated on Henderabi Island.

16 Henderabi Island, 6.5 km w.n.w. of Chiru.

17 Sheikh Ahmad.

18 Mohammad b. Sand? is probably meant here.

19 Rahmah b. Shahin is probably meant here.

From there, the next group: "the Al Haram inhabited Naband,[20] and Asalu.[21] They were governed by two sheikhs, Mohammad b. Majid (Mahometh Eben Maijd) and Abdol-Rahman." Because of their war with Bushehr about the control over Bahrain, a war they lost, the Al Haram were so weakened that their strength in 1755 was estimated to be not more than 40 vessels and all in all 300 men.

The Al Nasur were the Hula group that inhabited Taheri, Shilu[22] and Kangan.[23] They were divided into two groups that were "completely independent and apart from" each other. This group of Hulas is discussed more in detail later in this chapter.

THE HULAS, MOST KNOWN FOR THEIR MARITIME VIOLENCE

The Hulas of Nakhilu were not the only ones feared in the Persian Gulf, because other Arab tribal groups also wrought much havoc on others. One of the reasons for the lack of security in the upper Persian Gulf (apart from Portuguese-Omani hostilities) in the seventeenth century was the enmity that existed between the Arabs of Khark, Bandar-e Rig, Dowraq and Bushehr who went every year to Bahrain to take control over the pearl fisheries, and who opposed the 'interests' of the Huwalah or Hula Arabs from the lower part of the Persian Gulf such as those of Nakhilu.[24] Apart from ethnic enmity the main reason for their conflict was economic.

> The Arabs of Talanga [Lingeh], Chareque [Charak], Chyrou [Chiru], Kailo [Nakhilu], Aalu [Asalu?], Cheylo [Shilau], Kangon [Kangun], Verdostan [Bardistan], Monkailé [Nakhilu islet], Rishahr, Bushire, Bandar Rig, and Kharg, were all engaged in civil war with one another, and had armed more than eight hundred large dhows, which controlled all the sea from the Persian Gulf to Basra. The sea-route was therefore very perilous, for these Arabs gave no quarter to one another when they met. ... as all of these Arabs live mostly by rapine and deride the power of the Shah of Persia, recognizing only the authority of their sheikhs, who are as great thieves as themselves.[25]

The sheikh of Nakhilu told Carré that, "these Arabs from Kharg, Bandar Rig, Durack, and Bushire, go every year with fleets of armed vessels to the island of barem [Bahrein], where to our prejudice they try to make themselves masters of the pearl-fishery."[26]

---

20 Naband town is situated at 5 km from Asalu. The Al Haram came from Oman, according to Fasa'i, *Farsnameh*, vol. 2, p. 1616.
21 Asalu, a town nearly opposite to Cape Naband's low point at 6.5 km distance.
22 Shilu or Shilaw, near Taheri. There is no later report of Al Nasur living in Shilu. In 1674, Carré, *Travels*, vol. 3, p. 832 mentions "Cheylo, another colony of Arabs. It is half hidden by a large wood of all sorts of trees at the foot of high mountains, from which comes a spring of fresh water." For Shilaw's early role see Jean Aubin, "La survie de Shilau et la route du Khunj-o-Fal," *IRAN* 7 (1979), pp. 21-37.
23 Kangan, port at 32 km north-west of Taheri. It had good anchorage (5-8 fathoms) and protection against north-westers.
24 Carré, *Travels*, vol. 1, p. 101. In the 1670s, the Nakhilu Arabs were 3,000 men strong and had some 400 vessels. Ibid, vol. 1, p., 103. For the Portuguese-Omani hostilities see Floor, *The Political Economy*, pp. 371-75, 383-86, 395-98, 407-24, 469-75. On the early history of the Nakhilu Arabs see chapter one.
25 Carré, *The Travels*, vol. 3, p. 824; see also vol. 1, p. 111.
26 Carré, *The Travels*, vol. 1, p. 101. According to A. Aba Hussain, "A Study of the History of the Utoob," *Al-Watheeka* 1 (1982), p. 6, the 'Persians' incited the Hulas to attack the Otub and other tribes that lived on or near Bahrain, for which opinion he does not offer any historical evidence.

Vessels (*zowraq*) from Basra also frequented Bandar-e Asalu.[27] Thus "the Arabs of Chareck [Charak], Chiru, Kangun, and Asalu," had since March 1674 "joined with those of Kailo [Nakhilu], and made a descent with 400 dhows on Bandar-e Rig, where they committed a terrible massacre of its entire population, without sparing even women or children. This so terrified all the other tribes along the coast that they had armed themselves at sea."[28] Because of the war there was no trade, which meant reduced revenues. In March 1674 the shah, therefore, sent messengers, via the governor of Shiraz, to all coastal sheikhs, ordering them to come to Bushehr where the governor would attend to terminate the fighting. The governor of Shiraz arrived in Bushehr on April 7, 1674.[29] There is no information available whether, and if so, how, this conflict ended temporarily. What is known is that the enmity continued and led to renewed fighting later.

In 1684, the Dutch reported that Bandar-e Rig had been almost totally ravaged and plundered by marauding Arabs so that for a long time nobody dared to live there nor ships to call on it. Instead of going via Bandar-e Rig, as had been usual, vessels now went via Rishahr (Bushehr) to Basra.[30] The attackers may have been the Arabs of Bushehr, for Carré reported that the Hulas considered the people of Bushehr and Bandar-e Rig as mortal enemies. Most of the inhabitants of Bushehr were Arabs, the rest were 'Persians.'[31] The bitter enmity that existed between the Al Mazkur of Bushehr and the Hula Arabs may date from the mid-sixteenth century, when a group of Arabs settled at Nakhilu (i.e. Hula Arabs), because they had been ousted from Oman after they had lost the battle for the pearl grounds against their main rivals the *Alimoeiros* [Al Moheyr?].[32] The latter were also actively supporting the Safavids at a time when those of Nakhilu, for example, were hostile towards the Safavids. In 1602-03, Sheikh Musa Abu Moheyr assisted Emamqoli Khan with men and vessels to oust the Portuguese from Bahrain.[33] The Al Abu Moheyr, under their chief Sheikh Amir Mahin were living in the Bandar Deylam area in 1702, and most likely already much earlier; they still had contacts with their relatives in Oman at that time,[34] just like the Hulas had as well. These continuing contacts ensured that old enmities from the Arab side were transplanted to the Iranian side of the Persian Gulf.

The destruction of Bandar-e Rig did not mean the end of hostilities between the Hulas and the Arabs of Rig and Bushehr. Nor did the Hulas limit their hostilities to this Arab group, for they also were in conflict with other Arabs such as the Otub (عتوب) and the Khalifat, who were residing on Bahrain. Their war also continued and resulted in the ouster of the latter two groups from Bahrain. The Khalifat were living in the Bandar Deylam district in 1696. Their chief was Sheikh Majd at that time. Other Arab tribes

---

27 Mohammad Mofid Mostowfi-ye Yazdi, *Mokhtasar-e Mofid*. 2 vols. ed. Seyf al-Din Najmabadi. Wiesbaden: Reichert, 1989, vol. 1, p. 378. *Zowraq*, probably the same as *zaruqah*, a small one-masted coastal vessel with a sail and oars, 5-7 m long, crewed by 7 to 8 men. Lorimer, *Gazetteer*, vol. 2, p. 2324.

28 Carré, *The Travels*, vol. 3, pp. 829.

29 Carré, *The Travels*, vol. 3, pp. 828-29.

30 VOC 1406, van de Heuvel to Batavia (28/02/1684), f. 1161 vs.

31 Carré, *The Travels*, vol. 3, p. 834-35.

32 Francisco Rodrigues Silveira, *Memórias de um soldado da India*. ed. A. de S.S. Costa Lobo. Lisbon, 1987, pp. 45-46.

33 Mullah Jalal al-Din Monajjem, *Ruznameh-ye Abbasi ya Ruznameh-ye Molla Jalal*, ed. Seyfollah Vahidniya. Tehran, 1366/1967, p. 215.

34 Mohammad Ebrahim b. Zeyn al-'Abedin Nasiri, *Dastur-e Shahriyan*. ed. Mohammad Nader Nasiri Moqaddam. Tehran, 1373/1995, p. 154.

living in the same area at that time included the Al Zo`ab and the Al Abu Moheyr, whose chiefs were respectively Sheikh Khamis and Sheikh Amir Mahin. Part of the Al Zo`ab were still living at Masqat.[35] The Khalifat and other Arabs may have moved from Deylam to Bahrain shortly thereafter, because on 22 December 1701, Ali Pasha of Basra reported to Istanbul that two Arab tribal groups, the Otub and the Khalifat, with 150 boats, each with 2 or 3 guns and 30 to 40 armed soldiers, had arrived at Basra. They had been ousted from Bahrain by the Hulas. Their total number was 2,000 persons and they wanted to put themselves under Ottoman protection, and asked permission to live in Basra. Ali Pasha had not yet decided where to relocate them, but he asked that the Porte send an important official to mediate between the Hulas and the other Arabs to bring peace to the region, so that security and trade could return to the area. The Otub and the Khalifat also proposed the merchants of Basra to transport their goods for them. However, Ali Pasha did not want other Arabs in Basra to make his military situation even more insecure that it was already.[36] The Otub and Khalifat claimed that the conflict with the Hulas was due to 'Persian' (`Ajami) machinations, but this seems highly unlikely, because the Otub and Khalifat had been assisting the Safavids in Khuzestan against the Montafeq (1698) and in the planned invasion of Masqat (1697). In retaliation for their ouster from Bahrain, the Otub and Khalifat attacked the island killing many Hulas. Out of fear for revenge they then fled to Basra and Bandar-e Deylam, and later, of course, wound up respectively in Bahrain and Kuwait.[37]

The Hulas played also another role in the Persian Gulf, viz. that of auxiliary forces. When in 1672 the Imam of Masqat failed to obtain Dutch military support against Portugal he tried to obtain the support of the Hula pirates on the other side of the Persian Gulf. Carré reported that:

> Two Arabs with a large following which came to see me. Having learned that they were ambassadors from the Imam-king of Muscat, who had send them to Kailo, Asalu, and other places on this goes, to ask the Arabs to assist him against the Portuguese. They told them that they would never make peace was such an arrogant and proud people as the Portuguese, who wish to rule everywhere and seize rights to which they have no title, without wanting to carry on trade or commerce to the profit of the ports and other places they frequent, as do the other European nations.[38]

THE AL NASUR OF KANGAN

Throughout the eighteenth and the nineteenth century, one of the most active groups of Hulas were those of Kangan and Taheri. It would seem that prior to 1674 there is no

---

35 Nasiri, *Dastur-e Shahriyan*, pp. 154, 181 (*jama`at-e Khalefat va Bahrain*).

36 B. J. Slot, *Les Origines du Koweit*. Leiden: Brill, 1991, pp. 70-72; Aba Hussain, A. "A Study of the History of the Utoob," *Al-Watheeka* 1 (1982), pp. 25-42.

37 Slot, *Les Origines*, pp. 70-72; Aba Hussain, "A Study," pp. 25-42. Slot has rightly argued that the `Ajamis are not Europeans, as Aba Hussain had translated, but 'Persians'. Moreover, the Ottoman document mistakenly mentions that the Hulas were from Bandar-e Kong; it is more likely that they were from Kangan and elsewhere on the Shibkuh coast.

38 Carré, *The Travels*, vol. 3, pp. 830, 862; Foster, *English Factories* 1670-1677, p. 84 (attack on Bassein in February 1674).

record that makes mention of Bandar-e Kangan and its inhabitants.[39] For example, the detailed description of the shipping route from Bandar Abbas to Basra by the Dutch in 1645 makes no mention at all of Kangan, although it lists other small ports on the Iranian littoral as well as nearby Bardestan.[40] At about that time Mostowfi wrote his *Mokhtasar-e Mofid*, a geography of the Safavid Iran, where neither mention is made of Kangan nor of Taheri, although the nearby locations of Bardestan and Asalu are listed.[41] It is only in the 1670s that Kangan, in the form of Kangoen, for the first time appears on a Dutch map.[42] It is also at that time that the first description of Kangan is given. The French priest Abbé Carré who, in 1674, wanted to travel from Kong overland to Rig, was warned not to take the land route as he had to pass "Asalu, Kangoun [Kangun], and other places, where the sheikhs were dreadful people; that they would pillage my baggage, and otherwise annoy me, once they knew I was going to Bandar Rig, whose people were their greatest enemies."[43] Therefore, he hired space on a vessel sailing to Basra, and en route Carré's vessel anchored in the harbor of Kangan, which he described as:

> A large village on the seashore in a bay at the foot of high mountains. ... [they got some refreshments there, while the sailors drew water] from two ponds only about 400 feet from the sea, I rested in the first house I could fine. The sheikh and all the Arab inhabitants are very decent people and came to offer me a warm welcome. They also brought an excessive quantity of poultry, lambs, butter, eggs, cheese, and other such things, which I sent on to my boat, after rewarding the Arabs.[44]

Carré further reported that the Hulas and the people Bandar-e Rig were mortal enemies who in March 1674 had massacred the entire population of Rig.[45] Those of Kangan are again referred to in 1684, when the Dutch reported that Bandar-e Rig had been almost totally ravaged and plundered by marauding Hula Arabs so that for a long time nobody dared to live there nor ships to call on it. Instead of going via Bandar-e Rig, as had been usual, vessels now went via Rishar (Bushehr) to Basra.[46]

In the foregoing no mention is made that the Al Nasur and the population of Kangan were actually the same in the seventeenth century. However, that population was described as being part of the Hulas, and as we know that the Al Nasur clearly were part of the

---

39 According to Vincent, Kangan was ancient Gogana mentioned by Nearchus. Arrian, *The voyage of Nearchus, and the periplus of the Erythrean Sea*, translated by William Vincent. Oxford: OUP, 1809, p. 60; K. Lindberg, *Voyage dans le sud de l'Iran*. Lund: Gleerup, 1955, p. 181. However, there must also have been a settlement there in medieval times, because Kangan produced earthenware vessels at that time. D.B. Whitehouse, "Kangan: A Traditional Pottery in Southern Iran," *Medieval Ceramics*, 8 (1984) 11-26.

40 A. Hotz ed. "Cornelis Cornelisz Roobacker's Scheepsjournaal Gamron-Basra (1645); De eerste reis der Nederlanders door de Perzische Golf" *Koninklijk Nederlandsch Aardrijkskundig Genootschap* 1897, pp. 289-405.

41 Mostowfi-ye Yazdi, *Mokhtasar-e Mofid*, p. 378 (he mentions Shilu, which had a wonderful climate).

42 Zoltan Biederman, *Historical Atlas of the Persian Gulf*, Turnhout: Brepols, 2006, p. 193 and only later again in the 1730s (p. 217) as Congon, just like on French and English maps at that time. Biederman, p. 355 (in 1721). Congoon/Cogana is mentioned on maps by resp. Homan (Congon), Nolin (Cangon), d'Anville (Congon), Bellin (Congon) Tardieu (Congon), Le Rouge (Congon), de Vaugondy (Congon) and the de la Haye in the 1750s and given the addition to Gogana on the latter map, this map must have benefited from d'Anville's input. Mohammad Reza Saba et al., *Persian Gulf. Atlas of Old & historical Maps (3000 BC - 2000 AD)*, 2 vols., Tehran: Center for Documents & Tehran University, 2005, vol. 2, pp. 340, 371, 389, 397, 410, 412, 480.

43 Carré, *Travels*, vol. 3, pp. 828-29.

44 Carré, *Travels*, vol. 3, p. 832.

45 Carré, *Travels*, vol. 3, pp. 828-29.

46 VOC 1406, van de Heuvel to Batavia (28/02/1684), f. 1161 vs; Carré, *Travels*, vol. 3, pp. 836-37.

Hulas prior to the 1720s, it is obvious that those living in Kangan in the 1670s likewise must have been of the Al Nasur. Although data remain scarce about Kangan, it is reported that around 1700:

> Congoun stands on the South Side of a large River, and makes a pretty good Figure in Trade; for most of the Pearl that are caught at Bareen, on the Arabian side, are brought hither for a Market, and many fine Horses are sent thence to India, where they generally sell well.[47]

In the years thereafter Kangan and its inhabitants are mentioned with a certain regularity. The people who lived in Kangan as well as in nearby other places were known as the Al Nasur, at least since the early eighteenth century. During that time period the activities of Sheikh Jabbara Al Nasur dominated the 'news' about events in the Persian Gulf. Therefore, it seems right to continue the story of the Hulas by focusing on the Al Nasur.

Who were the Al Nasur?

According to an unpublished local history, the Al Nasur came to Iran from the Najd probably at the beginning of the eighteenth century. They settled at Kalatu, east of Bushehr, under Bin Khalid Bin Mohammad. After his death Banu Khalid Khawl b. Mansur a.k.a. Yaser took over the leadership of the group. Due to lack of pastureland at Kalatu he moved his people to Bambariyeh, some 5 km south of present day Gavbandi. Here the group split, one part went to Taheri and the other part remained in Gavbandi. The latter place was under the control of the Al Haram and the Bani Tamim. At Gavbandi the herds grew and it was at that time that the followers of Yaser b. Mansur became known as Al Nasurin.[48] According to Fasa'i, however, the Al Nasur (with *sin* not *sad*) came from Oman.[49] According to yet another tradition, the Al Nasur allegedly were a section of the Bani Khaled tribe, part of which lived around Mecca, and another part in Qatif in a quarter named al-Na`imah. In 1717 or early 1718, Sheikh Jabbara Nasuri Taheri took Bahrain from Seyf II Imam of Muscat, and thus this island fell into the hands of this family of Hulas or migrants.[50]

---

47 Alexander Hamilton, *A New Account of the East Indies* 2 vols. London, 1930, vol. 1, p. 59. Rory L. van Tuyl & Jan N. A. Groenendijk, *A Van Tuyl Chronicle: 650 Years in the History of a Dutch-American Family*. Decorah, IA: Anundsen, 1996, p. 110 mention an attack of Congo by British pirates in early October 1696, which port the authors misidentify as Kangan, whereas the port that the pirates attacked was Kong, see Floor, *Political Economy*, p. 471. These authors were not the only one who made that mistake, so did Reza Taheri, *Az Morvarid ta Naft. Tarikh-e Khalij-e Fars (Az Bandar Siraf ta Kangan va Asaluyeh)*. Tehran: Nakhostin, 1390/2011. Unfortunately, it is not the only mistake this author makes, and therefore, his book is not very reliable. Also, the author is rather free with his interpretations and opinions, hardly any of which are supported by references to primary or secundary studies and he mistakes Shamsi dates for Hijri dates, to name but a few of the many pitfalls that this book offers to the unwary reader.

48 Shahnaz Razieh Najmabadi, "The Arab Presence on the Iranian Coast of the Persian Gulf," in: Lawrence G. Potter ed., *The Persian Gulf in History*, New York: Palgrave, 2009, p. 137, citing an unpublished local history by `Abdol-Razzaq Mohammad Siddiq, *Sahwa al-faris, fi tarikh al-`Arab al-Fars*. It is not clear whether the Al Haram and Bani Tamim had already settled in Gavbandi in the early eighteenth century, and it may well be that this local oral tradition reflects the nineteenth century situation rather than that of eighteenth century.

49 Fasa'i, *Farsnameh*, vol. 2, p. 1616.

50 Ja`far Hamidi, "Al Nasur," in Idem, *Farhangnameh-ye Bushehr*. Tehran, 1380/2001, p. 55. This is reported by Muhammad b. Khalifa al-Nabhani, *Al-Tuhfa al-Nabhaniyya fi Tarikh al-Jazira al-`Arabiyya, Tarikh al-Bahrain*. Cairo 1342/1923, p. 112, which is not a very reliable source.

The alleged settlement of the Al Nasur in Gavbandi in the seventeenth century is not borne out by other sources, i.e. Gavbandi only is mentioned as an Al Nasur fief as of the mid-nineteenth century. In fact, Fasa'i makes it clear that the Nasuris only acquired it around 1860. Prior to that time it had been held by the governor of Lar, and before that time by an unknown chief, whose daughter married an Al Nasur chief (see below chapter three). The local history is right that the group split into two sections, one went to Taheri and the other to Kangan. This must have happened much earlier than ca. 1700 as reported in local oral tradition, because otherwise the Al Nasur could not have played such an important role already by the 1720s, as discussed in the previous chapter.

Also, the role of the Hulas in ousting the Omanis from Bahrain was less critical than local tradition has it. Rather than defeating the Omanis, these left of their own volition at the end of 1721, being needed in Oman due to the outbreak of a dynastic war, and Sheikh Jabbara simply took their place, as there was nobody to oppose him.[51] It is quite possible that the Hulas played a more critical role in defeating the Omanis during their earlier and unsuccessful invasions of Bahrain in 1715 and 1716, but not in 1717 when the Omanis actually took the island. They only left the island at the end of 1721, but without having been defeated; in fact, they defeated an invasion by Iranian forces, killing 6,000 of them in 1719, and only left two years later after having been paid 6,000 *tumans*.[52] The Hulas, since it is not reported that these were Nasuris, apparently were already living in Bahrain around 1700 and defeated the Khalifat and Otub at that time, when these wanted to settle there. The latter somewhat later retaliated against the Hulas, although they had to withdraw and wait another 80 years before they were more successful in seizing full control over Bahrain.[53]

In 1756 the Dutch wrote a report describing the people who lived on both littorals of the Persian Gulf. As to the people of Taheri, this report stated that they:

> are reckoned to be 50 vessels and more than 900 men strong, of whom more than half are armed. Their chief, called Sjeek Chatum,[54] is the richest of all Houlas on this coast, which gives him some influence. However, he is hated by them because of his pride and conceit. A Persian man-of-war that had run aground there has enabled him to build a *gallivat*,[55] which is the cause of his power and influence as well as the fact that the chief of Bouchier [Bushehr] pays him each year 14,000 rupees out of the revenues of Bahrehn in accordance with their agreement.

Of the Al Nasur of Kangan the same report states:

> Congon,[56] which is the last settlement of the Houlas. They are reckoned to be 60 vessels and about 1,000 men strong as well as the most peaceful of the Houlas. Some Jews and Banyans[57] who live there come here to buy goods,

---

51 Laurence Lockhart, *Nadir Shah*. London, 1938, p. 6.
52 Floor, *Political Economy*, pp. 418-24; VOC 1928, Isfahan 15/09/1718, f. 179; idem 01/10/1718, f. 186-87; KA 1856, Gamron to Batavia 05/04/1721, f. 357; KA 1875, Gamron to Batavia, 30/04/1722, f. 150.
53 Floor, *The Political Economy*, pp. 295, 585; and *The Rise*, p. 307.
54 Sheikh Hatem is meant here.
55 Gallivat, probably from the Portuguese *galeota*, and in Arabic became *qaliyat*. It was a small armed vessel with sails and oars.
56 Kangan, port at 32 km north-west of Taheri.
57 Indian traders.

do some business with upcountry [Persia] and start to make that place a bit flourishing to which end their chief Sjeeg Hutjer,[58] an old and peaceful man contributes his best [efforts].

The Al Nasur of Kangan were apparently independent of those of Taheri-Shilu, at least until about the 1780s.

Business as usual in the eighteenth century?

Due to dynastic problems and civil war between 1719-1749, Oman was unable to maintain its influence in the Persian Gulf. Because the Safavid dynasty had fallen in 1722 and the Afghan occupiers of Iran had neither the interest nor the power to impose their will on the sea lanes, the Hulas, therefore, made an effort to fill the power vacuum. The various Sheikhs smelled opportunities and those with the will and means took advantage of that situation. The most active among them (or is it because more is known about him than about the others?) was Sheikh Jabbara, the son of Sheikh Yaser Al Nasur, chief of Taheri, who, after his father's death in 1719, became the leader of the Al Nasur. A nominally Safavid, he subject he took possession of Bahrain on behalf of Shah Soltan Hoseyn in 1719, according to Persian sources, or in the fall of 1722, according to a Dutch source.[59]

The turmoil in Persian Gulf also effected the Iranian littoral. In 1727, the British intended to burn Asalu and to make a threatening naval demonstration at Bushehr, after Arabs from Asalu had badly treated the crew of a British ship.[60] On 11 October 1729 news reached Basra that rebellious Arabs threatened Bushehr, whose inhabitants had left in their boats to seek safety elsewhere.[61] The source does not indicate which Arabs attacked Bushehr, but in view of later developments and the movements of Arab tribes at that time they were most likely Hulas. One of those Hula groups, the Al Nasur was led by Sheikh Jabbara, who, in 1728, was further involved with a plan to attack and pillage the island of Qeshm. According to the Dutch, this was at the instigation of the British who wanted to use this act of violence as an argument to hold on to their recent occupation of the citadel of Qeshm. Ostensibly to dislodge Sheikh Jabbara, the British sent a party to Qeshm supported by Afghans on 24 November 1728. Sheikh Jabbara withdrew after a short skirmish that resulted in some casualties, but the British now could continue to maintain their force on Qeshm supposedly to protect it against future attacks by the Hula Arabs.[62] Despite this seemingly anti-Afghan action Sheikh Jabbara had credibility and easy

---

58 Sheikh Hajar.
59 Mohammad Hoseyn Qaddusi, *Nadernameh*, Mashhad: Anjoman-e Athar-e Melli-ye Khorasan, 1339/1960, p. 46, according to whom, in 1719 Shah Soltan Hoseyn appointed Sheikh Jabbar Taheri as governor of Bahrain. However, according to VOC 2009, Oets to Batavia (15/11/1722), f. 47, this was in the fall of 1722. According to Hamidi, *Farhangnameh*, p. 56, Sheikh Jabbara already took Bahrain in 1717 from the Omanis, while Najmabadi, "The Arab Presence," p. 137, gives the date of 1723/24. The latter two sources are not contemporary and thus are quite likely in error. Sheikh Jabbara's name also occurs as Jabbar in Persian texts. In European texts his name is found in various orthographies such as Tsjabar[a] or Thabaar. However, according to an Arabic Bahraini source, Sheikh Gheyth and Sheikh Nasr Al Mazkur were governor of Bahrain and Qatif and it was only in 1735 that they were expelled from Bahrian and went to Fars, which is not borne out by any other source. AliReza Khalifehzadeh, "Asnadi az pisihineh'i-ye tarikhi-ye Al Mazkur," *Pazhuheshnameh-ye Khalij-e Fars* 3/1390, p. 327.
60 B.J. Slot, *The Arabs of the Gulf 1602-1784*. Leidschendam, 1993, p. 263
61 VOC 2168, Extract uijt het Bassouras Dagverhaal (01/10/1728-07/01/1730), f. 409.
62 Willem Floor, *The Afghan Occupation of Persia, 1722-1730*. Paris: Cahiers Studia Iranica, 1998, p. 348.

access to the Afghans ruling in Bandar Abbas as is clear from the following events. On 12 November 1728, a serious conflict had broken out between the Dutch and the Afghans when the latter took the Dutch chief prisoner. To liberate their chief, after negotiations had failed, the Dutch attacked the Afghans on 8 January 1729. As a result, the Dutch chief died as did scores of Afghans. On 12 January 1729, Sheikh Jabbara offered himself as mediator to both parties. During the discussions a cease-fire was in force, and on 20 January 1729 both sides agreed to settle their differences amiably. Sheikh Jabbara told the Dutch that but for the English, who supplied the Afghans with lead and powder, although they denied this, the settlement could have been reached much earlier. As part of the agreement Sheikh Jabbara negotiated the payment of the considerable sum of 1,000 *tuman*s to the Afghan commander, Abdollah Khan.[63]

Sheikh Jabbara was rewarded by Shah Ashraf (r. 1725-1729) by appointing him as governor of Bahrain and by granting him the title of Bara Khan. At that time, Bahrain was in the hands of Sheikh Sanct [?] of Asalu.[64] In April 1730, the Dutch reported that Sheikh Jabbara, chief of the Hula Arabs of Bandar-e Taheri, was making the area around the islands of Larek and Qeshm insecure through his constant attacks. The Soltan (deputy-governor) of Bandar Abbas, Mir Mehr-e Ali, sent some men to Qeshm Island on 7 May 1730 who returned after one week without having been able to seize Sheikh Jabbara, whom they had engaged twice. On 21 June 1730 the Sheikh was again reported to be near Basidu (a township on Qeshm Island) with a great many vessels intending to attack British interests. The British therefore, sent the *Britannia Galley* to Qeshm, but found no sign of the pirate's presence.[65] According to the Dutch, Sheikh Jabbara nevertheless remained close to the English East India Company (EIC).[66] At that time (May 1730) some Dutch sailors deserted their ship in Bandar Abbas and took service with Sheikh Jabbara.[67]

Meanwhile, Sheikh Jabbara had decided to join the rebellion of his fellow Sunni, Sheikh Ahmad Madani of Evaz (Larestan). Apparently, to induce him to join forces with the Safavid party, Tahmasp Khan (the future Nader Shah), on behalf of Shah Tahmasp II, confirmed Sheikh Jabbara as governor of Bahrain in May 1730, who then was said to have sent troops to Lar to help to defeat Sheikh Ahmad Madani.[68] Sheikh Jabbara was also on the move at that time and was engaged by Mir Mehr-e Ali near Kalatu (Callatoe) on 17 November 1730.[69] Later the Dutch learnt that Sheikh Ahmad Madani, assisted by Sheikh Jabbara, who apparently had changed sides once again, had been defeated by Mohammad Ali Khan, *beglerbegi* of Fars and had been forced to withdraw into the citadel of Anak (?), which the *beglerbegi* had surrounded with his troops.[70]

One year later, we hear again about Sheikh Jabbara's activities, when some hajjis arrived in Bandar Abbas on 31 October 1731, who reported that Sheikh Ahmad Madani

---

63 Floor, *The Afghan Occupation*, pp. 348, 354-55, 357.

64 VOC 2152, f 7709; VOC 2034, f. 269, p. 270. According to Carsten Niebuhr, *Travels through Arabia, and other countries in the East* 2 vols. (Edinburgh, 1792), vol. 2, p. 152, at that time Bahrain was held by the Sheikh of Naband, which was in Harami hands, thus most likely Niebuhr's statement also refers to the Harami Sheikh of Asalu. He was expelled by the Sheikh of Taheri.

65 Willem Floor, *The Rise and Fall Nader Shah*. Washington DC: Mage, 2009, p. 196.

66 VOC 2254, f. 51, p. 277.

67 Floor, *Nader Shah*, p. 107, n. 23.

68 Floor, *Nader Shah*, p. 197; VOC 2254, f. 51, p. 277.

69 Floor, *Nader Shah*, p. 198.

70 Floor, *Nader Shah*, p. 198.

had taken Lar and had laid siege to its citadel assisted by Sheikh Jabbara and Sheikh Rashid of Basidu.[71] However, the rebels were defeated and were fleeing. To close the circle around him even more Mohammad Ali Khan asked the Dutch to patrol the shipping lanes and look out for fleeing enemies, specifically to guard the coast near Bandar-e Taheri and Morbagh. However, in April 1732 a peace agreement was reached and thus no further naval action was required.[72]

In June 1733, after Tahmasp Khan's defeat at Baghdad, one of his generals, Mohammad Khan Baluch rebelled, who was initially supported by Sheikh Jabbara and other Sunni leaders of the Shibkuh Coast and Larestan.[73] However, the rebellion was suppressed in the subsequent months. Sheikh `Allaq Huwala, perhaps a relative of Sheikh Jabbara, captured Mohammad Khan Baluch on the island of Kish and sent him to the royal court.[74] By May 1734 the last remnants of Mohammad Khan Baluch's rebels were mopped up. Some were said to hold out on Kish and, at Tahmasp Khan's request, a Dutch ship, two British vessels and Sheikh Rashid of Basidu with two ships and five other vessels contained the island. On 30 May 1734, Sheikh Jabbara, who had switched sides, had taken up position west of Kish. On 3 June 1734, at the request of Sheikhs Jabbara and Rashid, the European ships bombarded the redoubts and *tranki*s[75] on the beach, which showed that if they had to make a landing a pathway could be cleared. On 4 June 1734, a letter from Mohammad Latif Khan, the Iranian commander in charge of naval activities, arrived in which he ordered both Sheikhs Jabbara and Rashid to obey the orders of the European captains. His emissary went ashore on Kish to see whether the rebels were still on it. He returned on 8 June and reported not have seen any rebels except for three old men and an old woman, whom he had transferred to Sheikh Jabbara. He told the captains that they might as well return to Bandar Abbas.[76] Both Sheikhs Rashid and Jabbara emerged unscathed from their ordeal. Sheikh Jabbara was even appointed to collect 10,000 *tuman*s from all Arab Sheikhs who had participated in the rebellion, thus crippling them financially. Many of their followers were forcibly removed to Khorasan, which further defanged them.[77] Mohammad Taqi, the deputy governor of Shiraz, farmed out the customs of Bandar Abbas to both Sheikhs for the sum of 20,500 *tuman*s for a period of two and a half years. However, Tahmasp Khan (the later Nader Shah) did not agree with this decision and by October 1734 he had reappointed Mirza Esma`il Zamindavari, who had been on the point of leaving Bandar Abbas.[78]

As a result, relations between the Iranians and Sheikh Jabbara became somewhat strained. This was further reinforced by the preparations that Mohammad Latif Khan,

---

71 Floor, *Nader Shah*, p. 200.

72 Floor, *Nader Shah*, p. 202.

73 Sheikh Jabbara Kangani and Sheikh Ahmad Madani-ye Evazi supported Mohammad Khan Baluch, Fasa'i, *Farsnameh*, vol. 1, pp. 526; 286; Mirza Mehdi Astarabadi, *Tarikh-e Jahangosha-ye Naderi*. Tehran, 1368/1989, p. 286 (Sheikh Jabbar).

74 Mirza Mehdi Khan Astarabadi, *Dorreh-ye Naderi*, ed. Ja`far Shahidi. Tehran, 1341/1962, pp. 351-52; Reza Sha`bani, *Hadith-e Nader Shahi*, Tehran: Daneshgah-e Melli, 2536, p. 164. According to Bastaki, *Tarikh-e Jahangiriyeh*, p. 97 it was Sheikh `Abdol-Rahman Sheikh `Allaq, *zabet* of Nakhilu who captured Mohammad Khan Baluch.

75 *Tranki* is an oared vessel used in the Persian Gulf, possibly from the Portuguese *trincador*, a flat-bottomed coasting vessel with a high stern, see Hobson-Jobson.

76 Floor, *Nader Shah*, p. 215.

77 Lockhart, *Nadir Shah*, p. 79; Qadusi, *Nadernameh*, pp. 243, 352.

78 Floor, *Nader Shah*, p. 217.

Tahmasp Khan's *Daryabegi* or Admiral had been making in Bushehr in 1735 for an invasion of Bahrain. Latif Khan first asked the Dutch for support for the Bahrain operation, but they declined. Later he accused them of having alerted Sheikh Jabbara of the Iranian plans, but there is no evidence of that. The British were also asked to assist in the operation, but likewise refused. According to Mirza Mehdi Astarabadi, on learning of the plan to invade Bahrain Sheikh Jabbara fled to Mecca. In his absence, Sheikh Jabbara's deputy hardly opposed the invasion.[79] The good news that the conquest had been successfully achieved in April 1736 reached the recently crowned Tahmasp Khan, now Nader Shah, in June 1736. Having added Bahrain again to the Iranian kingdom, Nader, who had started to build a navy, positively reacted to a request from the Imam of Muscat in 1736 to assist him in suppressing a revolt. Nader clearly felt that having gained Bahrain, a navy and the opportunity to gain a foothold in Oman would give him easily control over the Persian Gulf.[80]

On 18 December 1737, Mohammad Taqi Khan came to Bandar Abbas with many troops and much pomp to begin the Iranian invasion of Oman. He was accompanied amongst others by Sheikh Jabbara, who rendered his services to Nader Shah in particular in providing support with vessels transporting troops and supplies, as did other Hulas.[81] However, this support was not given whole-heartedly. Sheikh Jabbara was still smarting from the loss of Bahrain, while a remark by Mohammad Latif Khan also did not enamor him more to the Iranian regime. In 1737, Jabbara Khan had married the widow of Sheikh Rashed of Basidu and farmed its customs. Mohammad Latif Khan told him that he had only married the old lady for her money, and had pressured him on that account to support the operation against Oman.[82]

He was not the only Arab chief who felt pressured, as the others were still smarting from Nader's punishment in 1734. Therefore, after the defeat of the Iranian fleet against the Omanis in 1738, there was a general uprising of the Hulas against the Iranians, in which Sheikh Jabbara participated. In July, or the beginning of August 1738 the latter retook the island of Bahrain, except for the fort.[83] As a result, Bahrain had been totally ruined, because the Hula Arabs ravaged and plundered it without leaving anything. They abandoned the island afterwards. In mid-August 1738, a royal grab (gurab) came from Bahrain to Bushehr, reportedly to fetch gun-powder and balls to assist the governor (*soltan*) of the island.[84] The Hula Arabs continued their depredations and took a *gurab* and a *gallivat* (both small sailing vessels) from the royal Iranian fleet at Bandar Taheri. Another had exploded by its own powder.[85] The rebelling Hula Arabs held Basidu on Qeshm Island and Kong (from which they later were ousted). They further preyed on shipping in that area where they had taken, for example, a vessel belonging to Sheikh Mazkur of Bushehr, which transported wheat for the army in Oman. Already, in June 1738, Hasan

---

79 VOC 2416, f. 308-09, 937, 1043, 1053; VOC 2417, f. 3039; Astarabadi, *Jahangosha*, p. 360 (Sheikh Jabbar); Mervi, vol. 2, p. 473, n. 7. Mohammad Taqi Khan was ordered to take Bahrain from Sheikh Jabbar Hula'i (هوله ای). Astarabadi, *Dorreh-ye Naderi*, p. 578 (Sheikh Jabbara); Qadusi, *Nadernameh*, p. 255.
80 Lockhart, *Nadir Shah*, p. 182.
81 Floor, *Nader Shah*, p. 128.
82 Slot, *The Arabs*, pp. 252, 283.
83 VOC 2448, f. 884-85; VOC 2510, f. 1097.
84 VOC 2476, Schoonderwoerd to Koenad, (17/08/1738), f. 1066.
85 VOC 2476, Schoonderwoerd to Koenad, (16/09/1738), f. 1077; Floor, *Nader Shah*, p. 133 (where I mistakenly wrote Masqat Arabs).

Ali Beg, the deputy-governor (*na'eb*) of Dashtestan, had asked Jacob Schoonderwoerd, the Dutch agent of VOC trade in Bushehr, to transport grain to Masqat, because Iranian vessels were seized by pirates due to the insecurity that prevailed in the Gulf. Not much was heard anymore about the robberies on the beaches, for it was said that the Hula Arabs had been told to lay low by Sheikh Jabbara (Sjeeg Sjabara). But it was all for appearance's sake, for Sheikh Jabbara (Sjeeg Thabaar) arrived at Qatif in November 1738, although it was unknown why. It was said that he wanted to retake Bahrain, where allegedly the entire royal fleet had concentrated to relieve the island from the Hula threat.[86] The new *vakil* of Bahrain, Mohammad Amin Khan, who was in Bushehr, could not even go there.[87] As a result of the general insecurity that prevailed at the head of the Persian Gulf, trade was and remained bad in Bushehr.[88] The Dutch merchant heading commercial operations there, Jacob Schoonderwoerd, could not sell the remainder of his iron and sugar stock, due to the ruin of Bahrain and the insecurity of navigation to Qatif.[89] Because of these developments the director of Dutch trade in Iran, Karel Koenad, who was based in Bandar Abbas, had written to Schoonderwoerd asking him whether there was cause to abandon Bushehr? He replied that there were no reasons to do so and he therefore, had decided to stay.[90]

A fleet under Mirza Taqi Khan's son, Mirza Reza, as commander of the pearling fleet to Bahrain, was not able to achieve anything.[91] This fleet possibly also had been intended to attack the Arabs at Qatif, who had supported the Hulas in their attack of Bahrain.[92] However, military setbacks in Oman and Makran made further Iranian operations against the Hulas at Bahrain impractical. When, therefore, Sheikh Qasem b. Jaber of Asalu of the Al Haram tribe came to Sheikh Jabbara's assistance the fort of Manama fell into their hands. The former's brother Mohammad b. Jaber Al Haram took control of the island and ousted Sheikh Jabbara.[93]

There was also interference with the Dutch in Bushehr by the local authorities, just as they did in Bandar Abbas. Schoenderwoerd was forced to allow the VOC ship that had called on Bushehr to transport troops to Nakhilu to suppress the mutiny of the Hula Arab crews of the royal fleet in the summer of 1740.[94] One of the reasons that the Iranian authorities wanted to make use of VOC ships was that the "mangoese and ghinoese arabs at Jifzeritt and keytz [Jazirat (al-Tawilah, i.e. Qeshm) and the island of Kish] had promised

---

86 VOC 2476, f. 183-84 (08/08/1738); VOC 2476, f. 1045 (14/06/1738); VOC 2467, f. 1058, 1063, 1066 (17/08/1738); VOC 2476, f. 1047, 1050-51, 1065-69, 1077 (14/06/1738); VOC 2476, f. 1097 (12/11/1738). Sheikh Jabbara had been ousted from Bahrain in 1736 and returned in 1738/39 to retake the island. Government of Great Britain, *Selections from the Records of the Bombay Government*. Cambridge, 1985, pp. 24-25.

87 Floor, *Nader Shah*, p. 134. According to an Arabic Bahraini source, Sheikh Mazkur II and Sheikh Nasr Al Mazkur, son of Sheikh Naser Abu Moheyr held the government of Bahrain from 1739 until 1800, which is contradicted by all other sources. Khalifehzadeh, "Asnadi," p. 327.

88 VOC 2476, Schoonderwoerd to Koenad (14/06/1738), f. 1045.

89 VOC 2467, Schoonderwoerd to Koenad (17/08/1738), f. 1058.

90 VOC 2476, f. 1084 (29/10/1738); VOC 2476, f. 1093 (12/11/1738).

91 VOC 2511, f. 992.

92 VOC 2511, f. 206; VOC 2476, 1097-98.

93 Captain Robert Taylor, "Extracts from Brief Notes," in Government of Great Britain, *Selections from the Records of the Bombay Government*. Cambridge, 1985, pp. 24-25; Niebuhr, *Travels*, vol. 2, p. 153.

94 VOC 2546 (08/10/1740), f. 1347. For the Dutch text of the official order see VOC 2546, f. 1849-51 (24/10/1740). Sheikh Mazkur had to provide the food supplies. VOC 2546, f. 1153-54 (24/10/1740). On the mutiny itself, see Floor, *Nader*, p. 139-45.

to subjugate themselves to me [Emamverdi Khan], and when seeing the VOC ships will do so quicker."[95] Sheikh Mazkur of Bushehr was given an important role in the suppression of the mutiny. He had been ordered to come to Shiraz on 28 January 1741 where he was instructed to go to the Hula rebels and induce them to return to their ships.[96] However, this yielded no result as he himself was taken prisoner by the Hulas in Kong in 1742, when they attacked that port.[97] In the years thereafter not much information is available, although the Hulas persisted in their revolt against the Iranians. They joined the Omani rebellion and supported those at Khasab. Although they were driven away from there in 1743, they nevertheless defeated the royal fleet in 1742 off Suwadi.[98] Thereafter, they threatened Iranian supply lines, reason why the Iranians pressed the Dutch to provide transportation, which at the same time meant, escort duty.[99]

Hulas and the Zands

After the death of Nader Shah in June 1747, there was no improvement in the troubled situation in the Persian Gulf. The battle for Nader's succession dragged on until 1756 when Karim Khan Zand successfully established his rule in southern Iran. In the meantime, as to the province of Fars there was a three staged conflict going on; one between Karim Khan and the governor of Lar, Naser Khan about who ruled in Lar. The other conflict was between both these rulers and the coastal petty rulers. The third conflict was between these various petty rulers, who locally vied for power. For with the disappearance of the power and authority of a central government in 1747, "every Arab chief has become an independent ruler."[100]

The situation at Bandar Abbas is an excellent case in point. The situation there was dominated by the conflict between the governor of the Garmsirat or Hot Countries, i.e. Lar and Bandar Abbas, Naser Khan and the deputy-governor of Bandar Abbas and vice-admiral of the fleet, Mullah Ali Shah. The latter wanted to remain autonomous, while the former wanted full control over the port, its revenues and the fleet. Mullah Ali Shah who had been a vice-admiral of the royal fleet controlled part of that fleet. However, in September 1747, a part of the fleet that was lying at Laft, a port of Qeshm Island, revolted led by Sheikh Abdol-Sheikh of the Banu Ma`in and Sheikh Ali b. Khalfan of the Al Ali of Charak.[101] The latter two contested Mullah Ali Shah's control over Bandar Abbas and a few ships of the royal fleet. After initially having been forced out of Bandar Abbas in 1748, Mullah Ali Shah was able to make his come-back in 1749 and re-establish his rule over that port. More importantly, he was able to induce the Al Ali chief to support him, as he needed troops to oppose Naser Khan of Lar.[102]

---

95 VOC 2546 (received 30/10/1740), f. 1760. Probably the Arabs from Moghu and Ganaveh, both Persian Gulf coastal settlements, are meant here.
96 VOC 2546, f. 1391 (31/01/1741).
97 Jean Otter, *Journal de voyages en Turquie et en Perse 1734-1744*. 2 vols. Paris, 1748, vol. 2, p. 145.
98 Otter, *Journal*, vol. 2, pp. 163-64, 169, 181-82; Lockhart, *Nadir Shah*, p. 217.
99 VOC 2610, f. 174-76.
100 ARA, VOC 2766 (Basra), f. 63.
101 Slot, *The Arabs*, p. 332.
102 Slot, *The Arabs*, p. 337.

At the other end of the Persian Gulf, Sheikh Naser of Bushehr and other coastal chiefs who had refused to pay taxes to Esma'il III nevertheless thought it prudent to leave to the islands at the end of 1750. Sheikh Naser left to Khark, while Sheikh Hatem of Taheri went to Bahrain.[103] Closer to home Bushehr was vying for control of trade in the upper part of the Persian Gulf with Bandar-e Rig, for both ports made efforts to attract merchants. Bushehr had the better cards in that it had been Nader Shah's naval base and shipyard, while it also had a better location for ships. Other contenders for regional power included the loose Hula mini-confederation of Jolfar, Lengeh, Taheri, and Kangan. By 1751, these Hulas were challenging the position of the Hulas of Charak, who were supported by the governor of Bandar Abbas. To the north of Bushehr were the Banu Ka'b in Khuzestan, and beyond Basra, the Otub of Kuwait both of whom had expansionist plans.[104]

THE AL ALI CAUSE TROUBLE

In March 1751, all of a sudden a war broke out among the Hulas about Sheikh Ali b. Khalfan's behavior and the control over shipping lanes. On one side were the Hulas of Jolfar (now Ras al-Khaimah), Lengeh (i.e. the Qavasem), Kangan, and Taheri (i.e. the Al Nasur) and on the other side those of Charak (Al Ali) and Bandar Abbas. The stakes became even higher when Naser Khan declared that he supported the Hulas against those of Bandar Abbas and Charak, while Abdol-Hasan Khan Shirazi, *begler-begi* of Fars supported Sheikh Naser of Bushehr in his bid to take Bahrain from the Hulas.[105] Sheikh Ali of Charak had taken 7 *tranki*s from the Huwala Arabs, who had attacked him and his forces.[106] To take revenge the Huwalas under Sheikh Hatem of Taheri and Sheikh Qa'ed of Jolfar had mobilized a force of 100 *tranki*s to attack Charak and Bandar Abbas. They seized a *qaliyat* that Mullah Ali Shah had lend to his ally Sheikh Ali of Charak. Things became worse when around 24 March 1751 Abdol-Sheikh the chief of the Banu Ma'in of Qeshm joined forces with the Hulas of Lengeh to participate in the attack of Charak and to seize Mullah Ali Shah's fleet. Mullah Ali Shah secured the support of the EIC in case of an attack on Bandar Abbas, because the British feared that such an attack would hurt the fledgling trade of the port. He also was able to come to an agreement with Sheikh Qa'ed or Rahma[107] of Jolfar in early April 1751 thus reducing the threat to Bandar Abbas. Moreover, an alliance with Mullah Ali Shah enabled Sheikh Rahma to control the Straits of Hormuz, as both parties controlled the coasts and the sea in that part of the Persian Gulf.[108] The alliance was facilitated by the fact that the Jolfaris or Qavasem had no conflict with Mullah Ali Shah, who just happened to be an ally of Sheikh Ali

---

103 Thomas Miller Ricks. *Politics and Trade in Southern Iran and the Gulf, 1745-1765.* unpublished dissertation Indiana University, 1975, pp. 198-99 referring to F. R. Gombroon VI (04/12/1750 and 04/01/1751).

104 Floor, "Description," p. 173.

105 Ricks, *Politics and Trade*, pp. 202-03 quoting F. R. Gombroon VI (12/02/1751 and 05/03/1751. About the Banu Ka'b, see Floor, "The Banu Ka'b," and for the Otub, see Ahmad Abu Hakima, *History of Eastern Arabia 1750-1800. The Rise and Development of Bahrain and Kuwait.* Beirut, 1965; Slot, *Les Origines.*

106 Ricks, Politics and Trade, p. 203.

107 The name of this Sheikh occurs as Rama Chaueed of Chaueed Rama or Tchaid, which I think indicates the word *qa'id* or 'chief, leader,' which becomes 'chaid,' due to the velarized pronunciation of hard consonants by Arabic speakers in the Persian Gulf.

108 Patricia Risso, *Oman & Muscat an early modern history.* New York, 1986, Oman, pp. 76-82; Slot, *The Arabs*, p. 331.

Charaki. This alliance between Mullah Ali Shah and Sheikh Rahma shows how strange some of these alliances were. Sheikh Rahma was on his way to invade Charak (Mullah Ali Shah's ally) as an ally of the Hulas. However, he promised to support Mullah Ali Shah against any attack by these same Hulas. Sheikh Qa'ed then left Bandar Abbas to join the gathering force to besiege Charak. However, the Hulas had not given up their designs on Mullah Ali Shah. Only a few days later he learnt that Abdol-Sheikh had sent letters to the governors of Qeshm, the Hormuz fort as well as to Qasem Beg, chief or *shahriyar* of Minab ordering them not to obey Mullah Ali Shah any longer. On 13 April 1751 the latter learnt that the Hulas had made common cause with Sheikh Mohammad Sayyed and Naser Khan of Lar against him.[109] On 16 April 1751, Abdol-Sheikh wrote to the British in Bandar Abbas informing them that the Hulas with 7,000 men were about to attack Charak and take that port within the following days after which they intended to take control of Bandar Abbas and Mullah Ali Shah's fleet. Further, that Sheikh Mohammad Sayyed had seized the brimstone mines in Larestan, from which Mullah Ali Shah drew part of his income, thus causing him financial trouble.[110]

On 2 May 1751, it was learnt in Bandar Abbas that Charak had fallen and that Sheikh Ali had been taken prisoner by Sheikh Hatem of Taheri. Sheikh Mohammad b. Salem became the new chief of Charak, who was a member of the Al Ali more acceptable to the attacking Hulas. A few days later the British received news that Naser Khan had hurried back to Lar when he learnt that Saleh Khan Bayat was once again in Shiraz and that Sheikh Mohammad Sayyed was operating independently from him. This meant that for the moment, a year it would turn out to be, that Mullah Ali Shah had nothing to fear from Naser Khan. However, the Hulas were not done with him yet. Although the Hulas had postponed their attack on Bandar Abbas, undoubtedly due to the influence of Sheikh Rahma of Jolfar, who persuaded them to invite Sheikh Naser's enemy and their intended next target, Mullah Ali Shah of Bandar Abbas to join them in their planned attack of Bushehr. In mid-May 1751, Sheikh Hatem of Taheri and Sheikh Chaueed of Jolfar let him know that they wanted to buy two of his ships. If he complied they would be good friends, if not they would just take them. On 18 May 1751, Sheikh Hatem came to Bandar Abbas and told Mullah Ali Shah that the Hulas would return to their own lands. On 28 May, Sheikh Chaueed came on behalf of all Hula chiefs to tell Mullah Ali Shah of their wish for closer ties. This meant family ties and therefore, Abdol Sheikh of the Banu Ma`in offered his daughter in marriage to his son, which Mullah Ali Shah refused, referring to his agreement with Sheikh Chaueed of April 1751 and by approving his daughter's marriage with Sheikh Chaueed on 8 June 1751, promising "to stand by each other on all occasions."[111]

In July 1751 Sheikh Ali b. Khalfan escaped from his captors in Taheri and with five large *tranki*s he landed near Kong, where he "cut off the whole village" and sought refuge with Mullah Ali Shah. He also went to Hormuz with four gallivats and *tranki*s that he had captured on raids against the Hulas near Hormuz. He then moved to Larek and sent Mullah Ali Shah two merchants and some merchandise that he had seized from a tranki returning from Mokha and asked Mullah Ali Shah permission to settle in Bandar Abbas or on one of the islands. Mullah Ali Shah refused, because he did not need new trouble

---

109 Slot, *The Arabs*, p. 337; Ricks, *Politics and Trade*, pp. 131, 203.
110 Ricks, *Politics and Trade*, pp. 131, 135, 204-06.
111 Abdul Amir Amin, *British Interests in the Persian Gulf*. Leiden: Brill, 1967, p. 28; Ricks, *Politics and Trade*, pp. 207-08.

with the Hulas. Seven months later Sheikh Ali, who meanwhile had settled on Qeshm, begged forgiveness from Naser Khan and permission to return to Charak, who acceded to his request.[112]

Battle for Bahrain

Another episode in the regular challenge to anyone who held the island so as to have access to its rich pearl grounds and its revenues happened in the second half of 1751, when Sheikh Naser of Bushehr and Mir Naser of Bandar-e Rig attacked Bahrain to oust the Harami Hulas from the island. However, the Bahrain expedition failed in September 1751 and the two Naser's fled back home.[113] As discussed above, the Hulas wanted to use this victory over their enemies of Bushehr and Rig to also destroy and conquer their home bases. On 26 September 1751, Mullah Ali Shah visited Danvers Graves, the EIC chief, at Naband (near Essin) to discuss the objective of the Hula chiefs returning to Bandar Abbas. The latter had intimated that they wanted Mullah Ali Shah's support against Bushehr and Bandar-e Rig to capitalize on their victory at Bahrain (see next section). The EIC Agent advised Mullah Ali Shah to refuse any cooperation with the Hulas, because the British feared that this only would result in more insecurity in the Persian Gulf. On 30 September 1751, Sheikh Hatem of Taheri and Sheikh Qa'ed (Chaueed) of Jolfar arrived in a very large *tranki* at Bandar Abbas.[114] They were followed by 12 more large *tranki*s with a force of 3,000 men, which caused great disquiet and worry among the local and foreign residents of that port.[115]

The discussions with the Hulas in October 1751 led to an alliance with the Mullah Ali Shah, who even appointed the Qavasem chief as deputy-governor of Bandar Abbas. Danvers Graves, the EIC chief, told Mullah Ali Shah that in doing so he was risking his authority, that merchants would not come to Bandar Abbas any longer, and that the central government in Shiraz and Lar would consider him a rebel and punish him severely. His task was to keep the roads open and maintain order in the district and port of Bandar Abbas, otherwise the EIC would depart if new troubles would occur. As a result, Mullah Ali Shah back-pedaled a bit and after some more and heated talks with his Hula allies reached a compromise. The Hulas had wanted the use of Mullah Ali's entire fleet and finally Sheikh Hatem left with one borrowed *gallivat*[116] and four months of supplies to Bushehr.[117] He was followed by Sheikh Qa'ed who left on 18 October 1751 with a token force consisting of one borrowed ship, one *gallivat*, a *dinghy*[118] and some *tranki*s[119]; as a

---

112 Ricks, *Politics and Trade*, pp. 208-09.

113 VOC 2546, f. 1272-74; Stephen R. Grummond, *The Rise and Fall of the Arab Shaykhdom of Bushire: 1750-1850 (Iran, Persian Gulf)* unpublished dissertation Johns Hopkins University (Baltimore, 1985), p. 76, n. 27; Floor, *The Rise*, pp. 31, 250, 327.

114 Ricks, *Politics and Trade*, pp. 211-12; J. A. Saldanha, *The Persian Gulf Précis* 8 vols. Gerards Cross: Archive Editions, 1986, *Précis*, vol. 1, p. xxxviii (LXI).

115 Ricks, *Politics and Trade*, p. 213.

116 An armed vessel, with sails and oars and small draught of water; it was also used on the West coast of India. The term may be a bastardization of the Portuguese term 'galeota', i.e. galiot or galley.

117 Ricks, *Politics and Trade*, p. 213.

118 Originally a small rowing boat or skiff, sometimes even a warboat; later often as a utility boat attached to a large vessel. In the Persian Gulf and Mekran Coast it seems to have been a rowing boat of varying size, small and larger, often use for warlike purposes. The word has been derived from the Hindi, *dingi* or *dengi*.

119 A very common large vessel, with sails and oars, used in the Persian Gulf and adjacent sea.

result, Mullah Ali Shah had only one ship left at Bandar Abbas. Also at that time, Abdol-Hasan Khan, *begler-begi* of Fars fell from power, due to excessive taxation and his role in supporting Bushehr in its endeavor to conquer Bahrain, which meant a loss of potential support for Bushehr.[120]

The allied force arrived at Bushehr in November 1751, but had to lift its siege by December 1751, having been totally ineffective and returned to Bahrain, where they had their families and possessions.[121] This did not put an end to the fighting for reports reached Bandar Abbas in mid-May 1752 that Bushehri and allied forces were attacking and pillaging the coastal settlements as far as Taheri. The Bushehr force consisted of two ships, four *gallivat*s and many *tranki*s and demanded that Sheikh Hatem and his Hula allies pay an old debt of 100,000 rupees (5,000 *tuman*s), in which the force was successful. Ricks has suggested that the debt may have been lost income due to Bushehr's failure to seize Bahrain from the Hulas in 1751, but this seems highly unlikely, because neither Bushehr nor Bandar-e Rig had control over Bahrain at that time.[122]

This success led to a renewed joint Bandar-e Rig-Bushehr attack on Bahrain between the summer of 1752 and the end of 1753 with three ships and three *gallivat*s. This time the attack was successful with little loss for the attackers. The Harami Hulas of Asalu, who controlled Bahrain, withdrew from the island, probably because the other Hulas, such as those of Taheri were fighting amongst themselves. Once the allies had seized the island, Mir Naser (or his two sons Mir Hoseyn and Mir Mohanna) was able to induce Sheikh Naser to return to Bushehr and then held Bahrain for himself; he did not pay Sheikh Naser anything, and was not even "willing to refund the cost he had made for this exploit." This was the cause of the enmity between the chiefs of Bandar-e Rig and Bushehr.[123] Mir Naser of Bandar-e Rig therefore, had to keep most of his men on Bahrain to hold the island. Mir Naser's neighbor, Qa'ed Heydar, chief of Ganaveh, seeing that Bandar-e Rig was weakly defended attacked the town. Mir Naser had to abandon Bahrain to come to the relief of Bandar-e Rig and thus was able to repel those of Ganaveh just in time. The Haramis of Asalu then immediately returned and re-established control over Bahrain, which they held without being challenged for two years. Sheikh Naser of Bushehr then approached the Otub of Kuwait to assist him regaining Bahrain, by promising them the right to fish for pearls without having to pay taxes. As most of the Otub were pearl divers this was a great incentive for them to agree to participate in the attack of Bahrain in 1753. Their combined fleet consisted of two ships and two *gallivat*s. The Haramis were supported by other Hulas and Mullah Ali Shah (with one *gallivat*) and put up such a fierce defense that during a sortie from the fort the Hulas surrounded 200 Bushehris and killed them all, despite the fact that they had surrendered.

Sheikh Naser being weakened significantly by this loss then focused on splitting the force allied against him. After six months he was able to induce Sheikh Hatem of Taheri

---

120 Saldanha, *Précis*, vol. 1, p. 74 (Bombay, 17/02/1752); Ricks, *Politics and Trade*, pp. 212-13; Amin, *British Interests*, p. 30; Saldanha, *Précis*, vol. 1, p. xxxviii (LXI).
121 Grummond, *The Rise*, p. 76-77, n. 28-29; Amin, *British Interests*, p. 28.
122 Ricks, *Politics and Trade*, p. 221.
123 Floor, "Description," pp. 170-71; Carsten Niebuhr, *Beschreibung von Arabien, aus eigenen beobachtungen und in lande selbst gesammleten nachrichten abgefasset nachrichten*. Kopenhagen: N. Möller, 1772, p. 331. Perry states that the sons of Mir Naser of Rig gained the controlling interest in the island, but were soon thereafter ousted by the Hulas. John R. Perry, *Karim Khan*, Chicago, 1979, p. 151.

(he had held Bahrain prior to those of Asalu) to defect and join him in exchange for an annual payment of 14,000 rupees from the revenues of Bahrain. The Haramis of Asalu, who thus had lost a major part of their defensive force, surrendered to Sheikh Naser and were allowed to leave the island. Sheikh Naser would hold Bahrain until 1783, although his position was attacked by the Ka'b in February 1761 and by the Hulas in September 1767.[124]

STRIFE IN THE BANDAR ABBAS AREA

In January 1752, Naser Khan of Lar swooped into Bandar Abbas and took Mullah Ali Shah with him to Lar as a prisoner. He also took hostages (Mullah Ali Shah's sons and Ali b. Khalfan's brother). This last hostage proved to be of less use, as the ruling Al Ali Sheikh, one of his relatives, killed Ali b. Khalfan in July 1752.[125] Sheikh Abdol-Sheikh bought off Naser Khan by sending him 150 *tuman*s as a present. Naser Khan left his brother-in-law, Masih Soltan, as his deputy-governor of Bandar Abbas with 200 soldiers, who were stationed aboard the *Rahmani* to defend the port against attacks from Arabs or Baluchis. In the absence of Mullah Ali Shah, his arch-enemy, Abdol-Sheikh, reinforced his fort at Laft on Qeshm. On 8 March 1751, he also took possession of Mullah Ali Shah's ship the *Fatta Soltanie*, which had gone to Bombay for repairs. When the ship returned and its captain learnt about the changes that had taken place in Bandar Abbas he sailed to Laft to Abdol-Sheikh. The other remaining ships of Nader Shah's fleet were out of repair and unusable, except for a few held by Sheikh Naser of Bushehr. Although it seemed that Naser Khan had favored Abdol-Sheikh above Mullah Ali Shah in the past, nevertheless trouble arose between Naser Khan and the chief of the Banu Ma'in about this ship. For when Masih Soltan asked for the ship several times, he was put off with fair words. Abdol-Sheikh, who was acting as governor of Qeshm for the Imam of Masqat, fortified his strongholds and mobilized his Arabs against Naser Khan. He furthermore incited the Hulas to take action against Naser Khan, who therefore, wanted to come to the coast to punish the Hulas and take possession of Mullah Ali Shah's ships. At that time, only the *Rahmanie* was lying in the roads of Bandar Abbas, but if the Arab crew would learn of Naser Khan's intentions the Dutch were convinced that this ship also would disappear.[126]

The EIC staff had been thinking about entirely relocating their factory away from Bandar Abbas to one of the islands in the Persian Gulf for the first time in 1750, when its hinterland had been ravaged by Ali Mardan Khan Bakhtiyari. These events and the threat of a direct attack of Bandar Abbas had been the reason why the Dutch had temporarily abandoned the port at that time. The EIC Agent, Savage had heard from a visiting Arab that Bahrain had a good fort, good water and that its revenues from taxes on date trees amounted to some 30,000 rupees or 1,500 *tuman*s and another 50,000 rupees (2,500 *tuman*s) in taxes from its subjects, which included 400 Hula Arabs. Savage liked this idea and proposed to London to move the EIC factory there, while he also proposed to seize

---

124 Floor, *The Rise*, pp. 251-52.
125 Slot, *The Arabs*, p. 341.
126 Floor, *The Rise*, pp. 58-59; VOC 2805, f. 28 (20/9/1752). On Nader Shah's navy see Willem Floor, "The Iranian Navy in the Gulf during the 18th century," *Iranian Studies* 20 (1987), pp. 31-53, or Idem, *The Rise*, pp. 1-22.

Mullah Ali Shah's fleet of three ships.[127] Bombay did not approve Savage's proposal, because it feared that the taking of the fleet would result in serious problems with whoever would take the throne in Iran. It further gave orders that relocating the factory could only be done with the approval of London. The EIC directors supported Bombay's position with regards to the seizure of the Iranian fleet, while it approved relocating the factory under certain conditions. The EIC staff was therefore, instructed not to leave Bandar Abbas until their life and the Company's merchandise was in danger and that the Company's goods had to be taken aboard in that case. "But should they find it impracticable to come to any agreement or to return to their Factory at least till the Government becomes settled under one head, and have any good encouragement to settle on any Island up the Gulph near Bunder, Bushire, or Bunder Rique where they are sure there is water and provisions & the inhabitants will permit them to land & join them for their mutual defence."[128] Furthermore, London stressed the fact that the Company was engaged in the business of trade and not in real estate and it was the former that had to be expanded not the latter.[129]

At the end of 1753 Naser Khan returned to Lar, after a visit to Bandar Abbas, where he reinstated Mullah Ali Shah as his deputy. The latter had been imprisoned in Lar until that time and had to send two of his sons as hostages to Lar. In spite of this, Mullah Ali Shah acted totally independently from Naser Khan, refused to support him against the Hulas, while he reinforced the citadel of Hormuz as a preventive measure against an eventual attack by Naser Khan.[130] He also continued to keep one ship at Bandar Abbas and one at Hormuz, so as to embark on the former if Naser Khan came. Naser Khan also had problems with the people of the Garmsir, in particular the Hulas. He had executed a holy man from Bastak and the Arabs therefore, hated him and caused him so many problems that he asked Karim Khan for the help of 4,000 veteran soldiers. By February 1754, without Zand troops which Karim Khan desperately needed himself, and after several defeats, Naser Khan negotiated a peace agreement with the Arabs, except for Sheikh Mohammad of Bastak who continued to plunder the Bandar Abbas region. During the remainder of 1754, Naser Khan just waited for the outcome of the battle between the Zands and the Afghans culminating in the October battle at Khisht. This victory gave Karim Khan breathing space and the opportunity to give Naser Khan and the Persian Gulf littoral his undivided attention. In January 1755 Karim Khan started making preparations to deal with Naser Khan, weakening the latter's back by making promises to Mullah Ali Shah and others. He also had made a "strict alliance with the Shaik of Bushire and the inhabitants of Dachtestown." As a result, Naser Khan promised to pay tribute, despite the fact that Karim Khan had to postpone his intention to pay a visit to Lar.[131]

In February 1755 Karim Khan finally marched into Larestan to enforce the promises made to him. He sought revenues and soldiers in Fars and thus had to subjugate all autonomous chiefs in the coastal areas. Quite a few, such as Sheikh Mohammad Bastaki, Mullah Abdol-Karim Gallehdari, Hajji Mohammad Amin Asiri, Sheikh Ali b. Khalfan, and Sheikh

---

127 Amin, *British Interests*, pp. 30-31; Ricks, *Politics and Trade*, pp. 200-01.
128 Saldanha, *Précis*, vol. 1, p. 73 (Bombay, 26/02/1751); Amin, *British Interests*, p. 31.
129 Amin, *British Interests*, p. 31.
130 VOC 2885, f. 7-8 (Memorandum by Schoonderwoerd; 28/12/55); Lorimer, *Gazetteer*, vol. 1, pp. 91-92; Amin, *British Interests*, p. 28.
131 Saldanha, *Précis*, vol. 1, p. 90 (Bombay, 17/10/1754); Ricks, *Politics and Trade*, pp. 276-77; Mehdi Roschan-Zamir, *Zand-Dynastie*. Hamburg, 1970, pp. 32-33; Perry, *Karim Khan*, pp. 58-59, 118.

Hatem Nasuri pledged their allegiance. Naser Khan was supposed to send 5,000 *tuman*s, 500 soldiers and Masih Soltan as a hostage in exchange for being recognized as governor of Lar. Once that was done Mullah Abdol-Karim Gallehdari, a staunch supporter of Karim Khan, would also come to Lar to serve as hostage for Karim Khan's end of the agreement. Mullah Abdol-Karim refused, however, claiming that Naser Khan would kill him just as he had killed his father. Karim Khan then stopped the negotiations and prepared for a siege of Lar. In April 1755 Mullah Ali Shah and the EIC received letters from Karim Khan asking for 3,000 *man* of gun-powder and lead, 350 "shot bombs" and orders to becalm the merchants who were daily leaving to Qeshm and Hormuz. On 10 April 1755 Naser Khan was still defending Lar against a Zand army of 15,000, while the population of Lar's hinterland was fleeing fearing Karim Khan's taxes. However, Karim Khan and Naser Khan reached an agreement at the end of April. On 2 May 1755 Naser Khan wrote Graves that Karim Khan had returned to Shiraz with Masih Soltan as a hostage and 5,000 *tuman*s in tribute. Mullah Ali Shah felt bolstered in his behavior towards Naser Khan by the latter's defeat at the hands of Karim Khan Zand. Having made peace with Karim Khan, Naser Khan could then give his undivided attention to the coastal areas. In June 1755 he began preparing for a campaign against Mullah Abdol-Karim, Sheikh Hatem and other Arabs who actively had supported the Zands. However, after the departure of the Zand army Naser Khan first attacked some of Karim Khan's possessions to seek compensation for his financial loss. For as soon as Karim Khan had returned to Shiraz, Naser Khan behaved as if he was still an independent ruler and attacked Gallehdar, which was Karim Khan's territory, to get compensation for his loss. However, he was again defeated in June 1755 by local forces loyal to Karim Khan, consisting of those led by Ali Khan Shahsevan, on of Karim Khan's commanders, Sheikh Hatem and Mullah Abdol-Karim, which signaled the end of the April agreement. Naser Khan had to flee for his life abandoning his entire army camp. As a result, it was expected that Karim Khan would infest the lower lands and also come to Bandar Abbas, which was bad for trade and everybody concerned. Indeed, in July 1755 the authorities in Bandar Abbas learnt that Karim Khan had ordered Sheikh Mohammad Bastaki and Ali Soltan to collect the taxes of Bandar Abbas. Ali Khan Shahsevan remained in the Lar area and sent a certain Soltan Mohammad Amin with 25 horsemen to Bandar Abbas to collect the annual revenue and *pishkesh*. However, he was given the cold shoulder by the local chiefs and sent back empty handed.[132] Karim Khan meanwhile recalled Ali Khan Shahsevan, because he needed his troops to oppose Azad Khan, the powerful Afghan contender for the throne. Ali Khan before withdrawing from Larestan to join Karim Khan at Isfahan ravaged the area around Lar. Out of fear for a possible visit to Bandar Abbas Mullah Ali Shah and the leading merchants fled to Hormuz. The Dutch and the English reinforced their garrison by hiring local Arab riflemen and kept a sharp watch.[133]

In early October 1756 Karim Khan marched to Kazerun and sent couriers to the chiefs in Larestan and Bandar Abbas to gather at Qir Karzin. Naser Khan wrote to the British on 2 November 1756 that he was on good terms with the Dashtestani Arabs who

---

132 Ricks, *Politics and Trade*, pp. 257; Perry *Karim Khan*, pp. 118-19; Mirza Mohammad Sadeq Musavi Nami, *Tarikh-e Giti-gosha* ed. Sa'id Nafisi. Tehran, 1363/1984, p. 50; Fasa'i, *Farsnameh*, vol. 1, p. 597.

133 Ricks, *Politics and Trade*, pp. 254-57; VOC 2885, Memorandum by Schoonderwoerd for his successor Gerrit Aansorgh (Gamron; 28/11/1755), f. 7-8 (the Dutch recorded the payment of tribute as being Dfl. 300,000 or 7,500 *tuman*s); Perry, *Karim Khan*, pp. 120-21.

had sent him their principal men to force an alliance against Karim Khan. The latter had written to Sheikh Hatem and other Hula chiefs to join him in the Dashtestan campaign. Naser Khan was to join with Sheikh Rahma of Jolfar to attack the pro-Zand Hula Arabs, although that alliance did not last long. Sheikh Rahma with a force consisting of the *Fath Rabbani* and some smaller vessels attacked Sheikh Hatem of Taheri. An additional reason for Sheikh Rahma's attack may have been Sheikh Hatem's involvement in the murder of Sheikh Mohammad b. Majd one of the Al Haram sheikhs in 1754. What followed was not war, but peace between Sheikh Rahma and Sheikh Hatem as well as between the Dashtestanis and Karim Khan, after they had been defeated by Ali Khan Shahsevan. The Dashestani chiefs then had promised to pay 3,000 *tuman*s and supply 2,000 soldiers, according to their assessment. And they did, for the crew of shipwrecked *Phoenix* met Sayyed Mansur, brother of Ra'is Ahmad, chief of the Tangestanis, who was collecting taxes for Karim Khan at Halla on the Dashestan coast. Naser Khan thus was on his own again.[134]

From the autumn of 1755 until mid-June 1757 Mullah Ali Shah had full control over Bandar Abbas, Hormuz and Qeshm. He continued to support the Qavasem in their expansion against Taheri and other Hula sheikhs. In mid-June 1757 Mullah Ali Shah began to flex his muscles again towards the Europeans. He imprisoned an EIC broker on Hormuz, claiming that he was more important than Mir Mohanna and therefore, he could do what he liked and expel them from Bandar Abbas as the former had done at Bandar-e Rig. Mullah Ali Shah changed his tone when Naser Khan's army approached in September 1757. Several meetings took place between the EIC, Sheikh Rahma and Mullah Ali Shah about the nature of his apology to the EIC and how to behave towards Naser Khan.[135]

FINAL CONFRONTATION AT BANDAR ABBAS

In the late 1750s four forces that would vie for power in the 1760s were solidifying their alliances. Mullah Ali Shah was faced by the Banu Ma`in supported by the Al Ali of Charak. The Al Haram and the Maraziq of Lengeh were allied with the Qavasem of Ras al-Khaimah. The Imam of Masqat-Oman and Naser Khan of Lar tried get one of the other parties on their side to impose their rule on Bandar Abbas area of the Persian Gulf.

In 1759, Naser Khan sent one of his commander, Mullah Hasan, to the coast to establish his rule there. Mullah Hasan came to an understanding with Mullah Ali Shah, and this was sealed with the commander's marriage with one of Mullah Ali Shah's daughters. This did not sit well with Mullah Ali Shah's son-in-law, Sheikh Rahma b. Matar of the Qavasem. In January 1760 he occupied the forts of Hormuz and Bandar Abbas. After holding both forts for 14 days he left taking all of Mullah Ali Shah's goods with him, including the ship *Fath Rahmani* and sailed to Laft. This falling out meant a significant weakening of Mullah Ali Shah's position at a time when he needed friends, although it was only a temporary rift.[136] These and subsequent events (the war that had broken out

---

134 Ricks, *Politics and Trade*, pp. 261-63; Perry, *Karim Khan*, pp. 119-20; chapter one.
135 Amin, *British Interests*, p. 42; Ricks, *Politics and Trade*, pp. 328-29.
136 Ricks, *Politics and Trade*, p. 330; Saldanha, *Précis*, vol. 1, p. 134 (Gombroon, 22/10/1759).

between the Imam of Masqat, the Hulas of Charak and the Banu Ma'in on the one hand against Mullah Ali Shah and the Qavasem on the other hand) upset the inhabitants of Bandar Abbas very much. On 15 February 1760, some sixty Hormuzi soldiers, followers of Sheikh Abdollah of the Banu Ma'in, and villagers revolted against Mullah Ali Shah and took the town and the fort of Bandar Abbas, which signaled the start of a three-year war. They "obliged his deputies and tribe of Conjees to fly the islands," who indeed went to Qeshm to seek aid from the Qavasem and the Al Haram Arabs, who had been settled on the island by Sheikh Rahma. That same day Mullah Ali Shah was arrested and imprisoned in the fort of Hormuz. The rebels also seized the ship the *Fath Rabbani*. They did not keep the Bandar Abbas for very long, because Ja'far Khan, the brother of Naser Khan of Lar, entered Bandar Abbas on 16 February 1760 and took possession of the citadel and the government. It remained quiet until 18-20 February when the Qavasem and Al Haram unsuccessfully attacked Hormuz to free Mullah Ali Shah, but they were repulsed. They were back on Qeshm on 29 February 1760 with the *Fath Rahmani*. The Banu Ma'in had given the *Fath Rabbani* (Furzarabioony) to the Charak Arabs, who delivered it to Naser Khan's brother when they both arrived in Bandar Abbas to support Ja'far Khan. Altough the latter took the side of the opponents of Mullah Ali Shah, these did not hand over their prisoner, fearing retaliation by the Qavasem. This local conflict as a consequence disrupted the entire surrounding area.[137] Fortunately, Sheikh Rahma's successor, his brother Sheikh Rashid b. Matar, was able to come to an agreement with Naser Khan. Things looked even better when Mullah Ali Shah managed to escape in May 1760 and fled to Qeshm. Some time thereafter, Mullah Ali Shah was able to reach a agreement with his enemies, including or especially the Al Ali. However, he had no ships anymore and was totally dependent of Sheikh Rashid b. Matar.[138]

Ja'far Khan was unable to make an alliance with the British, Omanis, and Banu Ma'in to attack the Qavasem. Thus, the initiative was left to Sheikh Rashed and Mullah Ali Shah, who attacked and plundered Bandar Abbas, but were unable to take the former Dutch factory, which had been turned into his fortress by Ja'far Khan. The Dutch Captain Eyken, the captain of *de Slot van Capelle*, who had arrived at Bandar Abbas to take in salt rock, brimstone and iron oxide on 8 October 1760 reported that the town had been besieged by the Qavasem from Jolfar, who had taken away all vessels, including fishing boats. This meant that loading and unloading of ships was not possible anymore. The Iranians, moreover, had taken possession of the Dutch factory at the orders of the new governor of Bandar Abbas, Ja'far Khan. The latter promised to help the captain get his goods aboard with the two small vessels that he had, if there was no hostile activity. Eyken tried to find bags to transport the brimstone, but was able to find only 70 bags. Moreover, at the slightest rumor about enemy activity Ja'far Khan recalled his porters so that loading the ship would take a long time. Eyken, therefore, in view of increased activity of maritime violence in the neighborhood decided to leave Bandar Abbas on 14 October 1760. He sent a letter to Khark requesting the director there to fetch the remaining goods.[139] A counter attack by Naser Khan against the Sheikh of Lengeh, an ally of

---

137 VOC 3027 (30/11/1760), f. 19; Saldanha, *Précis*, vol. 1, pp. 136-37 (Bombay, 15/04/1760); Amin, *British Interests*, p. 46; Ricks, *Politics and Trade*, pp. 331-32. His full name was Mohammad Ja'far Khan. VOC 3156, f. 51.

138 VOC 3027, f. 19 (30/11/1760); Amin, p. 46.

139 VOC 3027, Gamron to Batavia, f. 6-7 (14/10/1760); VOC 3064, Khark to Batavia, f. 40-41 (01/10/1761); Lorimer, *Gazetteer*, vol. 1, pp. 102, 107; Saldanha, *Précis*, vol. 1, p. 139.

the Qavasem, was defeated.[140] Meanwhile, the conflict between Bandar Abbas and Qeshm continued unabated. During October-December 1760 there had been some skirmishes at sea, in which the Omani fleet participated helping the Banu Ma'in of Qeshm. The combined Omani-Banu Ma'in fleet reinforced by the Hulas of Charak that had earlier dislodged Mullah Ali Shah from Hormuz now besieged his supporters the Jolfar Arabs in the fort of Laft at Qeshm. Oman feared that the Qavasem, their arch enemies, would gain control over the Straits of Hormuz, which was indeed their objective. Meanwhile, the situation of Bandar Abbas got worse with declining trade and the harsh rule by Ja'far Khan.[141] Although Oman and the Qavasem agreed to a truce, an effort to bring about a similar settlement between the Qavasem and the Al Ali-Banu Ma'in alliance proved to be impossible.[142]

In the fall of 1761 Sheikh Rashid again tried to gain control over Hormuz, but the Qavasem were defeated, when the Omanis hurried to the rescue of Sheikh Abdollah of Hormuz. The conflict dragged on for some time, marked by naval skirmishes. Peace became finally possible in the region when the Omani and the Banu Ma'in alliance fell apart.[143] In early 1763 Mullah Ali Shah and the Jolfaris made peace with the Banu Ma'in, who were to keep Hormuz, acquire the Laft fort as well as all their lands at Basidu, while the revenues of the islands were to be divided among the three parties. The Qavasem Sheikh of Jolfar would keep the *Fath Rahmaniyeh*. The Qavasem also reached a peace agreement with the Imam of Masqat and his Hula allies. Sheikh Abdollah was recognized as governor of Hormuz and Qeshm by Naser Khan, while his Banu Ma'in would serve Naser Khan as sailors. In short, those who benefited most were the Qavasem and the Banu Ma'in, while Mullah Ali Shah lost, for his role in the Bandar Abbas area was over.[144]

Kangan- Taheri in trouble

In the 1760s the Persian Gulf had become a dangerous place and this was not only due to maritime violence by the Banu Ka'b and Mir Mohanna. The Hula Arabs were traditionally also engaged in this activity, but they had limited themselves to attacking native shipping. It therefore, came as a major surprise that a group of Arabs, who had been hired as sailors at Basra to replace those of crew who had died during the voyage from Bengal and at Basra, murdered Captain Sutherland and his officers of the *Islamabad* and took the ship's cargo on 6 February 1765. Of the rest of the crew (all, but one, Indians), who had gone to Moghu in a longboat to fetch water and provisions, one was killed and some wounded on their return to the *Islamabad*. They therefore, fled and went to a town a league south of Moghu where the local sheikh stripped them of everything including the long boat. After the murder of Captain Sutherland the Arab perpetrators plundered the ship of its

---

140 Slot, *The Arabs*, p. 383.
141 VOC 3027, Khark to Batavia (30/11/1760), f. 19; Ricks, *Politics and Trade*, pp. 332-33; VOC 3027, Bandar Abbas to Khark, f. 6-7 (14/10/1760).
142 Slot, *The Arabs*, p. 384.
143 Slot, *The Arabs*, pp. 384-85.
144 VOC 3027, Khark to Batavia (22/06/1761), f. 4; Saldanha, *Précis*, vol. 1, p. 158 (Gombroon, 09/02/1763); Ricks, *Politics and Trade*, pp. 332-33. According to Niebuhr, Mullah Ali Shah had regained control again over Hormuz in 1764, but his statement must refer to an earlier situation as all other data say otherwise. He further reports that Basidu belonged to the Banu Ma'in, while Laft was held jointly by Mullah Ali Shah and the Qavasem. Niebuhr, *Beschreibung*, p. 329.

money and pearls and went to the island of Kish (Khisht), where they killed one of the Armenian merchants who were passengers on the ship. The Sheikh of Kish, when he learnt that they were murderers and pirates, arrested them and their goods, and sent them ashore in a small boat to the mainland.[145]

Allegedly Sheikh Jabbara was sent to Bambariyeh where he lived out the rest of his life, which, according to a local historian, is reported to have ended in 1773-74. His son Hatem took over tribal leadership and allegedly selected Gavbandi as his seat of government.[146] However, it would seem that Sheikh Jabbara had died quite some time prior to that date. In fact, after 1738 he is not mentioned anymore in published sources. Instead, his son Sheikh Hatem is mentioned regularly. In the fall of 1756, Sheikh Rahma with the *Fath Rabbani* (a large ship from the former royal fleet and bought from the British) and a number of smaller vessels sailed to Taheri with the objective to attack it, probably in revenge for Sheikh Hatem's murder of Mohammad b. Majid Al Haram. However, instead of fighting the two Sheikhs came to an understanding and returned home.[147]

Like Taheri, Kangan also had its share of outsider troubles. On 11 January 1757 somebody from Taheri arrived in Bandar Abbas reporting that Karim Khan had imposed the following taxes: on Sheikh Hajar of Kangan 4,000 *tuman*s and 400 soldiers.[148] It would seem that for a while at least the Arabs of Kangan had acquiesced in imposition of law and order. According to the Dutch in 1756, those of Kangan were considered

> as the most peaceful of the Houlas. Some Jews and Banyans[149] who live there come here to buy goods, do some business with upcountry [Persia] and start to make that place a bit flourishing to which end their chief Sjeeg Hutjer,[150] an old and peaceful man contributes his best [efforts].[151]

In 1756 a dispute arose with Sheikh Hajar about the salvage of the goods of two British ships, whose owners, being under EIC protection had complained to Bombay. "The owners of the *Pastorena* and the *Ali Rooka* had suffered considerably from the villainy of the Shaik at Congoone" the EIC Governing Council in Bombay concluded and it ordered its Bandar Abbas factory to send the *Swallow* and the *Drake* to demand satisfaction from him.[152] Francis Wood, the EIC chief in Bandar Abbas, replied that the owners' complaint was not borne out by the facts, while militarily the ordered operation did not look promising. He further reported that:

> In regard to Shaik Haijar at Congoon, many of the freighters as well as the Commander and officers of the Pasterenia signed an agreement with him to share equally all that might be saved, so that what he has done bears in some degree an appearance of Justice, though I can't say that this is my

---

145 Saldanha, *Précis*, vol. 1, pp. 184-85 (Bushire, 06/05/1765). In a note to this letter the Agent gave as his comments that the village on the island of Kish (Khisht) had no defenses and only a trifling force. He therefore believed that it could be easily taken by the *Tartar*.
146 Najmabadi, "The Arab Presence," p. 137.
147 Slot, *The Arabs*, p. 344.
148 Ricks, *Politics and Trade*, pp. 263-64.
149 Indian traders.
150 Sheikh Hajar or Hashar.
151 Floor, *The Rise*, p. 29. This is repeated almost verbatim by Niebuhr when he was in the Persian Gulf in 1764. Niebuhr, *Beschreibung*, p. 314.
152 Saldanha, *Précis*, vol. 1, p. 103 (Bombay, 17/07/1756).

Chiefest objection; but the village lies so straggling, and being extended along the Coast among date gardens as far in length as between Menelham's Point and Mallabar Hill, our cannonading it from the ships can give the inhabitants but very little annoyance it also ly's [sic] so near the mountains, that in case of landing, the Arabs can easily secure all their valuable Effects in less than half an hour's time, and after destroying a number of innocent People at the hazard of lossing [sic] many of our own, we should be obliged to return without any profitable satisfaction, leaving the Arabs so exasperated against us as to prove of very unhappy consequence to those of our nation who hereafter may chance to fall into their hands.[153]

Thus, it would appear that the Arabs of Kangan were indeed not very aggressive as the Dutch also had earlier intimated. But this may be only part of the story as the Al Nasur also showed a more violent side in their maritime activities. Because in 1766, when the Dutch left Khark in small boats, they decided not to go to Kangan, because by that time its population had acquired a rapacious reputation and earlier had caused them problems.[154] In 1765, the Kangan chief refused to suppress the piratical activities of Mir Muhanna of Bandar-e Rig, which seems to negate such as conclusion.[155] However, this refusal may have been due to the fact that Sheikh Hajar of Kangan was said to have been in league with Mir Muhanna, the scourge of the upper Persian Gulf at that time. For a contemporary history accuses Sheikh Hajar of displaying a behavior like that of Mir Mohanna, calling him "a second [Mir] Mohanna" (*thani athneyn Muhanna*) and that coastal people complained about him to the Zand court in Shiraz.[156] As a result, in late January or early February 1767, Zaki Khan Zand with about 6,000 men entirely destroyed Kangan. According to the Carmelites, this was a punishment for its disobedient behavior in 1765, but according to Persian sources it was in response to local complaints about Sheikh Hajar's violent maritime activities. Zaki Khan moved from Bandar-e Ganaveh, implying that at least part of his troops went by sea, which makes sense if he wanted to cut off Sheikh Hajar's escape route. He also must have marched the other part of his troops over land to Kangan, as is suggested by the fact that the port "was suddenly surrounded by his troops, who sacked it and after massacring the oldest and the infirm inhabitants took away the rest as prisoners to Shiraz." Among the prisoners was Sheikh Hajar, who together with his core retainers, who also had allegedly been involved in piracy, was executed.[157]

By May 1767 Bushehr was under siege by the Zand army. In August/September 1767, Sheikh Naser's only son went to Shiraz with gifts to get the siege lifted. Sheikh Naser offered to pay 1,000 *tuman*s which was refused.[158] Sheikh Naser's change of heart may have been brought about by the attack of Bahrain by the Hulas, which, although unsuccessful required that he had to rapidly resolve his problem with Karim Khan.[159] Thus, it would seem as if Bushehr was a rather peaceful place compared with its neighbors, due to the

---

153 Saldanha, *Précis*, vol. 1, p. 109 (in the Rig roads a/b the Swallow, 18/11/1756).
154 VOC 3159, f. 716r.
155 Nami, *Tarikh*, p. 165 (Mir Muhanna); Abu'l-Hasan Ghaffari, *Golshan-e Morad* ed. Gholamreza Tabataba'i. Tehran, 1369/1990, p. 276.
156 Ghaffari, *Golshan-e Morad*, p. 278.
157 Anonymous, *Chronicle*, vol. 1, p. 668; Perry, *Karim Khan*, p. 158; Nami, *Tarikh*, p. 168; Ghaffari, *Golshad-e Morad*, p. 278; Lorimer, *Gazetteer*, vol. 1. pp. 1802, 1824-25.
158 Anonymous, *Chronicle*, vol. 1, 668; Grummond, *The Rise*, p. 97.
159 Grummond, *The Rise*, pp. 77-78; Perry, Karim, *Karim Khan*, pp. 151, 157, 163.

fact that its Sheikh lived in peace with most of them. This also was due to the considerable power base that Sheikh Naser had been able to build. As a result, he had been able to easily oust and subjugate Baqer Khan, his Tangesir enemy, thanks to his solid relationship with the Arabs between Ganaveh and Asalu, who had supported him as well the government in Shiraz. At the same time, Baqer Khan had not been alone and also had supporters, such as the Banu Ka'b, some of the Hulas and in particular those of Taheri. Moreover, as earlier and subsequent events showed, to-day's ally could be tomorrow's foe and thus these alliances proved to be short-lived. Grummond therefore, seems to be correct in stating that Sheikh Naser's grip on the upper Persian Gulf began to slip as of 1782.[160]

The destruction of Kangan had only a short-lived impact on the willingness of the Kangan Arabs to follow the orders from the Zand regime. For in 1776 the new Kangan chief refused to render naval service to the Zand invasion of Basra in that year. Instead of obeying the royal orders those of Kangan ignored them.[161] The Zand government being engaged in the year-long invasion cum siege, followed by an uneasy two-year occupation, which was followed by the fractious succession problems after Karim Khan Zand's death in 1779, explains why no punitive action was undertaken against Kangan. Encouraged by the lack of constraining activities from Shiraz, the Al Nasur resumed their piratical activities. On 22 June 1771, three *gallivat*s off Kangan seized the *Britannia Galley*, owned by a private British merchant, and a country ketch from Gogo [?] under English colors, besides a Botella ketch and sundry boats from Masqat.[162]

Of course, too much maritime violence would invite retaliation from more powerful entities and thus, like other coastal dwellers, those of Kangan only were involved occasionally in such activities, i.e. it was not their main occupation. It also would seem that the growing power of the Al Mazkur of Bushehr, supported by the Zand regime, had a controlling influence of nearby ports. This is suggested by the fact that in 1784 Kangan was the staging area for a military operation against Bahrain. In September 1782, Bushehr had lost control over Bahrain to the Otub and the ensuing loss of revenues was sorely felt by Sheikh Naser Al Mazkur of Bushehr. Therefore, as of 1783 he tried to mobilize support for an expedition against Bahrain to regain control of that island. On 12 February 1785, he left Bushehr to travel overland to Kangan for a meeting with Sheikh Rashed Qasemi of Jolfar and Sheikh Abdollah of Hormuz in that town. The reason for the selection of Kangan was a logistical one, because the shortest distance from the Iranian littoral to Bahrain was from that port and it had an excellent roadstead. Sheikh Naser's fleet of vessels from Bushehr and Bandar-e Rig left on 21 February 1785, while a small force (not the 6,000 promised) from Shiraz had already arrived at Kangan. However, the unexpected death of Ali Morad Khan Zand in February 1785 led to the deferment *sine die* of the expedition to retake Bahrain. Sheikh Naser of Bushehr, therefore, had to accept the loss of Bahrain and did not try anymore to regain the island.[163]

Despite their occasional acts of maritime violence, the people of Kangan still had a good reputation. In 1787, Captain Plaisted went ashore at Kangan to visit the hot springs of Bardestan. He reported that Kangan

---

160 Floor, *The Rise*, p. 303f.; Grummond, *The Rise*, p. 111.
161 Nami, *Tarikh*, p. 133.
162 Floor, *The Rise*, p. 289.
163 Floor, *The Rise*, pp. 307-08.

is a Village seated on the eastward of Cape Verdiston about four leagues: it is inhabited by Arabs, as most of the Villages are along this part of the Persian Coast. It was governed by a Sheik who seemed to be good sort of a Man, and treated us very politely: it appeared to have no Share in the common Calamities of the Country; for the Ground about it, though very stony, was every where sown with Wheat while the most fertile Soil in other Places lay barren and uncultivated. Here is likewise Plenty of Sheep.[164]

At that time the major local players were Oman and the Qavasem at the entrance of the Persian Gulf, both of whom were quite weakened by the 1780s, while the Otub, after having ousted and trounced Bushehr, were the dominant force, with the Banu Ka`b, at the head of the Persian Gulf. The Hulas, in particular the Al Ali and the Al Nasur, who had played such a major role between 1720-60, were reduced to play a mere local and otherwise subservient role.

Dehu Fort Ruins

---

164 Bartholomew Plaisted, *A Journal from Calcutta in Bengal, by Sea, to Bussera: from thence across the great Desart to Aleppo … In the Year 1750*. London, 1757, pp. 17-18.

CHAPTER THREE

THE AL NASUR IN THE NINETEENTH CENTURY

In this chapter I discuss the vicissitudes of the Al Nasur of Kangan, Taheri and Gavbandi in relation to both the central government as well as to their neighboring Hula rivals.

The relationship between the various Hulas communities and their Sheikhs remained a fractious one in the nineteenth century. Intrigues, feuds, and fights were common, and there was jockeying for position, both between as well as within these groups. In 1818, Captain Taylor commented that "As far westward as Charak may be considered as in the possessions of the Joasim; then to the head of the Gulf they are in general enemies or friends, as necessity and their interests dictate."[1] It, therefore, would be helpful to have a description of the lay of the land to see who was where, and if possible, with whom? Such a short overview also serves to see whether there were any changes in the Arab groups inhabiting the Shibkuh coast in addition to the main groups of the Al Ali, Al Hamad, Maraziq, Obeydli, Al Haram and Al Nasur. The latter I don't discuss here as most of the chapter is about them.

WHERE WERE THE HULAS LOCATED?

Moghu was a small town, situated at the bay of same name. In the mid-1830s, it had a population of 260 men of the Qavasem (قواسم; Joasmee tribe), who owned a few trading boats, but mainly lived by fishing and pearl fishery, where they were mainly employed as divers.[2] Later it was mainly inhabited by 300 Maraziq or Marzuqis (مرازق), who had come from Oman. The Marzuqis also were in charge at Hasineh and Bandar Kondarun. The latter place was also called Marzuqi, after the people who lived there. In 1865, it had a population of 3,000 distributed over many villages that were partly hidden by date groves

---

1 Captain Robert Taylor, "Extract from Brief Notes," [prepared in 1818] in *Selections*, p. 20.
2 Captain George Barnes Brucks, "Memoir descriptive of the Navigation of the Gulf of Persia," in *Selections*, p. 598.

and cultivation and were situated around a 75 km long salt marsh.[3] Nearby Bostaneh was a small village, inhabited by 100 men of the Maraziq tribe, who were mainly fishers.[4]

The Al Hamadi (آل حمدي) had come from Oman, and settled in particular in Mogam, Morbagh, Kalat, Rostaq shib, and Gurzeh.[5]

The Al Ali (آل علي) also had migrated from Trucial Oman and were «of the same tribe as the pirates of Amulgavine [Umm al-Quwain], and were closely connected to them during the time they were in force.» Charak is situated at the bottom of the bay. Anchorage was good in easterly wind. Supplies as well good water were available there. The village had several towers and there were date groves behind it as well as a fort on a hill, 100 feet high. It was the strongest group of the Shibkuh coast and enabled the Al Ali to hold their own against the Marzuqi and Hamadi Sheikhs, their neighbors. In 1836, there were about 900 men of the Al Ali tribe, of which 360 were fighting men; the remainder fishermen and traders. It had some trade and in 1836 its people owned 6 *baqarah*s (buggalows) from 60-120 tons and 20 smaller trading vessels. The people were mainly employed in navigation and pearling, while a few were involved in trade; people also had some date groves.[6] The Al Ali were also involved in the slave trade, and even as late as the 1890s slaves were traded at Charak and Kish.[7]

Apart from Charak, the Al Ali also held sway over the island of Kish (variously referred to as Ghes, Ges or Kenn) that in 1836 was inhabited by ca. 100 men of the Al Ali tribe. By 1900, their number had grown to 2,250 people of the Al Ali mainly, who lived in 450 houses. It was well wooded island with plenty of good water and many wells near the beach. Barley and vegetables were cultivated, and off the island much fish was caught.[8] In the summer, more people lived on the island due to the influx of people from the Iranian and Arabian coast. There was some cultivation of dates as well as of wheat and barley by irrigation from wells and at Masheh by an inferior aqueduct. Onions, cucumber, water melons and marsh melons also were grown, but the main employment was fishing and pearling. The inhabitants had 26 large pearl boats, mainly *sambuk*s that went to the Arabian coast during the pearl season. Further, 27 small *baqarah*s and 40 *shu`ey*s used for fishing in the winter, and in the summer for coastal pearling. There also was some general trade with three trading *baghla*s to Basra, Bahrain, India and even Yemen. The bazaar of Mashah boasted of 50 shops and 9 commercial warehouses. About 12 Hindus with their families lived on the island making a living as shopkeepers and pearl merchants, and there were temporarily 10 more of them during the pearl season.[9]

Tavuneh (Tawoona) was a small town at the entrance of Charak bay. It was situated around a fort, which was built on a rock near the beach. In 1836, the place was inhabited by some 189 men of the Beni Baphar tribe. The town had a few trading boats and was in alliance with the Qavasem pirates prior to their pacification by the British in 1819. Djrd

---

3 Fasa'i, *Farsnameh*, vol. 2, p. 1618; W. H. Colville, "Land Journey Along the Shores of the Persian Gulf, from Bushire to Lingah," *Proceedings of the Royal Geographic Society*, XI (1866-67), p. 38.
4 Brucks, "Memoir," p. 599.
5 Fasa'i, *Farsnameh*, vol. 2, p. 1617.
6 Brucks, "Memoir," pp. 597-98.
7 *Administration Report* 1890-91, p. 10. On slavery in Qajar Iran, see Willem Floor, "Trade in and position of slaves in southern Iran, 1825-1925" *Studia Iranica* 41/2 (2012), pp. 255-94.
8 Brucks, "Memoir," pp. 596-87.
9 Lorimer, *Gazetteer*, vol. 2, p. 1473.

was a small village on the Charak side of the bay. It was home to 900 man men of the Al Ali tribe. It had a few small trading vessels, but they were mostly fishermen. Dovvan at the bottom of Moghu bay was inhabited by ca. 140 men of the Al Ali tribe, chiefly fishermen and farmers.[10]

The Bu Sumeyt (بو سميط; Aboosemate) tribe controlled the town of Nakhilu, which was situated on a point with about 800 inhabitants of this tribe. It had several trading boats. Its Sheikh was independent, although subject to the Iranian government. The Sheikh of Nakhilu also held Bu Sho`eyb island, which had 9 villages with 425 men of the Aboosemate tribe. Jezzar was a considerable village with 200 men of the Albubalal tribe, and was dependent on Nakhilu. Chiru and the island of Henderabi were also subject to Nakhilu until early 1836.[11]

Table 3.1: Principal inhabited places on the Shibkuh coast from north-west to south-east (1900)

Name	Houses and inhabitants	Remarks
Banak	20 houses	Administered from Kangan. Wheat, barley grown; 800 palms; 50 camels, 100 cattle, 3,000 sheep and goats
Kangan	-	See section on Kangan
Miyalu	50 houses/Shafi`i Sunnis	Fishermen, pearl divers, traders, date gardeners, cultivators, date growers
Tombak/Ayanat	225 stone houses/Shahfi`i Sunnis	Merchants, sailors, fishermen, pearl divers and cultivators, date growers; Customs house
Akhtar	80 houses/mostly Sunnis	Sailors, fishermen, pearl divers, cultivators, date growers
Bagh-e Sheikh	40 houses/Shafi`i Sunnis	Cultivators, fishermen, date growers; 6 small fishing boats
Taheri	-	See section on Taheri
Barak	100 stone houses/mostly Sunnis	Traders, sailors, pearl divers, cultivators, date growers
Ras al-Shajar	A dozen houses/partly Sunni, Shiite	Fishermen, pearl divers. Have their own pearl bank. Deserted since 1904 when charcoal burners killed 2 inhabitants
Nakhl-e Taqi	80 huts; 75% Sunni, 25% Shiite	Traders, fishermen, cultivators, date growers
Asalu	200 houses/Sunnis	4 *sambuqs*, 20 *baqarahs* for fishing, pearling; grain cultivation; date groves
Beyzeh Khan	15 huts; mostly Shiite; immigrants from Asalu	Cultivators (tobacco), date growers, fishermen with 10 *baqarahs*.
(Halat) Naband	50 huts; mostly Shafi`i Sunnis. 10 Al Bu Sumeyt families	A.k.a. Nakhl-e Hashem. Date growers, cultivators, pearl divers (6 *sambuqs*), 6 *baqarahs* and 5 *varjis* for fishing and local pearling; 100 date palms, 80 sheep and goats
Naband	200 stone houses and huts; Al Haram, now only 600 people; Sunnis	Fishermen and pearl divers, 28 small *baqarahs* and 20 *varjis*
Barku	A few huts; Shafi`i Sunnis. 10 Al Bu Samait families	16 *varjis* for fishing and pearling locally
Ras Ghorab	Half a dozen semi-permanent huts; Sunnis from Gavbandi valley	Some 26 *varjis* for pearling locally
Ghaf	Half a dozen houses	Dozen *varjis* for pearling locally

---

10 Brucks, "Memoir," p. 597.
11 Brucks, "Memoir," pp. 594-95.

Name	Houses and inhabitants	Remarks
Khovadan	8 huts/Shafi`i Sunnis	4 *baqarahs* and 10 *varjis* for fishing and pearling locally
Tibin	10 huts	Port of Gavbandi district. 3 sea-going *baqarahs* used for pearling on the Arabian side; *9 varjis*
Amariyeh	17 houses/Shahfi`i Sunnis	In summer fishing, in winter dive pearls; 3 small *baqarahs*, 5 *varjis*
Dastur	Dozen houses/Sunnis	4 *baqarahs*, 4 *varjis* for fishing in summer and pearling in winter
Kharabeh	Very small hamlet/Sunnis	Fishermen; 200 palm trees
Bostanu	100 houses/Sunnis	Port for neighboring districts and Tarakameh; under Nasuri Sheikh of Gavbandi; considerable trade with Bahrain; tobacco and sheep from Tarakameh; imports rice and piece goods; traders, cultivators, pearl divers
Borghaleh	45 houses/Shafi`i Sunnis	6 fishing *baqarahs*, used in summer for local pearling
Ziyarat	40 houses/Shafi`i Sunnis	6 fishing *baqarahs*, used in summer for local pearling
Kalatu	Nil	6 boats for fishing and local pearling
Shivu		See section of Shivu
Seyf al-Sheikh	10 houses/ Shafi`i Sunnis	Sailors, fishermen, divers; 4-5 small *baqarahs* for fishing and diving
Mogam	250 houses/Shafi`i Sunnis; mixed Persian and Arab population	Sailors, fishermen, divers, cultivators, date growers, some trade. 6 horses, 20 camels, 40 donkeys, 120 cattle, 100 sheep/goats. 12 *sambuqs*, 30 *baqarahs*, 5 *shu`eys*, 2 *varjis*
Nakhilu	80 houses; Hanbali Sunni Bedouins. Therefore, Nakhilu is known as 'Bedouin territory'	They fish, dive pearls, cultivate and grow dates; 2 *sambuks* go to Bahrain for pearling; 9 *`amilahs* for sea-fishing in winter and pearling in summer at Sheikh Sho`eyb.
Jazeh	100 houses; as above	Date growers, cultivators, fishermen, pearl divers, some trading; 2 *sambuks* go to the Bahrain pearl banks; 10 smaller *baqarahs* for fishing in winter and local pearling in summer
Makahil	50 houses as above	Date growers, cultivators, fishermen, pearl divers, some trading; 2 *sambuks* for trading in winter and pearling at Bahrain in summer; also 5 small *baqarahs* for pearling at Sheikh Sho`eyb
Chiru	200 houses; Obeydlis; Sunnis	Fort, date groves; 5 trading vessels all over Gulf; 5 pearl boats to Arabian side; dozen fishing *baqarahs* and *shu`eys* for sea-fishing and in summer for pearling; Customs house
Kalat	200 houses/Shafi`i Sunnis	Large fort; 14 *sambuks*, 20 *baqarahs*, 3 *varjis* of which 10 are trading vessels; 6 sea-going pearl boats, the rest used for fishing and local pearling at Henderabi. Some date growing and cultivation; some trade; there is a Customs house
Gurzeh	60 houses/Sunnis	7 *sambuks*, 16 *baqarahs*, of which 4 are trading vessels, 3 are large sea-going pearl boats, the rest for fishing and local pearling
Tavuneh	95 houses, mainly Bushris who at feud with the other Al Ali/ Sunnis	Mostly poor; some date growing and cultivation, but mostly sea-going operations. Some trading *sambuks*, 12 *baqarahs*, 6 *`amilahs*, 4 *shu`eys*, and 3 *varjis*; small craft used for local fishing and pearling

Name	Houses and inhabitants	Remarks
Charak	140 houses; Al Ali	Some cultivation; mostly sailors and divers; some traders. 8 trading vessels (*baghlahs*, *ghonchahs*, and *sambuks*), which occasionally visit India; dozen regular pearl boats that cross the Gulf, and a dozen smaller craft for local fishing and pearling; Customs house
Hasineh	200 houses of Maraziq; mostly Wahabis	Date growing and cultivation, but most engaged in navigation and trade; some employed as *nakhodas* on Lengeh vessels. 10 trading vessels (*baghlahs*, *ghonchahs*, and *sambuks*) sailing to Oman and in the Gulf; occasionally to India; 15 smaller craft for local fishing and pearling; depends on Sheikh of Moghu
Moghu	500 people; mostly Maraziq, Wahhabis (75%)	In 1899 fort built as protection against Charak; cultivators, date growers, pearl divers, and traders. 8 trading *sambuks*; 8 pearling *sambuks*, 4 `amilahs, 12 *shu`eys* used for local fishing and pearling; there is a Customs house
Kondarun	150 houses of Wahhabis, mostly Maraziq, and Shafi`i Sunnis of mixed origin	Cultivators, pearl divers; 20,000 date palms, 60 camels, 150 donkeys, 100 cattle, 4,000 sheep and goats; dependency of the Sheikh of Moghu
(Chah-e) Varzang	A large and ancient well with pasturage	Dependent on Charak; some cultivation by people from Golshan valley; grazing by those of Charak and Moghu in common

Source: Lorimer, *Gazetteer*, vol. 2, pp. 1790-1801

The Obeydli (عبیدلی) had come from Oman and settled in Hamiran (adjacent to Gavbandi) and environs.[12] They held Chiru and the island of Henderabi, first as subjects of Nakhilu, and then, as of early 1836, as independents, when the Obeydli Sheikh shook off the Nakhilu yoke. Their main settlement was in Chiru, which is situated at the bottom of the bay, which offered the best anchorage in a northwester in the Persian Gulf. Chiru had a fort and a large date grove. Ships could get reasonable supplies and ample water from five reservoirs filled by drainage of the hills. In 1836 it had a population of 150 men of the Obeydli (Abadaly) tribe and a few trading boats. The sheikh of Chiru always resided in another village inland.[13] Some 100 inhabitants of the Abadaly tribe lived in a village on Henderabi island, wo were subject to Chiru,[14] and they continued to do so throughout the period under study. Jella Abade was a small village inhabited by 300 men of the Bani Ahmaade tribe; they had a few boats, small quantities of cattle and poultry, and good water; it was well sheltered from northwester winds.[15] In 1865, the small district of Hamerun was under Sheikh Mohammad, who produced gunpowder, all of which (2-3,000 lbs annually) he sent to Lengeh by caravan. The sulfur came from Bostaneh, the charcoal from the hills, and the saltpeter from Bedeh, which he carried to Hamerun, where nitrate of potash was separated from sodium chloride by crystallization.[16]

Finally, there were the Al Haram (آل حرم), who were the sworn enemies of the Al Nasur and this feud would mark and define their history during this period. The Al

---

12 Fasa'i, *Farsnameh*, vol. 2, p. 1618.
13 Brucks, "Memoir," p. 596; Lorimer, *Gazetteer*, vol. 2, p. 355.
14 Brucks, "Memoir," p. 595.
15 Brucks, "Memoir," p. 596.
16 Colville, "Land Journey," p. 38.

Haram had come from Oman to Bandar Bidkhun, which is part of *boluk*-e Maleki, and developed Asalu (عسلو).[17] They shared the Maleki sub-district of Gavbandi with Tamimi and Maleki groups, who likewise had come from Oman and had become sedentary, and, apart from their chiefs, intermarried with non-Arabs.[18] However, the latter two groups were not subject to the Al Haram. Around 1785, Sheikh Khalfan Khan Al Haram was chief of Asalu; he was succeeded by his son Sheikh Abdollah Khan, and he by his brother Sheikh Ahmad Khan. The latter was succeeded by his son Sheikh Ebrahim Khan Asaluyeh Al Haram, who was the cause of much grief as is detailed hereunder.[19]

Asalu was one of the principal towns on the coast, situated at the NW entrance of the bay, which is almost one mile in length. The town is fronted by a reef, about 1 km offshore, within which is a basin with one and a half and two fathoms water, where their boats lay. Its anchorage was exposed to the *Shamal* winds, but small vessels could cross the reef and lie sheltered in front of the town. Supplies of fresh provisions and water were procurable. Behind the town dates groves were situated. The ruins of a town with two fortified hills belonging to it were situated near Asalu, and, as usual, wrongly identified as a Portuguese built settlement. In 1836, the population numbered 900 men, but by 1900 Asalu had 200 stone houses and a number of huts, which covered almost 2 km of coast. In 1836, 600 men were of the Al Haram and 400 of the Bu Sumeyt (Bosainut) tribes, who in 1833 had emigrated to this place from Bahrain 1833. They were all Shafi`i Sunnis. At that time, they had a number of trading and pearling vessels. By 1900, they had four pearling *sambuk*s and a score of fishing *baqarah*s, in which they went pearling at the banks near Naband; they also fished, and cultivated grain and dates. The only export was tobacco, brought down from the interior.[20] The Al Haram Sheikh also controlled the small town of Naband situated on southern side of the bay. In 1836, it had 240 men all of the Al Haram and Al Bakalif[21] tribes. Naband had 200 stone houses and huts of the Al Haram, but by 1900 it was partly deserted and not more than 600 people lived there, who were nearly all Sunnis. Cattle, poultry and good water were procurable, and in 1836 Naband had a few trading boats. Like in other ports people lived from fishing and pearling to which end in 1900 the town had about 28 small *baqarah*s and 20 *varji*s.[22] Ruffar, a village south side of bay near Cape Naband, in 1836 had a population of about 60 Al Haram men.[23]

The last group of Hulas were the Al Nasur who lived in Kangan, Taheri and Gavbandi, which is the main subject of the remainder of this chapter. Shilu seems to have been abandoned, at least in 1836 Captain Buckall reports that "Shillan [Shilu] is a small deserted village."[24]

The Al Nasur (آل نصور)

In the last two decades of the eighteenth century, published reports are almost silent about Kangan and Taheri, although in the first decades of the nineteenth century the

---

17 Fasa'i, *Farsnameh*, vol. 2, p. 1616.
18 Fasa'i, *Farsnameh*, vol. 2, pp. 1525, 1617.
19 Fasa'i, *Farsnameh*, vol. vol. 2, p. 1525.
20 Brucks, "Memoir," p. 593; Lorimer, *Gazetteer*, vol. 2, pp. 177-78.
21 I have not been able to identify this tribal group.
22 Brucks, "Memoir," p. 593; Lorimer, *Gazetteer*, vol. 2, pp. 1294.
23 Brucks, "Memoir," p. 593.
24 Brucks, "Memoir," p. 591. Later the village is not even mentioned anymore in, e.g., Lorimer and Adamec.

British Resident at Bushehr had occasional correspondence with the Sheikh of Kangan.[25] However, this silence came to an end in 1812, when the Qavasem, the arch-enemies of the Imam of Masqat, attacked Kangan and captured one or more of its vessels. This was due to the fact that Sheikh Allaq (علاق ; Ullag) Nasuri of Taheri, was «at variance with the Joasim.[26] Perhaps for that reason Sayyed Soltan, the Imam of Masqat and an enemy of the Qavasem, was able to call on the services of Iranian Hula ports such as Kangan to try and take Bahrain in 1816, and 1817/18; this temporary alliance brought these ports also some security.[27] Again, in a final outburst of Qavasem projection of power, in October 1819, they ravaged the Iranian coast, but failed at Kangan, although nearby Asalu and Dayyir suffered heavily in loss of life and property.[28]

The Qavasem of Ras al-Khaimah and Lengeh were not the only ones to engage in maritime violence, for so did those of Charak. In 1814 a British ship, the *Ahmad Shah*, shipwrecked near the island of Kish. If help had been forthcoming from the shore the ship could have gotten off and saved its cargo that belonged to the English East India Company (EIC). However, Sheikh Abdollah b. Ahmad of Charak seized the vessel and its cargo by force and then set fire to the ship. The EIC sent an agent from Bushehr to get compensation, who indeed received some of the recovered goods, viz. "treasure belonging to the merchants of Bushire and a few mares belonging to the Government." James Morier, the British Minister at Tehran at that time asked Fath Ali Shah to intervene, who promised to issue a *farman* addressed to the prince-governor of Fars to enforce restitution of the stolen goods from Sheikh Abdollah b. Ahmad. Although Captain William Bruce, the Bushehr Resident several times asked the governor of Fars to implement the *farman* nothing happened. In retaliation, in 1819, Captain Bruce ordered the destruction of boats lying on the beach of Charak. The Iranian government protested, asked for compensation and the replacement of Bruce. Captain Henry Willock, the British Charge d'Affaires supported Bruce's decision, because the Sheikh of Charak had refused to implement the royal order and Bruce had been authorized by Hoseyn Ali Mirza, the prince-governor of Fars to take punitive action. Also, he took it amiss that whereas the government of Iran asked for compensation of the trifling loss suffered by those of Charak, it did not raise at all the issue of the heavy losses that British subjects had suffered at the hands of the coastal dwellers. Bombay, therefore, refused to replace Bruce, although it did shortly thereafter because of Bruce's unauthorized agreement with Shiraz concerning the status of Qeshm island.[29]

I mention the events concerning Charak to underline the fact that at least nominally the central government held sway over the coastal chiefs and undertook action to either defend or punish them, depending on its own interests and capabilities.[30] For example, in August 1815, at the instruction of the Governor-General of Fars, Mohammad Khan laid siege to Kangan (Khangoon), at a time when a similar action was undertaken against Bushehr. Captain William Bruce, the British Agent in Bushehr commented on both these events, stating: "It would therefore appear that the policy of the Persian Government is to

---

25 Charles E. Davies, *The Blood-Red Arab Flag. An Investigation into Qasimi Piracy 1797-1820*. Exeter, 1997, p. 138.

26 Davies, *The Blood-Red Arab Flag*, pp. 169, 191; Taylor, "Extract," p.19.

27 Davies, *The Blood-Red Arab Flag*, pp. 180, 202.

28 Davies, *The Blood-Red Arab Flag*, pp. 203, 359 n. 47. The Al Nasur were at odds with the Qavasem. Taylor, "Extract," p.19.

29 Saldanha, *Précis*, vol. 2, pp. 133-34; Floor, *Bandar Abbas*.

30 For a similar reaction by the goverment of Iran after the British bombardment of Lengeh as well as the burning of Charaki vessels in the roads of Asalu and Kangan in 1819, see K. B. Kelly, *Britain and the Persian Gulf, 1795-1880*. Oxford, 1968, pp. 160-61.

withdraw the Arab tribes from the Coast and transplant them into the interior, a plan, however, they will not be able to carry into effect."[31] This and other events seem to have made Siddiq, a local historian of Kangan conclude that Sheikh Hatem of Kangan and his oldest son Jabbara together with other Arab tribes on the Iranian littoral opposed demands from Iran government to reduce their autonomy.[32] This statement does not appear to be borne out by the facts. True, like any other district chief at the outskirts of the kingdom of Iran the Al Nasur Sheikh and other Arab as well as non-Arab Sheikhs (e.g., Dashti, Dastestan, Tangestan) of the Iranian littoral tried to avoid paying taxes and rendering service to the central government in times of lax oversight or internal political turmoil. However, these were all temporary acts of defiance and invariably the negligent tax paying chiefs were called to account, paid and/or rendered the service asked from them. According to Captain Malcolm in 1800:

> These Shaikhs collect customs it is true, at their respective Ports but it is only as Officers of the Persian Government & they render a regular account. Whenever it happens that one of them during a period of anarchy & revolution withholds his Tribute, he is called to a severe account for his neglect, & he is generally plundered of double the amount.[33]

As we have seen above Kangan was destroyed in 1767, because of its refusal to assist the Zand rulers. The Al Nasur did not make that mistake again, for they participated with other Shibkuh and other coastal Arabs in Sadeq Khan Qajar Develu's attack on Oman in 1811.[34] The Al Nasur also paid their annual taxes as Malcolm noted; in 1812, the district of Kangan paid 1,000 *tuman*s yearly to the government of Iran.[35] Siddiq seems to be right, however, that these years under the early Qajars were a time of prosperity as is, for example, reflected in the high population figures (see Table 4.1). It is also clear from the strength of its number of fighters as well as from the Nasuri Sheikh's self-assuredness at that time. Whether the alleged prosperity at that time was due to Kangan's supposed autonomy is highly unlikely.[36]

Sheikh Jabbara does not seem to have made permanent alliances such as seem to have existed between, for example, those of Dashti and the Al Haram (see below), although his sons had good relations with the governor of Bastak. However, there appears to have been a good relationship with Bushehr such that when in 1827 a conflict arose between Sheikh Abdol-Rasul of Bushehr and the Imam of Masqat, the latter also attacked and seized Nasuri vessels. The two Sheikhs either had indeed cooperated militarily or the Imam felt that he had grounds to believe that the Nasuris were supporting the Al Mazkur of Bushehr. As the British were considered the arbiters of acts of violence at sea, Sheikh Jabbara of Kangan, accompanied by Sheikh Jamal, the treasurer of Sheikh Naser of Bushehr, on 12 May 1827, called on Captain David Wilson, the British Resident in the Persian Gulf. Sheikh Jabbara b. Mohammad Hatem informed him that his brother's vessel on its return voyage from Mangalore had been detained by the Imam of Muscat, although he was not at war with him nor with anybody else. Wilson expressed his regrets

---

31 FO 248/38, William Bruce, Resident Bushehr to Sir Evan Nepean, Governor of Bombay 16 August 1815.
32 Najmabadi, "The Arab Presence," p. 137.
33 Saldanha, *Précis*, vol. 1, p. 455 (Report of Capt. Malcolm 26/02/1800).
34 Bastaki, *Tarikh-e Jahangiriyeh*, pp. 208; Fasa'i, *Farsnameh*, vol. 1, p. 703.
35 Taylor, "Extract," p. 20.
36 Najmabadi, "The Arab Presence," p. 137 mistakenly, in my view, argues this position.

and stated that Great Britain regretted the seizure, but it could not stop independent states from declaring war. Sheikh Jabbara said that he also did not want war and had replied to a letter sent by Sayyed Sa`id, the Imam of Masqat, stating that his reason for being at Bushehr was because his superior, the prince-governor of Fars had sent for him. He further said that he hoped that the Sayyed would allow his vessel to continue its voyage, but if not he could not ignore this agression and he hoped the Resident would understand this. He therefore, wanted to know whether he had the Resident's permission to use force to get his vessel back or to take reprisal action against the Imam. Wilson replied that he could neither give nor withhold permission as the use of force against each other was a decision of independent states. He hoped that the Imam would react positively to Jabbara's letter. If therefore, the Prince-governor of Fars would give such permission he would inform the British cruisers in the area not to interfere. Sheikh Jamal asked whether the Resident would not mediate and write a letter to the Imam to arrange for the liberation of the vessel to avoid violence to take place. Wilson declined saying that Great Britain could not interfere and that the Imam knew perfectly well that it favored tranquility in the Gulf, not war. The Sheikh was satisfied with the reply, because he only wanted to know the Resident's position. Captain Wilson did not expect that Sheikh Jabbara would take retaliatory action, because his naval capacity amounted to 4 or 5 large boats, of which 2 or 3 had already been captured by the Imam.[37] The presence of Sheikh Jamal and the capture of 2 or 3 ships by the Omanis suggests close relations with Bushehr, while Sheikh Jabbara's bluster, although excuding confidence, at the same time was a sign of weakness in that he wanted British support to get his ship back.

The Family Tree

According to Fasa'i, the nineteenth century historian of Fars, Sheikh Mohammad Al Nasur, whom he considers to be the ancestor of the Al Nasur, turned Kangan, which had been destroyed by Zaki Khan Zand in 1767, into a thriving place. Given the fact that Sheikh Yaser was the earliest known ancestor of the Al Nasur a discussion on the family tree may be useful here. As noted in Chapter Two, Sheik Yaser (ياسر) headed the Al Nasur around 1700, and he was succeeded by his son Sheikh Jabbara (جباره), probably around 1717. In the 1740s, or earlier, Sheikh Jabbara b. Yaser was succeeded by his son Sheikh Hatem. The latter was already an old man in 1756, and his son Sheikh Mohammad or Mohammad Hatem (محمد حاتم) succeeded him, probably in the 1760s. Fasa'i is one of two sources that mention Sheikh Mohammad and it would seem that he ruled Kangan at the end of the eighteenth century. According to Fasa'i, Sheikh Mohammad's son Sheikh Hatem Khan became *zabet* of Kangan after him, and he, in his turn, was succeeded by his son Sheikh Jabbara Khan.[38] However, Sheikh Mohammad Hatem was succeeded by his son Jabbara, as all other sources confirm. Relations between father and son appear not have been always cordial. In July 1808, General John Malcolm instructed Bruce, the

---

37 FO 248/52, Wilson, Bushire to Bombay 12/05/1827; Idem, Substance of a conversation between Captain D. Wilson Resident in the Persian Gulf and Shaikh Jabbarah Chief of Congoon and Aga Jamal. Bushire, 12 May 1827; see also FO 248/52, Statement of Aga Hyder Ally 12 May 1827, which also indicates close collaboration between Sheikhs Naser and Jabbara.

38 Fasa'i, *Farsnameh*, vol. 2, p. 1463. The name of Sheikh Hatem, often occurs as Khatum, Khatim, Katun, etc.

British Resident at Bushehr, to send a present to Sheikh Jabbara as he had been helpful on several occasions. At that time, James Morier described Sheikh Jabbara as follows: 'The Sheikh of Congoon is represented as a young and spirited Arab, who can raise a body of two thousand cavalry, and who is able to lead them.'[39] However, soon thereafter confusion reigned at Kangan. Sheikh Jabbara was imprisoned by his father Sheikh Mohammad Hatem, who either took direct control of the government of Kangan or entrusted it to his other son Sheikh Ebrahim.[40] Bruce, therefore, wrote to Sheikh Jabbara that he could come and receive his present any time in the future. In 1809, Sheikh Jabbara was able to escape from his confinement and via Bahrain reached Bushehr and asked the British Residency for assistance. He was given 400 piasters in cash and 100 piasters in presents.[41] From Bahrain Sheikh Jabbara went to Bushehr, then to Bandar-e Rig, after which he returned to Bushehr. From there with a small group of followers he retook Kangan on the death of his father and ousted his brother.[42]

It is not known when Sheikh Jabbara b. Mohammad Hatem retook the government of Kangan, but in 1818, the British Captain Taylor reported that "Congoon is a large port and town belonging to Shaikh Mahomed Khatim Nusooree, uncle to Shaikh Ullag," who was in charge of Taheri.[43] Dupré's and Taylor's Sheikh Mohammad Hatem must be Fasa'i's Sheikh Mohammad. An anonymous Persian report only mentions Sheikh Mohammad (no Mohammad Hatem or Hatem) and Sheikh Jabbara at the beginning of the nineteenth century.[44] Whatever the truth of the matter, to confuse the issue even further, according to Siddiq, the author of a local history, Sheikh Jabbara b. Hatem (not Mohammad or Mohammad Hatem!) ruled until 1849-50 and was buried in Gavbandi. This information, however, is incorrect as Sheikh Jabbara was killed in 1844 (see below).[45]

In view of the above, it would seem that the succession of the Al Nasur Sheikhs must have been as follows: Sheikh Yaser, Sheikh Jabbara b. Yaser, Sheikh Hatem b. Jabbara, Sheikh Mohammad Hatem b. Hatem, and Sheikh Jabbara b. Mohammad Hatem. The latter had three sons: Sheikh Hasan, Sheikh Mazkur (مذكور) and Sheikh Hatem. The former apparently died without issue, and after his death in 1867, was succeeded by his brother Sheikh

---

39 James Morier, *A Journey through Persia, Armenia and Asia Minor in the Years 1808 and 1809*. London: Longman, Hurst, Rees, Orme, and Brown, 1812, p. 8.

40 Taheri, *Az Morvarid*, p. 291.

41 Saldanha, *Précis*, vol. 2, pp. 14-15. According to Adrien Dupré, *Voyage en Perse fait dans les annees 1807, 1808 et 1809*, 2 vols. Paris: Dentu, 1819, vol. 2, p. 490, the chief of Kangan was Mohammad Hatem Al Nasur (Muhammad-Katun-Ali-Nessour), whose son was kept as a hostage by the prince-governor of Fars.

42 Taheri, *Az Morvarid*, p. 291.

43 Taylor, "Extract," p. 20.

44 Anonymous, "Brief Account of the Province of Fars," *The Transactions of the Bombay Geographical Society* 17/1865, p. 185.

45 Najmabadi, "The Arab Presence," p. 137.

3 / THE AL NASUR OF KANGAN, TAHERI AND GAVBANDI IN THE NINETEENTH CENTURY

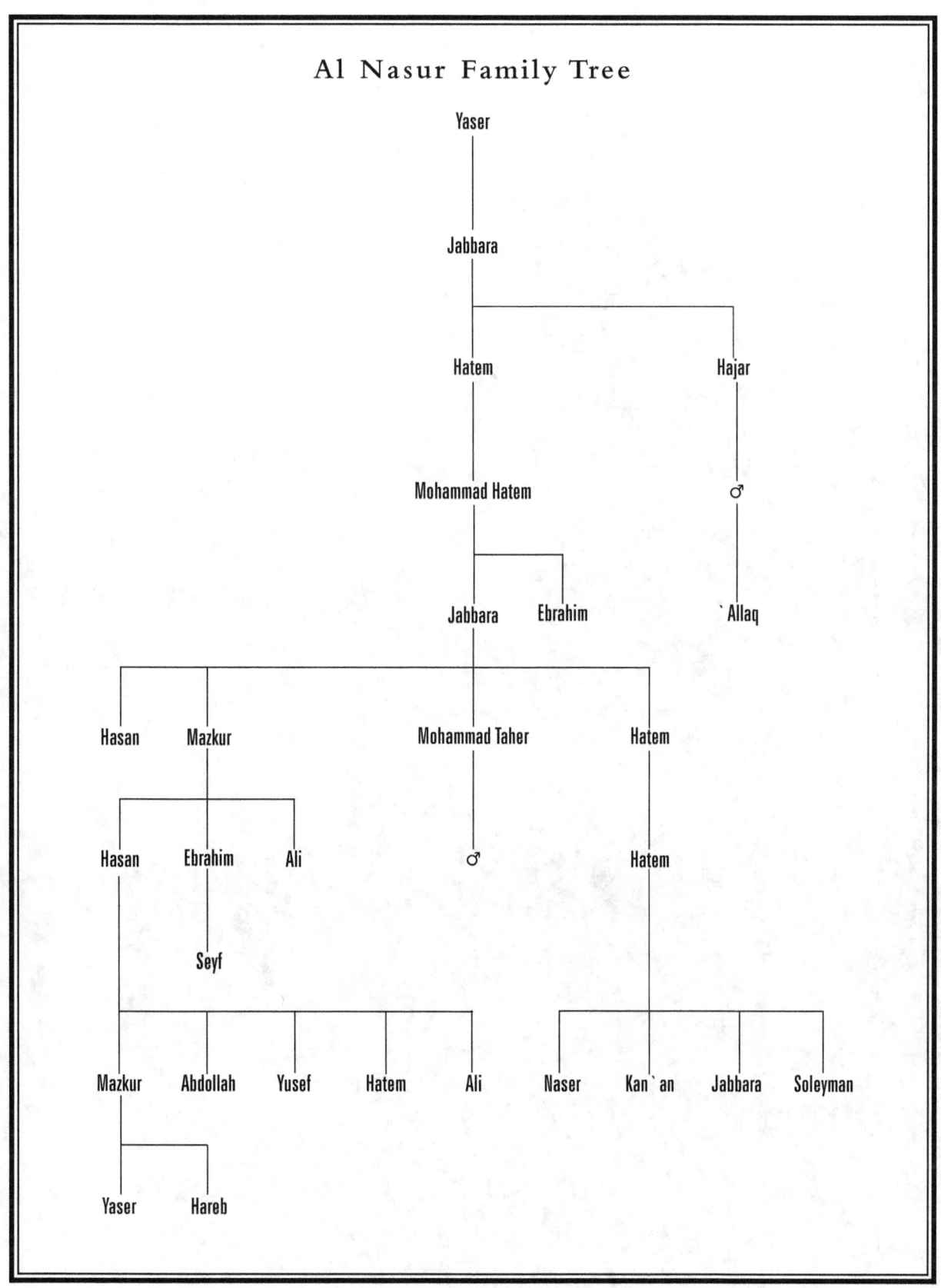

Kangan Fort

Mazkur. The latter had three sons: Sheikhs Hasan, Ebrahim, and Ali.[46] After his death in 1881, Sheikh Mazkur was succeeded by his eldest son Sheikh Hasan who remained in function until about 1908, because in 1906 it is reported that Sheikh Hasan b. Mazkur, who was a Sunni, had a wife, a daughter of Sheikh Taher of Gallehdar, who was a Shiite. His sons (Mazkur, Abdollah, Yusef, Hatem, and Ali) were raised as Sunnis and his only daughter as a Shiite.[47] Sheikh Mazkur Khan b. Sheikh Hasan Khan succeeded his father around 1908 as chief of Gavbandi. He was then 16, because in 1922 he said he was 30 years old. Sheikh Mazkur b. Hasan remained chief of Kangan and Gavbandi until 1931, when he was arrested and taken to Tehran where he died. His son Yaser was not appointed as his successor. It would seem that thereafter, his cousin Sheikh Soleyman b. Hatem, of the agnate line of the family, succeeded Sheikh Mazkur b. Hasan. Sheikh Hatem b. Sheikh Hatem, who was administrator of Taheri as of 1912, and was 40 years old in 1921, had three daughters and four sons: Sheikhs Naser, Kan`an, Jabbara, and Soleyman. Of these four, Sheikh Soleyman took over as *bakhsdar* of Kangan and Gavbandi, while his brother Sheikh Jabbara became *bakhsdar* of Taheri.[48]

The Al Nasur main branch initially was located at Taheri, while its agnate line held independently sway in Kangan. This was still the case at the end of the eighteenth century. It is not clear why the Jabbara–Hatem line of the Al Nasur instead of ruling in Taheri all of a sudden are mentioned as being in charge of Kangan. Perhaps this was because after the execution of Sheikh Hajar in 1767, who may have had no sons, Sheikh Mohammad b. Hatem took over there and rebuilt the port. In 1816, Sheikh Ullag (`Allaq), who either was the grandson of Sheikh Hatem by another son or the grandson of Sheikh Hajar (d. 1767), is mentioned as chief of Taheri. However, by then the relationship between the two ports had changed. Taheri was no longer independent of Kangan, because the Al Nasur chiefs were based in Kangan, not Taheri, probably as of the early 1800s, if not earlier.

---

46 When Sheikh Khalifah b. Sa`id of the Qavasem died in October 1874, he had four children: Ali, Mohammad, one whose name is not known, and a daughter named Kamala, of whom it was said that she had a bad aura. She was captured by Sheikh Mazkur b. Jabbara of Kangan, who later was killed by Farhad Mirza Mo`tamad al-Dowleh, the governor-general of Fars in 1880. Thereafter she was taken in marriage by Sheikh Yusof b. Mohammad Yusof, the usurper chief of Lengeh, who also was killed. Then Sheikh Qazib, the next chief of Lengeh, took her as a wife and with him ended the rule of the Qavasem sheikhs over Lengeh. Mohammad Ali Khan Sadid al-Saltaneh, *Sarzaminha-ye shomali-ye peyramun-e khalij-e Fars va darya-ye `Oman dar sad sal-e pish 1324-1332 h.q.* ed. Ahmad Eqtedari. Tehran: Jahan-e Mo`aser, 1371/1992, p. 195; Idem, *Bandar Abbas va Khalij-e Fars* ed. Ahmad Eqtedari. Tehran, 1342/1963, p. 605.

47 Lorimer, *Gazetteer*, vol. 2, p. 562. Starting with Sheikh Jabbara b. Mohammad Hatem, the Nasuri Sheikhs all were referred to as Khan, such as Sheikh Mazkur Khan (Kangani). Sheikh Jabbara was also sometimes referred as Sheikh Jabbar. In 1922, Sheikh Seyf Al Nasur is mentioned, who was then 25 years old, who was the son of Ebrahim, Sheikh Mazkur's brother, but this brother is nowhere else mentioned. Mohammad Baqer Vothuqi, *Tahavvolat-e siyasi-ye safahat-e jonub-e Iran*. Tehran, 1381/2002, pp. 49, 58.

48 Hamidi, *Farhangnameh*, p. 56; Vothuqi, *Tahavvolat*, pp. 43, 76, 79; Administration 1918, p. 12. For a short biography of Sheikh Kan`an b. Hatem and his brother Sheikh Naser b. Hatem (1913-77), see Gholamzadeh, *Me`mari*, pp. 462-63.

The Decline of Kangan and of the Al Nasur

After 1830 the history of Kangan is characterized by: (i) almost constant warfare with the Khan of Dashti as well as with the Harami arch-enemy of Asalu, resulting in multiple subsequent sacks of Kangan, (ii) resistance to the growing encroachment of the central government on the power of the Arab coastal chiefs, resulting in (iii) the reduction in the number of the Al Nasur.[49] Like other chiefs in the Garmsirat, the chief of Kangan often was in a semi-disobedient state with regards to the demands (especially fiscal) from the government of Iran. Therefore, in 1833 Hoseyn Ali Mirza Farmanfarma, the governor-general of Fars marched into the Garmsirat to put things aright in the districts of Gallehdar, Asaluyeh, Taheri, and Kangan.[50] This was but a first of several subsequent successful military 'campaigns' from Shiraz that, at least temporarily, curbed the authority of the chief of Kangan and the chiefs of other Shibkuh ports. Another such campaign may have been triggered by hostilities between Kangan and Asalu in 1838. Sheikh Jabbara accused Sheikh Khalfan of Asalu of attacking and seizing vessels from Kangan, sometimes in cooperation with the Bani Yas of the Arabian Coast. As a result, the two chiefs were summoned to Shiraz to explain their actions. Sheikh Jabbara complied with the summons, but Sheikh Khalfan did not. Given British interest in keeping the maritime peace in the Persian Gulf, the British Resident asked the governor-general of Fars to force the chief of Asalu to appear and punish him for his misdeeds. However, this request was very much resented by the governor-general, who replied that "the oppressor will be subject to punishment without the necessity of foreign assistance."[51] In early 1840, during another similar government campaign by Mirza Nabi Khan Qazvini, governor-general of Fars, "Sheikh Nasr Bakir Khan Tangestani, Sheikh Jabbarah Congoon, Sheikh Khalfan Asseloo, Mahomad Hassan Khan Brasgoon, the son of Mirza Houma Behaban, and Sherrif Khan Bawie" had been taken prisoner. However, when Mirza Nabi Khan Qazvini unexpectedly died in September 1840, the Sheikhs asked the *sartip* or general, the late governor's brother, to be released, because they had already been 8 months in Shiraz. Moreover, they were needed home where their affairs were suffering and therefore, asked for permission to leave offering all kinds of security for their behavior during their absence and return if they were needed in Shiraz. The general replied that they could not leave until the deputy (*navab*) of the new governor-general arrived.[52] The Sheikhs were released in early 1841, when Farhad Mirza took hold of the reins of government of Fars.

Sheikh Jabbara was not the only one who did not like to pay taxes, because when he was responsible for tax collection not only of his own district, but also of that of neighboring Jam. The chief of Jam and of the Modgomaris, Mullah Mohammad Taqi Khan reacted to his demand for payment by sending a camel loaded with refuse. Sheikh Jabbara

---

49 Anonymous, "Brief Account of the Province of Fars," *The Transactions of the Bombay Geographical Society* 17/1865, p. 185; H. W. Waver, "Report on the Bay and Fort of Shewoo on the Shore of the Persian Gulf," *The Transactions of the Bombay Geographical Society* 17/1865, p. 180.
50 Fasa'i, *Farsnameh*, vol. 1, p. 757.
51 *Gazetteer*, vol. 1, p. 1982.
52 FO 248/99, 3 October 1840, Shiraz news writer's report.

was infuriated by this insult and wanted revenge. However, he was not strong enough to attack the Modgomaris and waited for a suitable occasion to do so. This was offered by a conflict between Mullah Mohammad Taqi Khan and his brother Mohammad Hajji about, what else but taxes. As a result, the chief lost the support of the Modgomaris. Another neighboring chief, Mullah Hadi Gallehdari then invited him, where, on arrival, he was taken captive and brought to Kangan, where he was imprisoned in Qal`eh-ye Bariku. After a short imprisonment he was taken out to sea and drowned, an event attended by the entire population of Kangan that lives on in local poetry.[53]

There may have been good reasons for the rebellious attitude of the coastal district chiefs. When a government bureaucrat, who had been sent by Mohammad Shah (r. 1834-1848) to visit the coastal towns probably in the late 1830s, arrived in Kangan he reported that "everybody when seeing me started wailing and crying, complaining about injustice and oppression."[54] According to the same official, the oppression was not due to the 60-year old chief of Kangan, Sheikh Jabbara, whom he considered to be a good governor. The Sheikh complained much about the oppression by the officials of the government of Fars. He swore that under the two previous shahs he only had to pay 700 *tumans* in cash as present (*pishkesh*) and absolutely nothing in the form of regular taxes (*maliyat*)![55] This was not true, of course, as Kangan had been paying taxes under Fath Ali Shah (see above).

The chief of Kangan further told the unknown official from Tehran that at that time, when the number of his people had been reduced by plague and cholera in 1832 and subsequent flight, because they were unable to pay the government taxes, the tax collectors still demanded 1,200 *tumans*. The Nasuri chief said that it was not good to oppress people living at border of Iran, for if the pressure became too much they left to Arabia and lived there like their forebears did. To make the danger of losing Kangan altogether as a source of revenue even more realistic and threatening, the Sheikh further related that visiting British officials always told him that "from Iran you only get oppression, but if you were under us you would have it much better."[56] However, according to British sources the reverse was the case. In February 1809, Sir Harford Jones reported that "Yesterday accounts from Mahomed Nebee Khan [governor of Bushehr] arrived *informing the Minister that all the country from Kangoon to the southward was ready to join General Malcolm the moment he arrived and shake off the Persian yoke*."[57] I think one should not attach too much importance to either of these statements, as it is clear that the Sheikh of Kangan used the alleged British interest as a negotiating and pressure tool. He most certainly was not interested to put himself under British rule or protection, nor were the British at that time interested that he would do so. To plead his case for tax relief, Sheikh Jabbara sent a petition to Mohammad Shah with the fact-finding bureaucrat, who forwarded it to Tehran.[58]

---

53 Taheri, *Az Morvarid*, pp. 294-95.
54 Anonymous, *Do safarnameh az jonub-e Iran dar salha-ye 1256 -1207 AH*. ed. Sayyed Ali Al Davud. Tehran: Amir Kabir, 1368, p. 103.
55 Anonymous, *Do safarnameh*, p. 100.
56 Anonymous, *Do safarnameh*, pp. 100-01. It is highly unlikely that British officials ever made such remarks and it is more likely that Sheikh Jabbara used this as a ploy to get a lower fiscal burden.
57 Saldanha, *Précis*, vol. 2, pp. 14-15, italics in the original. The area referred to was the Shibkuh coast.
58 Anonymous, *Do safarnameh*, p. 102.

First sack of Kangan – 1844

Sheikh Jabbara of Kangan was scarcely back home for a year, having been released from internment in Shiraz as noted above, when having failed to pay his taxes Farhad Mirza, governor-general of Fars once again arrested him in April 1842.[59] It was believed that he was going to be sent to Tehran, because he stated that he was unable to comply with the prince's demand for money. Meanwhile, a high impost has been laid on the people of Kangan, payment of which they resisted. The prince was not only trying to exact money from Kangan, but from all districts in the Garmsir.[60] Sheikh Jabbara was apparently able to resolve his financial problems, because by 1844 he was back in Kangan. He had just returned, when he was killed during the sack of his port, which, at the end of August, or early September 1844 was totally destroyed and its inhabitants dispersed by a large Dashti force under Hoseyn Khan, son of Hajji Khan, the chief of that district. The reason for this attack was a dispute about the ownership of the fort of Gavbandi, which stood more inland from Kangan. Originally it was in the hands of Sheikh Jabbara's father-in-law. On his demise the district was seized by Nasir Khan Thani the *beglerbegi* of Lar, who held it until his death in 1839, when it fell into the hands of Sheikh Jabbara of Kangan, who placed his son Sheikh Hatem (Khatun) in charge of it. Sheikh Hatem died of the plague that ravaged the Iranian littoral. Hoseyn Khan of Galledar took advantage of this event and annexed the fort. Shortly thereafter the situation of the Kangan chief improved and he retook the fort, which continued to be contested thereafter. In early June 1844, Hoseyn Khan of Gallehdar had received information that he might surprise the fort and he therefore, made preparations to seize it. However, Sheikh Hasan, the son of Sheikh Jabbara b. Mohammad Hatem learned about this, and with some relatives and 40 followers laid an ambush and the Gallehdari 'surprise' party was "cut up to a man." On learning this, Hoseyn Khan's widow sent her veil throughout Dashti territory calling upon the tribe to revenge her husband. Many responded to the call and soon thereafter 2 to 3,000 men, sent by the Dashti chief Sheikh Hajji, under his son Hoseyn, ravaged Kangan. At first, their efforts to take the Kangan were thwarted because its fort was quite strong, but finally, through treachery, one of the gates was opened. The inhabitants immediately fled to their boats, but in the confusion 60-70 men drowned. How many were killed by the enemy is not known. The town was immediately plundered and the bazaar burnt and, as a result, the town became deserted and in ruins. Banak a small fort about 6 km from Kangan was also occupied by Hoseyn Khan Dashti.[61]

The British missionary Henry Stern visited Kangan shortly after the sack of the port. He wrote that Kangan,

> was formerly a large a populous town; but discord, anarchy, and war, have demolished the houses, destroyed the streets, and driven the poor inhabitants from their homes and fields. At present abject poverty prevails in the place, the land is uncultivated and covered with weeds, the farmers' cottages deserted and levelled to the ground; and the few inhabitants whom necessity detains here, are day and night in arms, in order to repel the Dashtees, their

---

59 Fasa'i, *Farsnameh*, vol. 1, p. 780.
60 FO 248/99, Resident Khark to Sir John McNeil 20 April 1842.
61 FO 248/271, Hennell to Sheil; 9 September 1844. It was probably also as of 1839 that the Al Nasur acquired control over Shivu. Mohammad Ebrahim Kazeruni, *Tarikh-e Banader dar Khalij-e Fars* ed. Manuchehr Setudeh. Tehran, 1367/1988, p. 102.

> most inveterate and powerful enemies. There are eighteen Jewish families in the town; a few years ago they exceeded triple that number, but the constant harassing feuds of the contending clans, compelled them to seek shelter in Geludar [Gallehdar], a place ten farsangs distant from Congoon.[62]

A year or so later other survivors of the massacre returned to Kangan and with new-comers tried to rebuild it. Sheikh Hasan Al Nasur, who had succeeded his father Sheikh Jabbara, tried to restore the family's standing and influence. It was at this time that the management of the district of Gavbandi was added his domain, perhaps to compensate him for the loss of income due to the sack of Kangan and/or, more likely, the good relations that he had with the governor of Bastak.[63] Gavbandi until that time had been managed by Mohammad Saleh of the Ra'isi family from the village of Fumestan for the Persian speaking population and the Bani Tamim and Maleki chiefs for the Arabic population of the district. Gavbandi remained part of the governorship of Bastak, which itself was under the jurisdiction of the governor of Larestan.[64]

Meanwhile, the old conflicts between the Nasuris and Haramis slumbered and only waited to be rekindled. This rekindling already happened in 1846, when "Ahmad Ananee Khargee" who piloted a Kangan *baghlah* (buggalow) was forced by the tide to anchor off the river of Basra when a *baghlah* from Asalu overtook it near the bar. As soon as the Haramis saw that it was a Kangan vessel they boarded and seized it and took it as far as Mooamie,[65] where they put the crew ashore, replacing them with Asalu men. Later the vessel was taken to Kuwait. On arrival in Kuwait a merchant of Bardestan, who had some goods on board the stolen vessel, went to see Sheikh Jabir and reported what had happened.[66] This event was but a symptom of the tense situation that existed between the population of the two ports, one that waited for a spark to explode, as events in the year thereafter show.

Conflict with Asalu

When the British had laid waste to Jolfar (Ras al-Khaimah) and other Qavasem settlements in 1819 and imposed a maritime peace on the various coastal dwellers, ports like Asalu and Dayyir, which are neighboring Kangan, that still had been attacked in 1819 were henceforth relatively safe from seaborne attacks. However, the maritime peace was challenged occasionally by this or that Arab chief. In mid-1835 the Sheikh of Amulgavine (Umm al-Quwain) wanted to assist the people of Charak, with whom his people had family ties. However, the British did not allow him to do so following the Maritime Truce of 21 May 1835 that all chiefs on the Arabian coast had signed. The British argued that "whatever claims he might formerly have possessed over the Charak people, now they had located themselves in Persia they had become Persian subjects, and consequently

---

62 Henry A. Stern, *Dawnings in the East; with biblical, historical, and statistical notices of persons and places visited during a mission to the Jews in Persia, Coordistan, and Mesopotamia*. London, 1854, p. 104
63 Fasa'i, *Farsnameh*, vol. 2, p. 1462.
64 FO 248/129, Major Hennell to Sheil, 9 January 1847; Bastaki, *Tarikh-e Jahangiriyeh*, p. 130; Najmabadi, "The Arab Presence," p. 138.
65 I have not been able to identify this place.
66 FO 248/271, Hoseyn Hajji acting governor of Khark to Hajji Ahmad, principal secretary Residency 10 Nov. 1846.

he could not, situated as he was, have any right to interfere actively in their quarrels."[67] The British could not, of course, prevent the outbreak of all forms of maritime violence thereafter, but they certainly put an end to most of them. One of those exceptions was a flare up between those of Kangan and Asalu in 1847.

Captain Hennell sent a copy of the arrangements agreed with the various so-called 'pirate ports' in what then called Trucial Oman to Hoseyn Khan Moqaddam Maraghe'i, the governor-general of Fars. In reply, the latter requested a similar agreement, be it of an incidental nature, to prevent maritime violence by the inhabitants of the ports on the Iranian littoral. This request had, among other reasons, come about by the piracy of Hajji Ya`qub's *baghlah* by the inhabitants of Khirrah[68] as well as other maritime violence against Iranian vessels. Sheikh Ahmad of Asalu claimed he had nothing to do with these acts of piracy. However, when the *nakhoda*s of the plundered vessels came to see him to complain about the treatment experienced by them, "Shaeen [Shahin] the headman of that place was sitting right next to him. The Sheikh then admitted that at one time they had been friendly with those of Khirrah, but at another time they were enemies. This could be no reason why he and his people could be hold responsible for the lawless behavior by Shaeen's followers." For this act Hoseyn Khan Moqaddam Maraghe'i, the governor-general of Fars fined him 402 *tuman*s, and also demanded that he gave an undertaking (*eltezamnameh*) that he would see to it that his people would not engage in such activities in the future. The Sheikh of Asalu was not the only one engaged in maritime violence, of course. For example, the Sheikh of Kenn (Kish) and Charak had taken a considerable part of property from Iranian merchants when the wrecked *Emily Schooner* was plundered in March 1845, and there were strong grounds to believe that these goods were in his possession. The Sheikh later refused to honor his agreement to restore these goods.[69]

In early December 1846 Hoseyn Khan, wrote to Hennell and intimated that he intended to leave Shiraz in January 1847 to make a tour of all the ports, asking that British ships be instructed to move along the coast shadowing the itinerary that he would make with his troops. Ostensibly this tour aimed to suppress piracy, but in reality, so Hennell believed, it was to show the various chiefs of Dashtestan that their retreat was cut off by British ships and that they had no choice but to submit to the Fars government.[70]

Meanwhile, Sheikh Hasan Nasuri, who apparently had good relations with the governors of Bastak and Lar, was able to persuade the *beglerbegi* of Lar to order Sheikh Mohammad b. Yusef, the chief of Nakhilu to return the strong fort of Behdeh near Gavbandi, which previously had been in the possession of Sheikh Hasan's father. Because Sheikh Mohammad b. Yusef refused to implement this order Sheikh Hasan killed him in early January 1847, while he was traveling from Lar to the coast. After the killing Sheikh Hasan immediately took possession of the fort.[71]

No punitive action was taken by the provincial or central government authorities, although the deed did not remain without consequences. Sheikh Mohammad b. Yusef was a cousin of Sheikh Ahmad, the chief of the Al Haram of Asalu, who were ancient

---

67 Saldanha, *Précis*, vol. 2, p. 200, note.
68 I have not been able to identify this village.
69 FO 248/129, Hennell to Sheil, 11 January 1847.
70 FO 248/129, Hennell to Sheil, 11 January 1847.
71 FO 248/129, Major Hennell to Sheil, 9 January 1847; Najmabadi, "The Arab Presence," p. 138. Qal`eh Behdeh is situated in Fumestan and was guarded by 10 men. Fasa'i, *Farsnameh*, vol. 2, pp. 1521, 1622.

enemies of the Al Nasur, as discussed above. In February/March 1847, despite many earlier warnings, a naval engagement took place between Asalu vessels and those belonging to Kangan. Hennell left Bushehr on 3 April 1847 and arrived at Asalu in the evening of 7 April "to learn what the cause was of the recent collision between Asalu vessels and those belonging to Kangan. Also, to make clear to the Sheikh that we intended to enforce the agreement entered into with the governor-general of Fars for suppression of piratical activities by Persian ports." The next morning Sheikh Ahmad came aboard the sloop. Hennell "expressed his surprise and regret that despite many warnings nevertheless a naval engagement had taken place between Asalu and Kangan a few weeks earlier. Sheikh Ahmad assured me of his and his entire tribe's submission to the agreement to suppress violence at sea." Sheikh Ahmad of Asalu blamed those of Kangan for the incident. He claimed that his oldest brother Sheikh Abdollah had wanted to return to Asalu and had directed him to send some vessels to the Dashti port of Dayyir (near Kangan) to take him home. Therefore, he had sent a *baghlah* and a *batil* with a few boats, but while passing Taheri they were suddenly attacked by those of Kangan, who took two of their *baqarah*s and killed and wounded a few of his people. Major Hennell, the British Resident doubted this story very much, because Sheikh Abdollah was still with the Dashti chief and as far as he knew had no intention to return immediately to his native place. Sheikh Ahmad, however, denied that his vessels had any other objective than related, but Hennell believed that those of Asalu showing up in force before Kangan gave the first provocation, at a time when this town was threatened by a large Dashti force, which suggests that there was collusion between the Chiefs of Asalu and Dashti. Given that those of Asalu got the worse of it during the naval engagement and had some people killed and wounded, besides the *baqarah* being captured, Hennell did not think it necessary to press this issue further. To make clear to Sheikh Ahmad that the British intended to enforce the agreement entered into with the governor-general of Fars for suppression of piratical activities by inhabitants of Iranian ports he made a formal point of it to remind Sheikh Ahmad under which condition the governor-general had forgiven him the payment of 402 *tumans* and to give an *eltezamnameh* that he would see to it that his people would not engage in such violent activities.[72]

Sheikh Ahmad submitted that Sheikh Shahin after having spent 40 days in chains had been mulcted of 200 *tumans* by Rashid Khan Sartip on account of the piracy committed by the people of Khirrah on Hajji Yaqub's vessel last year. Rashid Khan had been sent from Shiraz with a force of soldiers to execute a royal command ordering the punishment and arrest of those responsible for the piracy. Sheikh Ahmad promised Hennell to provide him with satisfactory proof of Rashid Khan Sartip's illegal exaction of 200 *tumans*. If this were true, Hennell reported, it would be injustice itself to demand that the chief of Asalu pay to the Iranian authorities twice for the same offense. Hennell promised to report the matter to Sheil, the British Minister in Tehran and to the governor-general of Fars.[73] Hennell kept his word and informed Hoseyn Khan, about the money illegally taken by Rashid Khan.[74]

Finally, after much hesitation and reluctance, Sheikh Ahmad signed the *eltezamnameh* on 8 April 1847, in which he stated that neither he nor his people would engage in

---

72 FO 248/129, Hennell to Sheil, 9 April 1847.
73 FO 248/129, Hennell to Sheil, 9 April 1847.
74 FO 248/129, Hennell to govern-general Shiraz 12 May 1847.

maritime violence. Sheikh Ahmad took the sealing of the document seriously as he said that he immediately had to warn his people at Biddah, Bahrain and Kenn (Kish) of this engagement entered into.[75] Hennell further reported that with the means available to the Residency he would hold the Sheikhs of Asalu and Nakhilu to their bond promise.[76]

Sheikh Ahmad also discussed with Hennell the death of his cousin Sheikh Mohammad b. Yusuf, chief of Nakhilu, who had been killed at the instigation of the chief of Kangan. After the murder, the latter had occupied the island of Bu Sho`eyb by force. He put out feelers to Hennell, by stating that supposing that the governor of Fars would appoint him chief of the island in stead of his cousin how would the British view this? Hennell replied that there would be time enough to reflect on this matter when a communication of that nature would arrive. Sheikh Ahmad then told him that he actually had been appointed chief of the island of Sho`eyb and that Hoseyn Khan, the governor of Fars, had written a letter to the Resident asking for his aid. Hennell said that he was unable to answer such a question until he had received a request of that nature from the governor of Fars. Sheikh Ahmad then left saying that he would come to Bushehr to see him to deliver this letter. The debt cancellation of 402 *tumans* must have been very welcome news to Sheikh Ahmad and an incentive, be it a temporary one, to show good behavior. Two days before Hennel's arrival the Company Schooner *Mahi* had arrived at Asalu to collect 50 *tumans* due to the British in connection with another case of indemnity. When Hennell arrived only 20 *tumans* had been received, but seeing that this was due to poverty (being unable to collect more) and not to opposition to the British claim Hennell contended himself by reminding the Sheikh that he had to bring the remainder with him on his visit to Bushehr. The poverty of the people of Asalu at that time was due to lack of rain, so that their crops had failed and even with their low consumption the price of grain had risen one-third higher compared with prices at Bushehr. Under those circumstances, Hennell argued, he could only expect the British claim to be paid in small amounts at irregular intervals.[77]

Conflict with Charak

Although the conflict between Kangan and Asalu seemingly had been settled for the moment, conflicts arose with other Hula groups, in particular with those of Charak. In fact, over time insecurity along the Iranian coast in general increased. In September 1849, Sheikh Mohammad, deputy governor of Kangan, reported to Hennell that his people had taken in a cargo of wheat and cash. While they were en route to Lengeh the *ghonchah* was attacked near Kish and plundered of everything. This act of maritime violence took place at the express order of Sheikh Hasan b. Abdollah, the chief of the Al Ali, based on the pretense that an inhabitant of Taheri living on his island had a claim on those of Kangan. Hennell wrote to Sheikh Hasan b. Abdollah that such behavior was not acceptable, as a claim or enmity towards another should not result in the use of violence to prevent a boat from pursuing its normal activity. The Residency (*sarkar*) would not permit this,

---

75 FO 248/129, Hennell to Sheil, 9 April 1847; FO 248/129, *Eltezamnameh* Sheikh Ahmad b. Kholfan of Asalu dated 8 April 1847/ 22 Rabi II. For the Persian text, see Appendix 2.
76 FO 248/129, Hennell to Sheil, 11 January 1847. For the Persian text, see Appendix 3.
77 FO 248/129, Hennell to Sheil, 9 April 1847.

and, therefore, on receipt of this letter the Sheikh either had to return all property to their owners or send him a reply so that he might take the necessary steps to rectify this matter.[78] Sheikh Hasan b. Abdollah replied that those of Kangan had been the first to commit irregularities in his territory. They had seized a small boat from Dayyir that came to Kish and after having exacted 200 *qrans* from it had released it. He had written to Hennell about this, who allegedly had not replied. Later the Nasuris seized another boat that was going to Taheri and that belonged to the Al Ali. Because of these acts of violence perpetrated against him and his people, Sheikh Hasan b. Abdollah had ordered to seize the boat about which Hennell complained. The wheat in the boat, which belonged to a Bushehri the Sheikh claimed to have restored to the owner. He only retained that part of the property that belonged to the people of Kangan. He ended his letter by stating: "If you decide justly against the people of that place we will abide by your decision, as we are under your authority."[79]

Despite Sheikh Hasan b. Abdollah's claim that he considered himself to be under British authority the issue of indemnity was not resolved, despite follow up demands by both Hennell and his successor Captain Kemball to show that the Residency had not forgotten about this issue. It was only in October 1858 that Kemball's successor, Captain Felix Jones, made a tour along the Iranian coast with the intention, among other things, to settle this affair. He visited Charak, where he met with the Sheikh's brother Abdol-Rahman. Jones demanded the settlement of the claim for the plundering of the *khonchah* belonging to Sheikh Hasan b. Jabbara of Kangan.[80] Under pressure, Sheikh Abdol-Rahman b. Abdollah b. Abdol-Rahman signed a bond in which he stated the following: "I give my word to Capt. Jones that in 6 months I will make good the 6,000 *qrans* that he demands on account of the plunder of the *ghonchah* of "Ali b. Nakdes" by the people of Kish (Ges) some 9 years ago. If I fail to do so Capt. Jones is free to take any steps to bring about the recuperation of this sum, i.e. permission to take any of their vessels."[81] Jones at the time of his visit to Charak also wrote a letter to the chiefs and people of the Bu Sumeyt and other lawless inhabitants of Kish who were warned not to repeat their violent behavior. He would seek out and find any individual who disobeyed and fled the island.[82]

After his return to Bushehr, Captain Jones received a letter from Sheikh Hasan b. Abdollah, in which he asserted that he was not aware of this and other claims by the Sheikh of Kangan and he declared them to be false. He wrote: "We are people under authority and can commit no disorder at sea." Therefore, he and his people were careful in their dealings and actions. As to the claim that his people had seized a boat belonging to Kangan, Sheikh Hasan b. Abdollah wrote: "let him prove it, and if proven right we will be forthcoming. I hope you will not believe the report of our enemies." To make the point who was the real injured party the Al Ali Sheikh reported the fate of a *baghlah* that belonged to him. While en route to Basra it was driven by storm to Kalatu, where it came at anchor. Then 3 *baghlah*s came with a crew of 50 who attacked and seized the *baghlah*

---

78 FO 248/183, Hennell to Sheikh Hasan b. Abdollah of Charrak 9 October 1849/21 Zu'l-Qa`deh 1265.
79 FO 248/183, Sheikh Hasan b. Abdollah to Hennell, 1 November 1849/23 Zu'l-Hijja 1265.
80 FO 248/183, Sheikh Hasan b. Abdollah chief of Charrak to Felix Jones, n.d. rec. 25/10/1858
81 FO 248/183, Bond given by Abdol-Rahman brother of Sheikh Hasan b. Abdollah to Felix Jones dated 1 June 1858/18 Shavval 1274.
82 FO 248/183, Extract of a report of the proceedings of Captain Felix Jones.

and drew it ashore, while the crew was confined. This was done by Hasan b. Jabbara's orders and was further evidence who was the real perpetrator of maritime violence.[83]

According to the British Agent in Lengeh indeed a Charaki vessel had been driven ashore near Kalatu and people from Shivu, who were under Sheikh Hasan b. Jabbara sent news to him in Gavbandi, from where he ordered to seize it. The boat was put ashore, the cargo unloaded, its captain sent to Gavbandi, while the sailors were released and returned to Charak. Having been informed of this event by Sheikh Hasan b. Abdollah, the Lengeh Agent sent someone to Gavbandi with the advise to release the captain, cargo and vessel and to commit no further disorder at sea. In reply Sheikh Hasan b. Jabbara wrote that the Sheikh of Charak had seized two of his men on land, inhabitants of Baada[?], and that 8 years ago when Yusuf b. Mobarak was chief of Naband he had seized a *ghonchah* at Kish belonging to his dependents with a value of 3,000 *qran*s. If Sheikh Hasan b. Abdollah released the two men and returned the value of the vessel he would release the seized captain, vessel and its cargo. The Agent warned the Charak chief not to cause any disorder.[84]

In January 1859, Sheikh Hasan b. Jabbara acceded to British pressure and released the vessel, its captain and cargo. Captain Jones, therefore, considered it necessary to ensure that the chief of Charak would respond in kind, if need be by force. He asked the Shah's government to give him permission to exact compensation in its name.[85] However, Tehran did not give its permission, and in fact, it was totally uninterested in what happened in the Persian Gulf. This despite the fact that in the first half of 1859, "almost every town and tribe is by land in hostilities with each other, and here also instigated by the Chief of Amulgavine, who has become restless and a patron of those desirous of exciting the public distemper on both shores." In spite of these developments, Jones noted that the Iranian government seemed to be totally blind to the rapine and bloodshed on its own littoral, because it did nothing whatsoever to keep order and did not react to all representations to take action.[86]

The situation at Charak had taken a turn for the worse. Both its Sheikh and its people were known for their "ill disposition towards all other tribes in their neighborhood." At that time it was beleaguered on all sides by those who had suffered the rapacity of the late Sheikh Hasan b. Abdollah, who recently died of cholera. A year had passed since Captain Jones's visit and payment still had not taken place. The Resident ascribed Charak's indifference to the presence of British war ships in the Persian Gulf to the apathy of the Persian government, as his remonstrations to the Legation in Tehran had no effect, in fact there was no reply. As a result, acts of maritime violence increased, because the coastal population of the Iranian littoral realized that without action by the government of Iran the hands of the British were tied. The Resident therefore, had to listen to their claim that Charak had no money, as it had spent it on defense against those on which it preyed upon. The new Sheikh, Abdol-Rahman b. Abdollah, offered an unseaworthy *baghlah* as

---

83 FO 248/183, Sheikh Hasan b. Abdollah chief of Charrak to Felix Jones, n.d. rec. 25/10/1858.
84 FO 248/183, Ahmed Moollah Hussein, Lingeh agent to Jones, 15 October 1858/7 Rabi I 1275.
85 FO 248/176, Jones to William Doria, charge d'affaires, 2 February 1859 plus Persian letter from Hasan b. Jabbara and its translation, stating that on receipt of Jones's letter he released the captain and vessel; now he awaits the Charak chief to release his men and pay compensation to show that your government give realm justice and to prevent further disorder.
86 FO 248/176, Capt. Jones to Willim Doria, charge d'affaires, 14 June 1859.

security appealed for further delay and clemency, because the act was done by his brother. He made further efforts to avoid compliance and the Resident, given his limited power, had to give in, and allowed a delay of the bond till autumn of 1859.[87]

On 21 May 1859 the Resident anchored at Asalu, where recently passing vessels had been plundered. The acts of plunder included that of a *baqarah* belonging to Rashid b. Mohammad, whose cargo was taken Jaber b. Rajab of Naband. Rashid b. Mohammad complained to the Harami Sheikh's representative, Seyf b. Abdollah, who ordered Jaber b. Rajab to make full restitution. Although the latter complied with the order, the goods returned were 150 *qran*s and 19 German crowns, some coffee and frankincense short. Another case concerned that of a vessel from Taheri en route to Lengeh, which, due to winds, had to shelter at Tibi. Sheikh Ahmad b. Khalfan's dependents plundered everything on aboard, representing a total value of 1,000 *qran*s. Captain Jones exhorted Sheikh Ahmad that he should forbid his subjects to perpetrate such acts. To put pressure on the Harami chief he wrote that he would seek redress in Tehran, so that he might be punished if he didn't indemnify the claimants.[88]

For without express orders from Tehran, Jones could hardly demand indemnity from Sheikh Ahmad b. Khalfan as he lived in Iranian territory. The Asalu chief was sorry about what he heard, but claimed innocence as he was away at Shiraz when all those plunderings happened. If he had been there it would not have happened, or so he claimed, and to show his sincerity he offered to make good the indemnity demanded for the plundered vessels. However, as there was uncertainty about what had been taken from the vessel he asked that an inquiry be made as to this question. He claimed to have sequestered all arms and property that he had been able to ascertain, and if proof was given he would satisfy the Resident's demand if something was missing among the sequestered goods. This seemed fair and more than Jones expected, but later he learned that the Sheikh and his people intended to flee from the coast to Bu Sho`eyb to avoid having to pay arrears to an Iranian official who was then in their neighborhood. Therefore, the Asalu Sheikh had shown himself very conciliatory to the Resident who took a bond from him.[89]

Second sack of Kangan – 1858

Meanwhile, the future looked promising for the Al Nasur. In early 1852, the governor-general of Fars, Firuz Mirza, had mounted a military expedition in the Garmsir to make the various chiefs pay their arrears, which had been very lucrative for him and his high-ranking executive officers. In July 1852, the British Resident in Bushehr reported that had heard that in gifts (*pishkesh*) and arrears Firuz Mirza collected twice the normal amount of revenue. He further reported that he had learnt that local sheikhs on the Iranian littoral had been confirmed in their posts by Firuz Mirza, although all of them were subordinate to either Mostafa Khan of Bastak or to Sheikh Hasan Khan of Kangan, which was quite a boost for the latter's standing.[90] Therefore, in 1851, when Mostafa Qoli Khan of Bastak

---

87 FO 248/176, "Extract From Your Report" section on Charak.
88 FO 248/176, Letter from Jones to Sheikh Ahmad b. Khalfan re the plundering by Naband and Assalu re passing vessels.
89 FO 248/176, "Extract From Your Report" (section on Asalu).
90 FO 248/113, Capt. Kemball, Resident to Sheil, 14 July 1852.

was supporting Mirza Na'im, the vizier of Fars, he was not alone in doing so, because he ordered the chief of Charak and other coastal chiefs to assist Mirza Na'im to put down the troubles in Lar.[91]

Since the sack and occupation of Kangan by Dashti in 1844, the port had remained a bone of contention between the Khan of Dashti and his neighbors in the south, resulting in another Dashti attack on Kangan in 1847.[92] Thereafter, it did not remain quiet between the two sides. In 1856, Sheikh Hasan of Gavbandi had destroyed the Dashti village of Bardestan, while he also since the sack of Kangan had twice burnt Dayyir. To protect his port, Heydar Khan of Dashti built there "a large fort with four towers, two right-angled, one six and one ten sides." He also built a fort on the ruins of the village of Bardestan, which fort had "one or two rooms overloaded with guildings and painting of women drinking wine."[93] Both sides, it would seem, were only looking for an excuse to attack the other once again. Such an opportunity presented itself around 1858, when Sheikh Hasan Nasuri of Gavbandi put the *kadkhuda* of Kangan to death on suspicion of an intrigue to hand over the place to the Khan of Dashti. In reaction, the latter "attacked and destroyed Kangan, ravaging the coast and destroying all the date-groves as far as Taheri."[94] A contemporary anonymous Persian source ascribed the attack by Jamal Khan and Hoseyn Khan Dashti to jealousy.[95]

After the attack the Dashti Khans induced people to settle at nearby Bardistan in Dashti territory.[96] Referring to the year 1857, Khormuji mentions the desolate state of the port.[97] Stiffe writes that in 1859 Kangan was totally abandoned and that Sheikh Hasan Nasuri had gone to the island of Sheikh Sho'eyb and only returned many years later. According to others, Sheikh Hasan Nasuri went to Gavbandi.[98] It was, however, Sheikh Mazkur b. Jabbara of Kangan who had sought asylum at Sheikh Sho'eyb and its population made him their chief.[99] Very likely, quite a few of those fleeing from Kangan went to Lengeh, where they settled or joined those already settled in a quarter known as Kangani; its inhabitants were all sailors.[100] The British Navy in the Persian Gulf reported in October 1860 that all was quiet on the coast and that reportedly Sheikh Hasan b. Jabbara was at Lengeh.[101]

---

91 FO 248/146, Hennell to Sheil, 15 March 1851.
92 FO 248/129, Hennell to Sheil, 9 April 1847.
93 Also, the chief of Dashti's new and large fort in Khormuj, his residence, had rooms that were richly decorated in the style of Shiraz; in addition to many mirrors, "gilding and painting of flowers, nightingales, wild animals, and Persian beauties, on a panel of a door in one of the chief rooms is the double-headed eagle of Russia." Colville, "Land Journey," p. 37
94 Adamec, *Historical Gazetteer*, vol. 3, p. 387.
95 Anonymous, "Brief Account," p. 185. Colville, "Land Journey," p. 37 calls him Jamil Khan, chief of a subdistrict who had his residence in Kaki, which was twice the size of Khormuj (which had 150 mud and stones houses), but not so well built. In 1866, he was building a new fort.
96 Waver, "Report," p. 180. According to Adamec, *Historical Gazetteer*, vol. 3, p. 387, "The Khans are taking great care to improve it. Many of the people of Kongun have settled here." C.M. MacGregor, *A contribution towards the better knowledge of the topography, ethnology, resources & history of Persia*. Calcutta, 1871, p. 65.
97 Khormuji, *Haqayeq al-Akhbar-e Naseri*, p. 232.
98 Waver, "Report," pp.186-90.
99 FO 248/189, Inhabitants Bu Sho'eyb to Jones 9 February 1860/17 Rajab 1276.
100 Floor, *Bandar-e Lengeh*, pp. 6-7.
101 FO 248/189, Letter from Chief Naval Officer commanding the Persian Gulf squadron to Jones 26 October 1860.

Kangan was not the only target, because Taheri was also attacked on 3 January 1860 (9 Jomadi II 1276). Sheikh Hatem b. Jabbara Nasuri commandeered a *ghonchah* that had just arrived, because he, his family, and servants wanted to flee from the enemy whose attack was imminent. When the boat was fully laden and ready to sail a number of vessels from Asalu suddenly appeared and took Taheri. They plundered the boat, which together with its gear was destroyed resulting in a loss of 4,000 *qrans* (including 345 *qrans* of the boat's cargo). All of them were taken prisoner by those of Asalu, who had made common cause with those of Dashti.[102] What is interesting is that, according to Sheikh Seyf b. Abdollah of Asalu (who had succeeded Sheikh Ahmad b. Khalfan), the attack on Taheri was the result of the recent adoption by the government of Iran of a policy to oppose tribe against tribe, which, according to Captain Jones, only had led to indiscriminate mischief. Likewise, when Jones raised with Sheikh Seyf b. Abdollah his involvement with the plundering of a vessel from Khark and the disturbance of the peace of the inhabitants of Bu Sho`eyb by those of Asalu and Naband, the Sheykh declared that everything was done at the orders of Iranian officials who had their own objectives. What these were Jones didn't know, but he concluded that it led to the detriment of the welfare of Taheri and anarchy followed on the coast, which was "as fatal to friends as to foes."[103] Likewise the people of Bu Sho`eyb mentioned that Sheikh Mazkur had fled "from the Persians." Moreover, they wrote that they were oppressed by the coastal people and had no means "to keep them far from us." Therefore, they sought the Resident's protection expressing their trust in him. However, they wanted something in return for their trust it appeared, because they informed Jones that they had some property in Naband that Sheikh Ahmad b. Khalfan took from them. Because they knew that the British tried to suppress any maritime violence they 'innocently' informed him that they wanted to retaliate by seizing the vessel from them, but had not done so until they would get Jones's permission. They clearly wanted Jones to do the heavy lifting for them.[104]

In his report to the British Minister in Tehran, Captain Jones commented that the shah was indifferent to the disasters that had befallen the coastal people and had declined British cooperation. As a result, anarchy prevailed on the littoral as well as insecurity to trade and both trends signaled the defeat of "our humane policy." He further observed that Iranian disregard and apathy would eventually hurt British interests. Because, if disorders were not controlled their number would increase and so far only British policy has kept it so. A show of HM ships would deter Arab chiefs from committing irregularities, or so he believed.[105] The Iranian government twice appointed a commission to report on the sack of Kangan, but on both occasions the Commissioner was bought over by the Khan of Dashti and no result followed."[106] The result of these actions was that Kangan was made subordinate to a central government appointed governor. In 1860, Tahmasp Mirza Mo'ed al-Dowleh was appointed governor-general of Fars and he appointed his son Abdol-Baqi

---

102 FO 248/189, Statement of oath before Sheikh Abdollah b. Ebrahim Sunni mojtahed of Bushehr by Nakhoda Feerooz of the ghoncha of Mohammad b. Homud Taheri.

103 FO 248/189, Jones to Rawlinson, Tehran 4 March 1860.

104 FO 248/189, Inhabitants Bu Sho`eyb to Jones, 9 February 1860/17 Rajab 1276 (one page with the names of the signatories).

105 FO 248/189, Jones to Alison. 15 September 1860; FO 248/249, Jones to Soltan Morad Mirza Ehtesham al-Saltaneh, govenor of Dashtestan, 10 Jomadi II 1276/2 January 1860 (proposal to cooperate with the British naval squadron to reduce the violence on the coast of Fars and make its small ports thrive again).

106 Adamec, *Historical Gazeteer*, vol. 3, p. 387.

Mirza as governor of Bushehr, Dashti, Dashtestan, Gallehdar, Asir, Alamarvdasht, Kangan, and Asuliyeh.[107] It would appear, however, that these districts were subcontracted to local chiefs, such as Kangan to Sheikh Hasan Nasuri.

THIRD SACK OF KANGAN – 1862

Despite the crushing defeat suffered at the hands of the Dashtis and those of Asalu in 1858, Sheikh Hasan b. Jabbara assumed an aggressive stance to regain his position. At that time the government of Iran was interfering in the situation in Bahrain and even contemplated invading the island. Apparently, Sheikh Hasan Nasuri, who had good contacts with Bahrain offered his services to the government of Iran. According to Sheikh Seyf b. Abdollah of Asalu, Sheikh Hasan b. Jabbara told Ehtesham al-Dowleh, the governor-general Fars that assistance in troops and boats were needed and that all those of Bahrain residing in Iranian territory would have to return to Bahrain, i.e. all those that wore the *Mahurramath* (cloth headdress) such as Khalifah b. Abdollah Ebrahim b. Yusuf al-Monsharee and all merchants. But, according the Sheikh of Asalu, Sheikh Hasan asked the Iranian authorities to do things that were beyond his power to perform, and having received permission Sheikh Hasan Nasuri began to maltreat the Haramis contrary to prior usage. A *baqarah*, a small vessel of 15 tons, from Lengeh, whose *kadkhoda* and crew were from Asalu, were sailing from Asalu to Dayyir when a vessel belonging to the Al Ahneeyat seized it on the high sea and maltreated the crew, because they were from Asalu and friendly with those of Lengeh. Moreover, Sheikh Hasan Nasuri sent troops to take Asalu and seeing a *baghlah* of theirs to the north sent a *baqarah* to take it. Sheikh Seyf's people ran their vessel ashore and the pursuers took it. While the Haramis were preparing to leave Asalu for Dayyir, Sheikh Hasan's people followed them in four boats and although they had women and children with them the Nasuris constantly fired at the fleeing Haramis and only stopped when they were tired. They also suffered injury as the Haramis defended themselves. He, therefore, told Jones that if Britain wanted the Haramis to keep the maritime peace they would obey if Britain would revenge their injuries. When the Haramis left Asalu three *mashwash* remained behind; these were plundered. Therefore, Sheikh Seyf wanted Jones's permission to retaliate against the Nasuris. If not, Britain which had control over the sea had to demand compensation for their loss and punish their oppressors.[108]

At that time there were quite some occurrences of maritime violence along the Iranian coast. In October 1860 four such events alone were reported. (i) An Omani *baqarah* was plundered off Tibin Bandar by a Tangesir boat; all cargo was taken; the crew swam ashore; (ii) Four slaves took an Abu Dhabi vessel and went to Chiru whose Sheikh took the slaves and the vessel; (iii) Sheikh Hasan b. Jabbara of Kangan was engaged in attacking the fort of Suffur[109] on the Iranian coast in which the people of Tibin had take refuge. He attacked by land, while he directed an ally from Bahrain, named Khalil, who was sent from Bahrain in the boat of Ali b. Khalifa to fire on the fort from sea. Sheikh Hasan apparently had sufficient funds and/or equipment, because he placed a gun in this

---

107 Fasa'i, *Farsnameh*, vol. 1, p. 823.
108 FO 248/189, Sheikh Seyf b. Abdollah of the al-Haram tribe of Asalu to Capt. Felix Jones, 12 September 1860/25 Safar 1277.
109 Probably *qal`eh-ye Saffar*.

boat, and (iv) Elsewhere, the Al Ahneeyat tribe [the port of Kangan] seized a *baqarah* of Nakkee Bushehri and took her to Taheri where it was drawn ashore and plundered.[110]

Despite his aggressive actions, Sheikh Hasan b. Jabbara was also at the receiving end of maritime violence. In October 1860, a *baghlah* belonging to "Jaber Jassen al-Basateen" laden with 110 bags of dates at anchor at Nakhl Hashel was seized by the Al Haram tribe and plundered. He asked Captain Jones redress for this outrage.[111] Sheikh Hasan clearly did not like this development, because in early January 1861 Sheikh Hasan wrote a letter to Captain Jones, alerting him that the people of the Harami tribe in Dayyir, who were under Sheikh Seyf, together with the people of Dashti had laid an ambush for 2 boats, one belonging to the chief of Qeshm, the other to some other port. He reported that it was their intention to take them and equip them with canon and armed men, and then to send them with mischievous intent into the direction of Mayalu. Sheikh Hasan argued that the Dashti people should be brought to account and he was counting on the British to do so.[112] Not only the Nasuris were a target of Harami violence, but also innocent traders such as an Indian subject, "Congoo Hindoo Multanee" from whom Sheikh Seyf of Naband seized 11 baskets of dates, 30 *man* of madder, sugar and piece goods on 27 March 1861. He then went to Nakhilu and Mogam, where he was robbed by Sheikh Hatem (Khatum), Sheikh Saqr (Sugur) and Sheikh Abdollah of 11 basket of dates and piece goods. Continuing his journey to Bu Sho`eyb Island, Sheikh Mazkur, brother of Sheikh Hasan of Kangan, plundered 50 baskets of dates and piece goods from him. Arriving in Lengeh he complained to the British Agent, who wrote to the Sheikhs concerned calling on them to restore the stolen goods. The Sheikhs wrote that "Congo" had to come to them and receive his goods in person. He then went, spent 100 *qran*s in cash and bought a *baqarah* that went to pieces on the way. On arrival he received nothing from the Sheikhs and he left empty handed.[113]

Sheikh Mazkur took his new position of Sheikh of Bu Sho`eyb seriously, certainly to amass goods, because when on 11 September 1861 a person absconded from the island of Bu Sho`eyb and went to Chiru, Sheikh Mazkur went in pursuit but those of Chiru refused to give him up. Mazkur returned to Sho`eyb Island, seized Hilal the father the absconder and branded him to get money from him, and failing to do so he plundered his house and left the island. Sheikh Saqr (Suggur) with Hilal and a party from Jazeh (Jizza) and Chiru went in pursuit. They overtook him near the shore in a *baqarah* and a fight ensued. Sheikh Mazkur struck first and 4-5 of the pursuers were killed and 15 wounded. The boats of the fighting parties drifted ashore and Sheikh Mazkur fled on foot.[114]

As Captain Felix Jones had foreseen, the anarchy and disorder in the ports on the Iranian coast, which he repeatedly had brought to the attention of the authorities, assumed a most appalling form in September 1862. The Dashti tribe again devastated the territory of the chief of Kangan. "Villages were destroyed, date plantations, teeming with fruit, have been ruined. Houses have been burnt. At Mayaloo and Tahiree, minor seaport towns, defenceless women and children have been cruelly butchered." The Chief of Kangan's

---

110 FO 248/189, Report Agent Lengeh October 1860.
111 FO 248/189, Letter from Sheikh Hasan b. Jabbara received on 11 October 1860 by Jones.
112 FO 248/198, Sheikh Hasan b. Jabbara to Capt. Felix Jones, rec. 22 January 1861.
113 FO 248/198, Congoo Hindoo Multanee to Jones, 16 May 1861/15 Zu'l-Qa`deh 1277.
114 FO 248/198, Mohammad Bushehri, Agent Lengeh to Capt. Felix Jones. 18 September 1861/ 12 Rabi` I 1278.

brother with some retainers, their wives and families, who trying to escape by boat via the sea, were chased by those of Asalu, who had espoused the Dashti side, overtook them and after having shot two of them took the rest captive and brought them to Asalu. Captain Jones considered this behavior "worse than the barbarous treatment given by the Tangestanis to shipwrecked boats and the maritime violence by other groups." Therefore, he argued, "there is a need to put an end to such atrocious activities, or else piracy would be revived. The swift and decisive action taken against Arab chiefs committing maritime violence stands in stark contrast what we allow their kinsman on the Iranian coasts do and will hurt our reputation of impartial justice. Now I can only reports such deeds, as I did to the kargozar. I hope you agree with its tenor." A number of escapees of the Dashti horror came to Bushehr, where they still were, "naked and hungry," dependent on the food charity of the Sunnis of Bushehr, who but recently owned valuable date plantations and property. Other refugees have fled to Bahrain.[115]

The Iranian authorities seemed not to have been greatly shocked by these atrocities. Captain Disbrowe, the officiating Resident, wrote to the *kargozar* of Bushehr about the atrocities done by the Dashtis on those of Kangan. He stated upfront that he didn't want to interfere in internal Iranian affairs, but he noted that this violence now also extended to the maritime sphere and that the Shah like the Queen favored the suppression of violence at sea. Caught between those of Dashti to the north and of Asalu to the south the people of Taheri and Mayalu people tried to escape by sea. Then they "were pursued, attacked, seized, and carried captives" to Asalu. Given the interest of both states to suppress this kind of violence he expressed the hope that the *kargozar* would obtain the necessary farmans to punish the offenders of these atrocities.[116]

Such orders did not come. The *kargozar* merely confirmed receipt of Disbrowe's letter and informed him that he would report the Resident's grief and expressions of good will towards the government of Iran to the Ministers.[117] For a few years Kangan remained a heap of ruins, to the material advantage of the neighboring Dashti port of Dayyir.[118] An anonymous Persian report written in 1865 states, "Bunder Congoon was once well inhabited."[119] Although Kangan formally was under an appointee from Shiraz, this did not mean that the local Sheikh was no longer in charge, for by 1865, Sheikh Hassan Khan, aided by the Iranian government, was "trying to put the port into order again."[120] Sheikh Hasan resumed his function of *zabet*, i.e. that of tax collector and district administrator. In practice this meant that locally his authority basically remained in tact. Also, the central government was still far away and its reach was short and intermittent. Therefore, the old local problems remained unresolved and festered.

---

115 FO 248/206, Capt. H. F. Disbrowe, Officiating Resident to Alison, Tehran 3 September 1862; see also FO 248/206, Bushehr to Bombay 30/09/1862 reporting the arrival of refugees in Bahrain.

116 FO 248/206, Disbrowe to Mirza Mehdi Khan, kargozar 25 August1862/28 Safar 1279 plus Persian text, see Appendix 5.

117 FO 248/206, Mirza Mehdi Khan to Disbrowe 29 Safar/26 August 1862 plus Persian text, see Appendix 6.

118 Colville, "Land Journey," p. 37 ("The prosperity of Dayyir dates from the destruction of Kangan 7 years ago"); Adamec, *Historical Gazetteer*, vol. 3, p. 387.

119 Anonymous, "Brief Account," p. 185.

120 Anonymous, "Brief Account," p. 185.

The Fourth Sack of Kangan – 1867

Apart from the threat of those of Dashti, the people of Kangan feared most those of the Al Haram of Asaluyeh or Asalu, who were allied with those of Dashti.[121] Since more than one century there was enmity and bloodshed between the Nasur and the Al Haram of Asalu. In 1866, Sheikh Hasan Khan Nasuri marched from Taheri to Gavbandi. Between Gavbani and Asaluyeh, but close to the latter, there was fort Maleki, where he arrived at sunset and made ready for prayer. At that moment his horse bolted and his servants were dispersed trying to get it; one Asalu man reported this to Sheikh Ebrahim Khan Al Haram who sent some men to capture Sheikh Mohammad Khan Kangani. They took him to Asaluyeh where he was killed. He was succeeded by his younger brother Sheikh Mazkur Kangani, who in 1867 with levies from Gallehdar and Gavbandi and government soldiers and guns besieged Aasaluyeh. After having taken it he killed Sheikh Ebrahim as well as Sheikh Seyf Khan and Sheikh Mohammad Khan, both paternal cousins of Ebrahim, in addition to all Al Haram males and destroyed Asaluyeh.[122] Ebrahim Harami had tried to flee dressed as a wife, but he was captured. Sheikh Mazkur told him: "my brother was a man when he was killed and you're not and killed him."[123] Those from Asaluyeh who were at sea escaped the massacre and allegedly only returned in 1879. In that year Sheikh Ahmad Khan Asaluyeh Al Haram, son of Sheikh Seyf, a paternal cousin of Sheikh Ebrahim brought the scattered Al Haram together and settled at Asalu and became its *zabet*.[124]

There was, of course, no government retaliation for this atrocity, as government troops had participated in the massacre. However, it seems that the Khan of Dashti took offense, or saw an opportunity, for it is reported that in 1867 the Khan of Dashti suddenly took and sacked Kangan, which had almost 700 households. He uprooted its houses, walls, trees, and date groves due to enmity that previously already existed between them, so that, according to Khormuji, "now some 40 years later still nobody wants to live there."[125] However, this cannot be correct. For after the fourth destruction of Kangan in 1867 the Al Nasur not only returned to the port, but Sheikh Mazkur remained governor of Kangan, which he tried to develop, and Gavbandi (plus Banak, Tombak, Ayenat, Akhtar, etc) as well as of Taheri, where he appointed his brother Sheikh Hatem as his deputy.[126]

The Dashtis and Haramis continued to attack and plunder ships that belonged to Sheikh Mazkur's subjects. In March 1869, he complained that a vessel from Dayyir, but crewed by 50 armed Haramis living in there, was cruising along the coast in search of boats belonging to Nasuri dependents and landed their booty in Naband. Sheikh Mazkur asked Colonel Pelly, the Resident via his Agent at Lengeh, whether his government had given up to protect shipping in the Persian Gulf, if so, he would take steps himself to rectify the situation. When he received no reply Sheikh Mazkur wrote again in April informing the Agent at Lengeh that a *ghonchah*, taken from Abdol Hoseyn Bahraini, with 400 men from Dayyir landed at Ayenat (Ayeenah) a.k.a. Tombak and continued to plunder his subjects. He once again asked Colonel Pelly whether the British had given up protecting

---

121 Waver, "Report," p. 189.
122 Fasa'i, *Farsnameh*, vol. 2, pp. 1462, 1525.
123 Hamidi, *Farhangnameh*, p. 59.
124 Fasa'i, *Farsnameh*, vol. 2, pp. 1525-26, 1564.
125 Mirza Ja`far Khormuji, *Haqayeq al-Akhbar-e Naseri*, ed. Hoseyn Khadivjam. Tehran: Zavvar, 1344/1967, p. 232.
126 *Administration* 1875-76, pp. 16, 20 (for a full list of places under his jurisdiction).

the shipping lanes. On 11 July 1869 the Agent at Lengeh again received a letter from Sheikh Mazkur who noted that he had not heard from him for a long time, while the Dashtis were still cruising the coast with their stolen *ghonchah* plundering his subjects, and even one large *baghlah* belonging to Sheikh Mazkur himself. Through intercession of Abdol-Fath Khan of Morbagh the vessel was returned but its cargo of barley was not. The Sheikh wanted to know whether those of Dayyir were allowed to act at liberty alone by the British, or "are all others permitted to act as they choose?" He wanted the Agent to bring this issue quickly to the notice of the Resident and to send him an answer that he was free to act as he liked or not. He preferred not to attack, but something needed to be done quickly. However, those of Dashti did not fear to be brought to account by the British, whereas he did.[127]

Problems at Charak

Kangan and Asalu were not the only districts that were in turmoil and at war at that time, but so was the so-called district of Shibkuh-e Larestan. Its chief place was Charak, and the *kalantar* or chief of the district was sometimes selected from the Hamadi and Obeydli, who lived to the west of this place, and sometimes from the people of Charak.[128] In 1869, after the death of Sheikh Soltan Obeydli, Hamad Esma`il of the Sheikh's agnate kin, took control over the entire district and Chiru and called himself Sheikh and *zabet*, and opposed the governor of Bastak and neglected *divani* matters, i.e. he did not pay his taxes. As this district was part of Hajji Mostafa Khan of Bastak's governorate he wrote that Hamad Esma`il had to pay the regular taxes that he had totally neglected to do. If these taxes would have been paid Hajji Mostafa Khan probably would have acquiesced in the new situation, as is clear from what follows. However, this changed when Sheikh Mohammad Sheikh Abdol-Rasul Obeydli came to complain in Bastak about Mohammad Esma`il saying that he was erecting fortifications in Chiru and Khalafani. Moreover, he considered himself an independent governor and was not going to pay any taxes. Mostafa Khan then sent his brother Abu'l-Fath Khan with 1,000 *tofangchi*s to Shibkuh and with help of the Hamadi and the Marzuqi Sheikhs, in addition to other neighboring sheikhs, he attacked Chiru and took it after a short fight. Mohammad Esma`il fled with many men to Fort Omm al-Hogum in the direction of Khalafani which was besieged. After some fighting he surrendered and paid his taxes. Then Abu'l-Fath raised the siege and returned to Bastak. However, after some time Mohammad Esma`il again took Chiru and some other villages from Sheikh Mohammad and Sheikh Abdol-Rasul and the trouble began all over again. Then Qavam al-Molk, governor of Lar, with an army arrived, and the governor of Bastak informed him about the rebellion. In 1870, Qavam al-Molk then marched with his army to Ashkenan via Tang-e Ahlan and the Barand pass to Shibkuh and asked Hajji Mostafa Khan, the governor of Bastak to join him to lay siege to Omm al-Hogum or Omm al-Hokum, at one *farsakh* from Nakhl-e Khalafan. Khalafan was the

---

127 FO 248/255, Bottomway, Ass. Resident to Pelly, Resident. Bassidore 26 May 1869; Ibid., Report Agent Lingah 26 March 1869/12 Zu'l-Hijjah; Ibid., Agent Lengeh to Resident 7 April 1869; Sheikh Mazkur of Naband to Agent Lengeh, 31 March 1869; Ibid., Sheikh Mazkur to Agent Lengeh 24 April 1869; Sheikh Mazkur to Agent Lengeh, rec. 11 July 1867 plus Persian letter, see Appendix 7. In the translations Sheikh Mazkur is in all cases mistakenly referred to as governor of Bastak.

128 Fasa'i, *Farsnameh*, vol. 2, p. 1519.

Qalat-e Sorkh

old residence of the Obeydli Sheikhs, which Sheikh Hamad Obeydli had constructed as his own refuge and rose up with his cousin Sheikh Mohammad Sheikh Abdol-Rasul and took control over the entire Obeydli district. Mohammad Esma`il and his men erected barricades in high narrow places and opposed the advance of Qavam al-Molk's army through the pass. As a result, Qavam al-Molk had to withdraw with his army to the village of Amiran. From the other side Mostafa Khan with Arab and Iranian chiefs had marched to Shibkuh and took control over Chiru and Obeydli villages and also took Khalafan.[129]

This and other events had consequences for the distribution of power among the various Hulas groups. Sheikh Mazkur Al Nasur held the entire coastal area from Banak to Nakhilu and the island of Bu Sho`eyb. However, Shatvar was not included and together with Jazeh and Basatin remained under unknown local chiefs. Chiru, Ras Mansura and Henderabi island remained in the hands of Sheikh Abdollah b. Mohammad. A separate group was formed by Kalat that was under the Bani Hamad, Jirzah[130] under Sheikh Abdollah Hamadi, Tavuneh under the Albin Beshi,[131] and Charak and Kish remained under the Al Ali led by Sheikh Mohammad b. Hasan. Together these places constituted the Ashkanun district which was under Ra'is Ali. Moghu and Bostaneh continued to be

---

129 Bastaki, *Tarikh-e Jahangiriyeh*, pp. 278-81.
130 This must be Gurzeh, 23 km east of Chiru.
131 I have not been able to identify this tribal group.

governed by Soltan b. Hasan of the Ali Saudan[132] tribe and with Farur island was part of the governorate of Bastak.[133]

However, this re-arrangement of power did not have the desired results. For example, in April 1875 Abdollah Musabbeh, former chief of Charak, wrote to the Agent at Lengeh, informing him that when going from Morbagh via Tavuneh on his way to Hoseyni, Mohammad b. Hasan, the then chief of Charak pursued him in a *batil* and a *baqarah* with a crew of 70-80 men. Apparently, their encounter at Laz on Bu Sho`eyb in the past, when Abdollah Musebbeh was still chief of Charak, had not gone well for Mohammad b. Hasan and this seemed to be pay-back time. Like Sheikh Mazkur a few years earlier, Sheikh Abdollah wanted to know whether the British still maintained the peace at sea, if not he would like to know as he did not lack the means to take action.[134]

Downfall of Sheikh Mazkur

Having gained more power and territory and not being interfered with by the Fars authorities, Sheikh Mazkur felt that he could return to the old ways and ignore the dictates of the central government, because the administrators of Fars were neglectful. This situation lasted until Mo`tamed al-Dowleh Hajji Farhad Mirza became governor of Fars in 1877, who wanted to put an end to what was called the 'rebellion' of chiefs such as Sheikh Mazkur Khan Kangani, Mohammad Hasan Khan, chief of Borazjan and Mohammad Taher Khan, chief of Gallehdar. Mo`tamed al-Dowleh therefore, sent his son Ehtesham al-Dowleh, governor of Behbahan to deal with the disobedient local chiefs. According to the British news writer in Shiraz, their rebellion consisted of ignoring government directives and not giving enough presents (*ta`arrofat*) to the government.[135] On 16 March 1877, Ehtesham al-Dowleh left Bushehr and arrived at Kangan on 21 April 1877, where he arrested Sheikh Mazkur and Mohammad Taher Khan Gallehdari, and he left Kangan on 1 May 1877. Ehtesham al-Dowleh appointed Mohammad Hasan Khan Mafi, brother of Hoseyn Qoli Khan Sa`d al-Molk and governor of the Gulf Ports, as governor of Gallehdar, Kangan, Taheri, Bandar-e Nakhl-e Taqi and dependencies, Asaluyeh, and the district of Gavbandi. Sheikh Mazkur was imprisoned in the Karim Khan prison in Shiraz, while Sheikh Mohammad Taher Khan Gallehdari was executed.[136] Although Sheikh Mazkur's districts were made over to Mohammad Hasan Khan Mafi, the latter "was detected in treasonable practises, and after administration of the usual course of sticks, or bastinado, was sent to Shiraz as prisoner, 'to encourager les autres.'"[137]

---

132 The Al Sudan, see Lorimer, *Gazetteer*, vol. 2, p. 1248.

133 Saldanha, *Précis*, vol. 7/2, pp. 3-4.

134 FO 248/290, Agent Lengeh to Acting Resident, 8 April 1873/5 Safar 1290; Ibid., Sheikh Abdollah Musebbeh to Agent Lengeh, 28 Moharram 1290 plus Arabic letter, see appendix 8. Ibid., Rahma b. Saleh, chief of Tavuneh to Agent Lengeh, 22 Moharram 1290/11 March 1873 plus Arabic letter (see Appendix 9), confirming Sheikh Abdollah's story and asking the same rhetorical question; finally noting that those of Tavuneh and of Charak were enemies, although they were of the same tribe, and he was prepared to go after them, if they went to Kish. Sheikh Mohammad b. Hasan continued to be a problem for shipping in the Persian Gulf, see, for example, FO 248/232, Bushire to Tehran, 17 July 1889 concerning his behavior towards a stranded British ship.

135 Sa`idi Sirjani, *Vaqaye`-ye Ettefaqiyeh. Gozareshha-ye khafiyeh-nevisan-e englisi*. Tehran, 1361/1982, p. 69 (3 Rabi` II till 1 Jomadi I 1294).

136 Fasa'i, *Farsnameh*, vol. 1, pp. 851, 854; Sirjani, *Vaqaye`-ye Ettefaqiyeh*, p. 69.

137 *Administration* 1877-78, p. 6.

3 / THE AL NASUR OF KANGAN, TAHERI AND GAVBANDI IN THE NINETEENTH CENTURY

In June 1877, Sheikh Mazkur was released from prison after he had promised to pay a large amount of *pishkesh*,[138] which, according to the British amounted to the huge sum of 100,000 *qran*s.[139] Although released from prison, Sheikh Mazkur was not yet free, for he remained under a kind of house arrest. In February 1878, Sheikh Mazkur was taken to Bushehr under armed guard for unknown reasons.[140] It may have been to make it appear as if he might return to Kangan if he made this worthwhile to the Fars authorities. This indeed seems have to been the case, because in early March 1878, Sheikh Mazkur was said to have promised to pay 12 or 14,000 *tuman*s to be released.[141] In May 1878, through mediation by Hajj Abdol-Nabi, a leading Bushehr merchant, Sheikh Mazkur was again appointed as governor of Kangan, Taheri, Gavbandi as well as of the districts of Gallehdar, Asir, and Ala Marvdasht.[142] After his reinstatement as governor, the British were encouraged by the fact that "He has since paid up a longstanding claim for indemnity to some Indian subjects who were wrecked on his coast."[143]

According to Fasa'i, this period of good behavior only lasted one year, because thereafter Sheikh Mazkur stopped paying taxes.[144] However, other sources indicate that soon after his return relations between the Shiraz administration and Sheikh Mazkur deteriorated and that he was again in conflict with the Fars authorities. These were not the only problems that Sheikh Mazkur had. In that same year Sheikh Mazkur due to a feud with Abdollah b. Mohammad, chief of Charak and Hamad b. Esma`il, chief of the Obeydli of Chiru attacked and plundered the village of Morbagh, killing 17 men. Qavam al-Molk, the governor of Lar, sent of a force of 200 infantry and 700 levies under Fath Ali Khan of Garash with one gun against Sheikh Mazkur in July 1878, who surprised the invading force and defeated it.[145] In August 1878, the two sides had not yet settled their dispute and shots were exchanged between the forces of Sheikh Mazkur and Fath Ali Khan Jarrashi.[146]

In June 1879, Sheikh Mazkur's tax arrears amounted to 12,000 *tuman*s. The governor of Fars, Ehtesham al-Dowleh, sent his *farrash-bashi* Mohammad Ebrahim Beg to Gallehdar to collect this sum and was instructed that if the Sheikh did not have the money to take him to Shiraz. However, he returned without the Sheikh as it was difficult to get him.[147] In that same month Sheikh Mazkur was reported to be 6,000 *tuman*s in arrears (does this mean that he had paid already 6,000 *tuman*s?), but that he did not react to any of the tax collectors (*mohassel*s) or other signals sent to him to pay. Therefore, the governor-general of Fars promised to pay 100 *tuman*s to anyone bringing his head, while in addition he would receive 200 *tuman*s as a gift (*an`am*).[148] In September 1879, Sheikh Mazkur still refused to come to Shiraz to pay last year's tax arrears. In reaction, Ehtesham al-Dowleh appointed

---

138 Sirjani, *Vaqaye`-ye Ettefaqiyeh*, p. 73 (1-6 Jomadi II 1294)
139 Sirjani, *Vaqaye`-ye Ettefaqiyeh* 1877-78, p. 6.
140 Sirjani, *Vaqaye`-ye Ettefaqiyeh*, p. 81 (20 Moharam-17 Safar 1295).
141 Sirjani, *Vaqaye`-ye Ettefaqiyeh*, p. 83 (18 Safar-13 Rabi I 1295).
142 Fasa'i, *Farsnameh*, vol. 2, p. 1463. According to the British newswriter in Shiraz, Sheikh Mazkur was given governorship of Gavbandi and Bandar-e Jam. Sirjani, *Vaqaye`-ye Ettefaqiyeh*, p, 89 (17 Rabi` II-17 Jomadi I 1295).
143 *Administration* 1877-78, p. 6.
144 Fasa'i, *Farsnameh*, vol. 2, p. 1463.
145 *Administration* 1878-79, p. 9; Fasa'i, *Farsnameh*, vol. 2, p. 1463.
146 Sirjani, *Vaqaye`-ye Ettefaqiyeh*, p. 96, (19 Rajab-20 Sha`ban 1295).
147 Sirjani, *Vaqaye`-ye Ettefaqiyeh*, p.108 (18 Rabi` II-28 Jomadi II 1296).
148 Sirjani, *Vaqaye`-ye Ettefaqiyeh*, p. 111.

his *farrash-bashi* Ebrahim Mohammad Beg as governor of Gavbandi and Gallehdar.[149] In late October 1879, Ebrahim Mohammad Beg was ordered to arrest Sheikh Mazkur and his brother Mohammad Taher Khan. Ebrahim Beg left with 400 horse and foot from Kuhgiluyeh, commanded by Khoda Karam Khan of the Buyer Ahmadi tribe and 400 soldiers and two guns, to take the Red Fort (Qalat-e Sorkh) as well as Sheikh Mazkur and his brother. To that end he invited the two Sheikhs to a friendly meeting. Mohammad Taher Khan arrived before his brother, and then sent news to him that the purpose of the meeting was to arrest him on arrival and thus Sheikh Mazkur did not come. Ebrahim Mohammad Beg then ordered to arrest Mohammad Taher Khan, but he had many riflemen with him who then started to shoot killing two and wounding four persons, and on his side there also were some wounded. However, Mohammad Taher's resistance was in vain, because he was arrested. Sheikh Ahmad, a claimant against Sheikh Mazkur, who in 1878 had demanded that he be imprisoned in Shiraz, sent armed men to come and take Mohammad Taher Khan to Shiraz. When taking Mohammad Taher Khan the guards also wanted to take Hoseyn Qoli Khan, the son of Baqer Khan Gallehdari, who resisted and was killed. Sheikh Mazkur then mounted a rescue operation to try and set his brother free, but Ebrahim Mohammad Beg let them know if he tried to do so he would immediately behead Mohammad Taher Khan.[150]

In December 1879, news arrived in Shiraz that Sheikh Mazkur intended to flee with his family by sea. When he heard this Ebrahim Mohammad Beg sent a body of men to prevent this, which was able to capture Sheikh Mazkur's daughter and some of his retainers. Mohammad Taher Khan was taken to Shiraz and put into prison. One group of soldiers was sent to Gallehdar with a gun to take Sheikh Mazkur, with the message that if he came out of the fort with the Koran and his sword around his neck his blood would not be shed.[151] In January 1880, Ebrahim Mohammad Beg still had not been able to take Sheikh Mazkur who sat behind the safety of the walls of his fort with supplies of all kinds and 200 riflemen. Ebrahim Mohammad Beg, the governor of Gallehdar had another setback because little rain had fallen in Gallehdar and it was feared that the harvest would fail. As a result, people were much upset and intended to move away. It was believed that even if good rains would fall half of the taxes would not be collected.[152] On 1 March 1880 news arrived from Gallehdar that on 20 February 1880 that Sheikh Mazkur had died during a sortie. The government ordered to cut off his head and bring it to Shiraz. Ebrahim Mohammad Beg was given as a reward the title of Khan and the rank of colonel.[153]

Shortly thereafter, in April 1880, news arrived in Shiraz that Sheikh Mazkur was only wounded and that he had withdrawn into the Red Fort, which he was strengthening and assembling riflemen from all around. Colonel Mostafa Qoli Khan was ordered to

---

149 Sirjani, *Vaqaye`-ye Ettefaqiyeh*, p. 113 (28 Shaban-1 Shavval 1296); Administration 1879-80, p. 6.
150 Fasa'i, *Farsnameh*, vol. 2, p. 1463; Sirjani, *Vaqaye`-ye Ettefaqiyeh*, pp. 115-16 (2 Zu'l-Qa`deh-3 Zu'l-Hejjeh 1296).
151 Sirjani, *Vaqaye`-ye Ettefaqiyeh*, pp. 116-17 (4 Zu'l-Hejjeh-8 Moharram 1297).
152 Sirjani, *Vaqaye`-ye Ettefaqiyeh*, p. 119 (8 Moharram-7 Safar 1297).
153 Sirjani, *Vaqaye`-ye Ettefaqiyeh*, p.120.

march with 10 guns from Shiraz to Gallehdar to take him.¹⁵⁴ The result was a serious fight between Sheikh Mazkur and Ebrahim Mohammad Beg during which 35 persons were killed on both sides. Sheikh Mazkur took four men of the enemy prisoner and burned them in the fort with oil. Ehtesham al-Dowleh, who was in Bushehr at that time, was very upset and almost decided to go there himself.¹⁵⁵ However, the tide turned into his favor, because in May 1880, Sheikh Mazkur was taken without a fight. He was betrayed by Khoda Karam Khan Buyer Ahmadi who promised him safeguard and then arrested him. On hearing the news the governor-general of Fars immediately ordered 15 salvos to be fired and the drums to be beaten.¹⁵⁶ Ehtesham al-Dowleh who was still in Bushehr, on hearing the news of Sheikh Mazkur's capture left Bushehr on 19 May 1880. Although sorely wounded, Ebrahim Mohammad Beg forced Sheikh Mazkur to post ride in fetters to Ehtesham al-Dowleh's camp in Kazerun, and from there in the same condition to Shiraz.¹⁵⁷

On 29 May 1880, Sheikh Mazkur with seven retainers arrived in Shiraz; all officials were gathered in Government House to see the 'show.' On 1 June 1880 Sheikh Mazkur was forced to swallow a copper coin that he himself had struck in Gallehdar and Kangan and then he was strangled and hung from the gibbet in the *Meydan-e Tavileh*, at the orders of Mo`tamed al-Dowleh. Two of his men were also strangled at the foot of the scaffold; two men were released, one of whom was the son of Mohammad Taher Khan and the other his masseur. Three others had a hand cut off. Ebrahim Mohammad Beg was rewarded with the appointment as governor of Kangan, Galledar and Gavbandi and the honorary rank of colonel (*sarhang kharej az fowj*).¹⁵⁸

According to the British, public opinion almost universally condemned Mo`tamed al-Dowleh for executing Sheikh Mazkur, who after all was driven into rebellion by sheer desperation. "When a prisoner in Shiraz he had bought his release by promising to pay a sum far beyond his means of raising, and when pressed, met force by force and fled to a mountain fort."¹⁵⁹

---

154 Sirjani, *Vaqaye`-ye Ettefaqiyeh*, p. 121 (12 Rabi` I-5 Rabi` II 1297); Sheikh Mazkur after some skirmishes fled to Kalat-e Sorkh. *Administration* 1879-80, p. 6. Shahin Kuh a.k.a. Kalat-e Sorkh 7 km south of today's Gavbandi. Najmabadi, "The Arab Presence," p. 137; the impregnable fort Qalat-e Sorkh. Fasa'i, *Farsnameh*, vol. 2, 1463, 1630 (*qal`eh-ye qalat-e sorkh* two *farsakh* south of Gavbandi; it had a rainwater cistern and 50-60 *tofangchi*s as guards). For a photo of this fort, see Gholamzadeh, *Me`mari*, p. 417.

155 Sirjani, *Vaqaye`-ye Ettefaqiyeh*, p. 122 (5 Jomadi I-12 Jomadi II 1297).

156 Sirjani, *Vaqaye`-ye Ettefaqiyeh*, p. 123 (5 Jomadi I-12 Jomadi II 1297); *Administration* 1879-80, p. 6. According to Fasa'i, *Farsnameh*, vol. 2, p. 1463, Ibrahim Beg took the fort in a few days and arrested the Sheikh. According to the British, Sheikh Mazkur "was lured out by treachery." *Administration* 1880-81, p. 8; Hamidi, *Farhangnameh*, p. 60.

157 Fasa'i, *Farsnameh*, vol. 2, 1463; *Administration* 1880-81, p. 8.

158 Fasa'i, *Farsnameh*, vol. 2, p. 1463; Sirjani, *Vaqaye`-ye Ettefaqiyeh*, p. 123 (13 Jomadi II-17 Rajab 1297); *Administration* 1880-81, pp. 8-9 (Strangling is usually reserved for Khans and persons of some distinction, "more vulgar offenders being dismissed by cutting the throat with a knife"). For the alleged coin struck by Sheikh Mazkur, see Morteza Qasem Beglu, *Sekkehha-ye Siraf*. Tehran, 1385/2006. These coins bear the inscription of 'Kangan' on one side, and 'Zarb' on the other. However, the coins bear no date and might belong to a period prior to that of Sheikh Mazkur.

159 *Administration* 1880-81, pp. 8-9.

Did the Fall of Sheikh Mazkur Meant the End of Arab Authority?

When Sheikh Mazkur was executed in 1880 this signaled, according to Curzon, that "Arab authority throughout this region has been successfully disintegrated by the Government, and yielded to centralization supported by guns."[160] This sentiment is repeated in modern scholarship such as by Larry Potter, who writes:

> The late nineteenth century was the end of the era of autonomous Arab principalities along the Iranian coast. The leases by which Arab shaikhs were authorized to rule, and paid to Tehran to do so, were now a relic of the past. …As the Qajar government modernized and centralized, it was inevitable the Gulf coast, as other parts of the country, would be increasingly subject to the will of Tehran.[161]

However, as is clear from what follows, actually not much changed on the Shibkuh coast and the tributary relationships of the Arab Sheikhs with the government of Iran continued on the same footing as before. Potter and others were misled by the successful ouster of the Al Mazkur from Bushehr in 1850 and of the Qavasem from Lengeh in 1887. However, these were important ports and major revenue earners and also much easier and much less costly to take over by military force than the small ports on the Shibkuh coast.

It is true that there was a decline of the Arab element on the littoral, but not of Arab influence. The decline or rather the dilution of the Arab element had begun much earlier than the fall of Sheikh Mazkur in 1880 signaled. Whereas in the eighteenth century the various Shibkuh ports were dominated by strong, sizable and recognizable Arab tribal groups, this was no longer the case by the early 1800s. For by that time not everybody belonged anymore to the original tribal Hula groups that had settled the various Shibkuh ports. According to Malcolm, in 1800 the Hulas were composed of the: "Ben Jouassim, Ben Ahmed, Ben Nasir, Ben Saboohil, Ben Houl, and Houl.[162] The fading away of the original Arab groups became even more pronounced in later years, and was very evident locally. Concerning the people of Taheri, Parak, Kangan, and Nakhl-e Taqi, Captain Brucks reported in 1835:

Its inhabitants are Mahomedans, Arabs of the Beni Husan, Beni Khalid, Albuya, Albusnarif, Albuyareh, Alyia, Beni Ahmood, Abadaly, Kasheanaria, and Nussoor Tribes, and its present Shaikh's name is Jubarra. The number of inhabitants is about fourteen hundred.[163]

Some of these tribal groups were not mentioned before and are an indication that there was still ongoing migration between the two littorals, but also that some, if not most of the old Hula groups were not receiving fresh inflow from their parent tribes in Arabia anymore. By 1900 only the Al Ali of Charak still intermarried with members of their tribe in Trucial Oman. Because of the plague and cholera that carried away many people during the nineteenth century, in particular the 1832 epidemic, as well as because

---

160 G. N. Curzon, *Persia and the Persian Question*, 2 vols., London, 1892, vol. 2, p. 406.
161 Lawrence G. Potter, "The consolidation of Iran's frontier on the Persian Gulf in the nineteenth century," in: Roxane Farmanfarma, *War and Peace in Qajar Persia: Implications Past and Present*, London-New York: Routledge, 2008, p. 143.
162 Anonymous 1828, *Sketches of Persia, from the journals of a traveller in the East* 2 vols. London, vol. 1, pp. 32-34.
163 Brucks, "Memoir," p. 590.

of constant warfare with their neighbors the composition of the coastal Arab population changed significantly over time.

Officially, there were six Arab groups still living on the Shibkuh coast by 1900. However, to paraphrase the bard, an Arab by any name is still an Arab. For as is clear from Table 3.2, the Al Hamad, the Al Haram and the Al Nasur were mostly Hamadis, Haramis and Nasuris in name only. Many were Persian speakers who had become Arabicized and called themselves, e.g., Nasuri because their Sheikh was one. In fact, the only real Nasuris that still were around in 1900 were the family of the Al Nasur Sheikh and a few other families.[164] Things were not as bad with the Hamadis and Haramis, but here also many just named themselves after their Sheikh. It would seem that only the Al Ali still had strong links with the parent tribe in Trucial Oman. Nevertheless, all groups to varying degrees relied mostly on population influx from the interior of Iran.

Table 3.2: Distribution and size of Arab tribes of the Shibkuh Coast in 1900

Name	Est. no.	Where	Remarks
Al Ali	3,500	Charak, Tavuneh, Qays, Dovvan	Sunnis from Trucial Oman with whom they intermarry. Sections: Al Bu Khazam, Al Bu Muflih, Al Bu Yamish, Al Bu `Abdollah b. Ahmad. At Tavuneh the Bushri section is at enmity with those of Charak.
Al Hamad	200	Muqam, Marbakh, Kalat, Gurzeh	Claim descent from the Qahtan. Many call themselves Hamadis because they are subjects to the Hamadi Sheikh.
Al Haram	2,000	Asalu, Naband	Sunnis. Claim to be of the Raziyeh tribe and to have come from Mecca area 6 generations ago. Many call themselves Haramis because they are subjects to the Harami Sheikh.
Maraziq	1,500	Moghu, Hasineh, Kondarun, 300 in Bostaneh	Wahhabis. Claim to be branch of the Ajman. The Sheikh at Moghu belongs to Al Soleyman. Supposed to be the same as the Maraziq of Oman. Many are Maraziq in name only.
Al Nasur	A few	Gavbandi village	Mostly exterminated due to constant wars with Haramis.
Obeydli	1,500	Chiru, Henderabi	Sunnis. Claim to be of Ahmadah tribe that is derived from the `Abdah Shammar of Najd. Also, that `Abadilah of Trucial Oman are connected with them.

Source: Lorimer, *Gazetteer*, vol. 2, pp. 1782-84

As a result, by 1900, "the bulk of the people [of Shibkuh] are of mingled Persian and Arab blood and the tribes to which they belong are of no consequence."[165] However, neither the fading away of the pure Arab elements in the population nor the ouster of the Nasuri sheikhs from their historical lands meant a diminishing of the influence of the Arab Sheikhs. To demonstrate this point, I first discuss what happened with the Nasuri Sheikhs and then how the situation developed throughout the Shibkuh coast after 1880.

At the end June 1881, Sheikh Hatem, brother of Sheikh Mazkur was released from prison. It was said that some of his brother's properties would be given to him, but that did not happen.[166] For to show the intention of the central government that it

---

164 In 1865, the population in Sheikh's Mazkur district, except in Asalu and Naband, called themselves Nasri or Nasriya Arabs. Colville, "Land Journey," p. 38.
165 Lorimer, *Gazetteer*, vol. 2, p. 1779-84.
166 Sirjani, *Vaqaye`-ye Ettefaqiyeh*, p. 139 (3 Sha`ban- 4 Ramazan 1298).

meant business and wanted to impose its rule on the unruly coastal Arab sheikhs, Tehran appointed Nowzar Mirza in 1882 as governor of Gallehdar, Taheri and Kangan. However, as an indication that the seemingly tough government policy was without any punch, the new governor sublet the rule over the latter two places to Sheikh Hasan, oldest son of Sheikh Mazkur with security from Hajj Mohammad Hasan Tajer-e Shirvani.[167] Fasa'i, a man who for many years had been intimately involved in the reshaping of the political and administrative realities of Fars, unlike Curzon, did not know about the effective end of Arab rule, for he wrote in 1882 that "since old times the rule of this district was in hands of the Sheikhs of the Al Nasur and it still is."[168] In November 1882, it was further reported that one of the sons of Sheikh Mazkur, presumably Sheikh Hasan, had also been given the governorship of Gavbandi. Apparently, old scores needed to be settled there, for the newly appointed district chief invited six old beards to a party, who after entering were all shot. In reaction the government of Shiraz sent a military force to arrest him.[169] Sheikh Hasan b. Mazkur then fled to Bahrain. A few months later, in April 1883, he landed at Taheri and caused considerable disturbances in Gallehdar and adjacent districts and Fath Ali Khan Garrashi, governor of Lar was ordered to suppress it. Sheikh Hasan b. Mazkur fled and escaped. Further disturbances followed when the people refused to accept the new governor Na'eb Ebrahim Khan, one Ahmad b. Seyf being the ringleader. Na'eb Ebrahim went to Jam with a force of tribal levies and regular infantry to suppress the revolt of the people of Jam, who resisted and several of his Baharlu tribesmen were killed. In retaliation his troops plundered Jam; 30-40 men of Jam were seized as being guilty of killing the Baharlu tribesmen. The captured men were given to given to the Baharlu levies, who cut them into pieces. They also took large flocks of animals from Jam.[170] By March 1883, Nowzar Mirza the new governor of Gallehdar was 1,000 *tumans* in arrears that the son of Sheikh Mazkur (presumably Sheikh Hasan) owed him.[171] To underline how shaky the situation was a severe earthquake occurred 16 October 1883, which caused much damage at Kangan and other coastal villages.[172]

Whether Nowzar Mirza received his money or not, a fact is that although the Nasur Sheikhs had lost control over their ancestral homes of Taheri and Kangan, they held on to Gavbandi. For Sheikh Hasan b. Mazkur returned three years later, i.e. about 1886.[173] According to a recent local history, Sheikh Hasan went to his brother-in-law, Ali Akbar Khan Gallehdari, who notified Ra'is Ali Fumestani that Mullah Mohammad Ali, who then held the governorship of Gavbandi, had to go. If he was not willing to leave voluntarily he had to be forced, even, if need be, killed. Sheikh Hasan's maternal uncles, who had married women from the Ra'isha family, went to Gavbandi and had Mullah Mohammad Ali killed while he was reading the Koran in the Sheikhi mosque. On being informed about the murder, Ali Akbar Khan, accompanied by Sheikh Hasan and his brother Soleyman, went

---

167 Sirjani, *Vaqaye'-ye Ettefaqiyeh*, p. 161 (May 1882); However, according to Fasa'i, *Farsnameh*, vol. 2, p. 1463, the two sons of Sheikh Mazkur, Sheikh Ebrahim Khan and Sheikh Hasan Khan Kangani jointly were *zabet* of Kangan in that year. According to Siddiq, quoted by Najmabadi, "The Arab Presence," p. 137, Sheikh Mazkur had three sons, who allegedly all disappeared, which is not borne out by the facts.
168 Fasa'i, *Farsnameh*, vol. 2, p. 1463.
169 Sirjani, *Vaqaye'-ye Ettefaqiyeh*, p. 175 (3 November 1882).
170 *Administration* 1883-84, p. 8.
171 Sirjani, *Vaqaye'-ye Ettefaqiyeh*, p. 186 (22 April 1883).
172 Saldanha, *Précis*, vol. 7/2, p. 11.
173 Najmabadi, "The Arab Presence," p. 137.

to Fumestan, where people welcomed him carrying green banners. Sheikh Hasan then remained in Gavbandi; however, he needed an official appointment as governor. He wrote to Hajji Salem, chief of Dashti asking to supply him with pistols. He then sent Ali Akbar Khan and his brother Soleyman to the Khan of Bastak and made him a present of these pistols and asked to arrange that he was appointed governor of Gavbandi. As a result of the Khan of Bastak's intercession Sheikh Hoseyn was reinstated as chief of Gavbandi.[174]

Sheikh Hasan's brother, Sheikh Ebrahim was in charge of Taheri until 1895, when he opposed the appointment of a successor and holed up in the fort. The government sent a force to expel him, after which Taherim was held by the Dashti chief.[175] Around 1903, Sheikh Soleyman b. Sheikh Hasan b. Sheikh Jabbara, a nephew of Sheikh Hasan b. Mazkur, the Gavbandi chief was able to acquire the district of Taheri, Bagh-e Shah, Barak, Ras al-Shahr, from which he was ousted by force in 1904 by the Khan of Dashti, the family's old nemesis. The reason for this fight was that the Khan of Dashti believed that the district was his by rights. In fact, others like Sadid al-Saltaneh even wrote that Sheikh Soleyman held: Parag, Taheri, Akhtar, Mayalu. The ensuing quarrel was fomented by Salar-e Mo`azzam when governor of Bushehr. Many sympathizers of Sheikh Soleyman Nasuri then left for Shivu, which was part of Gavbandi and was held by his uncle Hasan b. Mazkur Nasuri.[176] In 1903 Teben, Naband, Bidkhun, and Asalu were governed by the Al Haram. Nakhl-e Hashem, Ghamareh, and Barku between Naband and Asaluyeh were under the Bani Malek, in the jurisdiction of Sheikh Hasan b. Shaikh Mazkur. Ten years later it was held by the Bu Someyt.[177]

WAS THE SITUATION IN THE OTHER SHIBKUH PORTS DIFFERENT?

Having established that the Al Nasur still held on to their old position and influence, granted that temporarily they had lost Kangan and Taheri, it is necessary to have a look at the other Arab districts along the Shibkuh coast. Because the return of the Al Nasur could have been an exception to the rule. Therefore, it is important to know whether the other Arab Sheikhs also had been ousted or whether nothing had changed.[178]

Around 1900, the Shibkuh coast boasted of some 8,500 houses with an estimated population of 42,500, including the valleys of Gavbandi, Darveh Asuh and Golshan. In 1906, its nominal revenue was 21,960 *tumans* excluding Gavbandi. This amount represented the official nominal revenues, because the Sheikhs did not always pay or, when

---

174 Abdollah Darya'i, *Goftarha va Revayatha az Sargozasht-e Al-e Nasuri va Al-e Haram*. Shiraz: Novid, 1379/2000, pp. 25-26. This intercession is not mentioned by Bastaki (*Tarikh-e Jahangiri*), but given the good past relations between Bastak and the Nasuris it seems likely. In 1893, Sheikh Hasan b. Mazkur is mentioned as governor of Gavbandi, whose Bani Malek dependents had seized and plundered a Bahraini vessel at Bisatin. FO 248/567, Complaint against the Bani Malik tribe.

175 Administration Report 1895-96, p. 8.; Saldanha 1986, vol. 7/2, p. 14-15.

176 Adamec, *Historical Gazetteer*, vol. 3, pp. 707, 729; Lorimer, *Gazetteer*, vol. 2, pp. 1786, 1789 (Sheikh Soleyman Nasuri died at the end of 1907); Sadid al-Saltaneh, *Sarzaminha*, p. 56.

177 Sadid al-Saltaneh, *Sarzaminha*, p. 57.

178 In 1889, Sheikh Mohammad b. Hasan, chief of Charak and Kish defied the Iranian government with regard to the conflict that had arisen about his behavior in connection with a stranded British vessel, the *Transition*, see FO 248/484, Sheikh Mohammad b. Hasan to Ross 4 April 1889, and Idem, Ross to Tehran, 17 July 1889.

they did, did not necessarily pay the full amount.[179] Despite the fact that the 'pure' Arab element was diluted among the population of the Shibkuh coast this did not mean that the political and administrative influence of the hereditary Arab Sheikhs had been reduced as well. At the end of 1906 the Shibkuh coast districts were administratively organized as follows:

Table 3.3: Administrative districts of Shibkuh at the end of 1906

Name	Attached to	Villages	Local authority
1. Kangan	Fars	Banak, Kangan, Miyalu, `Ayanat, Akhtar	In 1905 farmed by the Khan of Dashti for 1,800, and sublet to his cousin for 1,500 *tumans*. In 1906 the sea customs of districts 1-3 were transferred to Customs Admin. who paid him 2,300 *tumans*/year compensation. He appears to collect the other revenues, but not to pay anything to the government. Total former revenue of nrs. 1-3 was 8,000 *tumans*/year of which 4,910 *tumans* was for the government.
2. Taheri	Fars	Bagh-e Sheikh, Taheri, Barak, Ras al-Shajar	In 1904 the Dashti Khan replaced Sheikh Soleyman Nasuri; he farmed it for 1,900 tumas/year
3. Asalu-Naband	Gulf Ports	Nakhl Taqi, Asalu, Baydhah Khan, Halat Naband, Naband, Barku, Ras Ghurab, Ghaf, Khodavan, Tibin and `Amariyeh	Till 1905 these were under Sheikh Ahmad b. Seyf Harami under the Dashti Khan who farmed them. Ras Ghurab, Ghaf and Khodavan were under the Nasuri Sheikh of Gavbandi. In 1906 the entire district was transferred from Fars to the Gulf Ports. The Tamimi Sheikh of Gavbandi was placed in charge. Before the change the Harami portion was 4,400 *tumans*; the Nasuri share was not separately assessed.
4. Gavbandi-Shivu	Bastak	Dastur, Kharabeh, Bostanu, Boragleh, Ziyarat, Kalatu, Shivu, Seyf al-Sheikh + Gavbandi and Darveh Asu valley villages	Till 1906 under the Nasuri Sheikh of Gavbandi who paid 12,000 *tumans*/year. In 1906, the Tamimi, Maliki, and Harami villages in Gavbandi came under Tamimi Sheikh paying 3,500 *tumans* to the Customs Administration and 5,000 *tumans* to Bastak. Nasuri Sheikh revenue was 7,000 *tumans* from Nasuri villages in Gavbandi and Darveh Asuh, and places on the coast.
5. Mogam	Bastak	Mogam, Nakhilu, Jazeh, Makahil + villages in Mogam valley	Under the Hamadi Sheikh of Mogam who also holds Kalat. Revenue of Mogam is 800 *tumans*/year.
6. Chiru	Bastak	Chiru, Henderabi and Golshan in the valley	Under the Obeydli Sheikh of Chiru who pays 1,600 *tumans*/year as taxes.
7. Kalat	Bastak	Kalat, Gurzeh, Sho`eyb and Shatvar islands	Under the Hamadi Sheikh of Mogam, who is represented by his brother Ebrahim b. `Abdollah. Revenue is 1,400 *tumans*. The Qavams of Shiraz claim Sho`eyb.
8. Charak	Bastak	Tavuneh, Charak, Kish, villages of Golshan valley, Baverdun, part of Dovvan	Under the Al Ali Sheikh of Charak; annual revenue 1,600 *tumans*. Chief of the Bushri section holds Tavuneh and Nakhl-e Mir in Golshan valley and defies his Al Ali chief.
9. Moghu	Bastak	Hasineh, Moghu, Farur island, Kondarun, part of Bostaneh	Under the Marzuqi Sheikh of Moghu; annual revenue to Bastak is 1,000 *tumans*.

Source: Lorimer, *Gazetteer*, vol. 2, pp. 1786-88.

---

179 Lorimer, *Gazetteer*, vol. 2, pp. 1462, 1782, 1790.

As Table 3.3 shows, the largest groups of the Shibkuh coastal Arabs were the Hamadis and Haramis, who were in alliance against the Nasuris, while the Hamadis and Marzuqis were allied against the Al Ali. However, the Bushri section of the Al Ali was allied with the Hamadis and Marzuqis against their own kinsmen. The Obeydlis were on bad terms with the Al Ali. Although fighting all the time, sometimes they reconciliated to face a common foe, but despite oaths on the Koran these reconciliations did not last long. Moreover, the power of the Sheikhs had dwindled due to internecine fights that were encouraged by the central government. Despite this, the Iranian government had little and uncertain control over the *zabet*s or district governors, who were mostly Sunni Arab Sheikhs. Moreover, the government could only replace a Sheikh by a member of his own family, if not, the outsider was murdered, as is clear from the following example.[180]

Until his violent death in 1906, Sheikh Ahmad b. Seyf ruled over Nakhl-e Taqi, Asalu, Baidheh Khan, Halat Naband, Naband, Barku, Tabin and Amariyeh in subordination of the Dashti Khan who held their farm. In 1906, however, this group of ports was brought under the governor of the Gulf Ports and the connection with the Dashti Khan was ended. The imperial customs also established a post in Asalu in that year.[181] Abdollah b. Mohammad Abdol-Rasul Obeydli was the chief of Chiru and Henderabi. However, he normally lived in Baikheh Armaki a village 30 miles in land, and left his brother in Chiru to look after his interests there. The revenue was 1,600 tumans payable to Bastak. The imperial customs had a customs post in Chiru.[182] Like those of Chiru, the *kalantar* or chief of the Shibkuh-e Larestan district (main town Charak) also were part of the governorate of Bastak. The *kalantar* was sometimes from the Hamadi and Obeydali, who lived to the west of this place, and sometimes from the people of Charak. The revenue of Charak, Tavuneh and Kish amounted to 1,600 tumans and was payable to Bastak. Around 1905, the Sheikh of Charak, Tavuneh, Gulshan, Bavirdyun and part of Dovvan was Saleh b. Mohammad Saleh. He was childless and was grooming a nephew in his government. Saleh b. Mohammad Saleh was noted for his greed and his control over his subjects was insecure. The imperial customs also had a post at Charak.[183] Until 1906, Kish was under Charak, hence the wealth of its Sheikh, but as of that year Qavam al-Molk and his family claimed ownership, because in 1878 Naser al-Din Shah had deeded it to them. The Qavamis claimed a revenue of 800 *tumans*, mainly from pearling.[184]

From Table 3.3 it is also clear that all Shibkuh districts were still controlled by the hereditary Arab chiefs as *zabet*s, despite efforts to end their rule. Despite the changes in 1906, most of the Shibkuh coast districts still remained part of Fars, except for the Asalu-Naband district that was transferred to the Gulf Ports. This was due to lobbying by the Customs Administration that wanted the bring all Shibkuh districts under the governor of the Gulf Ports for administrative and revenue reasons. Although these plans failed in case of other ports, the Customs Administration nevertheless was able to take over the control over the customs revenues at some of the other ports as well. The imperial customs had a

---

180 Lorimer, *Gazetteer*, vol. 2, p. 1466.
181 Lorimer, *Gazetteer*, vol. 2, pp. 177-78.
182 Lorimer, *Gazetteer*, vol. 2, p. 355.
183 Lorimer, *Gazetteer*, vol. 2, p. 355; Fasa'i, *Farsnameh*, vol. 2, pp. 1519-21, 1587-89 (detailed description of Kish).
184 Lorimer, *Gazetteer*, vol. 2, p. 1474; Fasa'i, *Farsnameh*, vol. 2, p. 1589 (in 1879, Mirza Ali Mohammad Khan Qavam al-Molk received Kish as *soyurghal*)

post, for example, at Kangan, whose customs revenues until 1905 were farmed by Dashti chief, as well as at Asalu, Chiru and Charak.[185]

Not only were the Arab sheikhs able to hold on to most of their territory and authority, but where it was usurped they fought back and sometimes regained it again. For example, the changes in allotment of the districts is a case in point. The influence of the Khan of Dashti, who, since the early nineteenth century, had been encroaching on the territory of his neighbors, notably that of the Nasuris, was reduced to the villages north of Asalu by 1906. The rest of the district then was under the Tamimi Sheikh Saqr b. Mobarak who resided in Chah Mobarak in Gavbandi valley. Residing in Gavban village in the Gavbandi valley, Hasan b. Mazkur Nasuri's wings were also clipped as he lost control over the Tamimi, Maleki and Harami villages to his neighbor, the Tamimi Sheikh, Ahmad b. `Abdollah, while the Hamadi Sheikh continued to hold sway over Mogam, and so did Abdollah b. Mohammad Abdol-Rasul the Obeydli Sheikh over Chiru. The Al Ali chief, Sheikh Saleh b. Mohammad's influence was reduced by internal opposition within his tribe by the chief of the Bushri section who resided at Nakhl-e Mir in the Golshan valley, who also held Tavuneh. The latter further sided with Ahmad b. Rashed the Marzuqi Sheikh of Moghu the traditional enemy of the Al Ali.[186]

Another case is that of Kangan, which had been in the hands of the Al Nasur until 1886 or thereabouts. It finally passed into the hands of the Khan of Dashti, who had tried to get control of Kangan since the 1840s. Kangan remained Dashti territory until 1904, when once again it fell into Al Nasur hands. However, one year later Sheikh Soleyman was driven away by the Khan of Dashti, who, in his turn, lost the district again in 1906. Kangan was later restored to the Dashti Khan, but due to political changes in Bushehr in 1911, the governor of the Gulf Ports, Movaqqar al-Dowleh sent Sheikh Hatem Khan Al Nasur with the *Persepolis* and *Mozaffar*, who expelled Ahmad Khan Dashti from Kangan and took control of the town. On arrival Sheikh Hatem found that Ahmad Khan of Dashti had not left any inhabitants in Kangan, and destroyed many buildings; whatever was built since then was done by Sheikh Hatem, or so he claimed.[187]

The Local Authority of the Hula Sheikhs

What this rearrangement of districts shows is that the central government tried to get more control over the Garmsir and the Shibkuh. However, it was a rather feeble attempt as the Sheikhs kept most of their territory and their revenues. It further shows that the central government realized that without the cooperation of the local sheikhs it would have great difficulty collecting any revenues. For the Sheikhs were not only the local 'governor' they also were the tax farmer. Each of the hereditary local sheikhs exercised considerable powers in their own district.

> He settles all civil disputes – except those that are religious or semi-religious in character, according to what he thinks is proper. His disposes of all criminal matters, inflicting at his discretion imprisonment and bastinado, but not the penalty of death; and without his permission no stranger dare engage

---

185 Lorimer, *Gazetteer*, vol. 2, p. 972.
186 Lorimer, *Gazetteer*, vol. 2, pp. 1785-89.
187 Vothuqi, *Tahavvolat*, pp. 44-45.

in pearl diving in his territorial waters. He is the exclusive revenue farmer of his own territories.[188]

If the government would have auctioned the districts to the highest bidder, as it is did elsewhere in Iran, those who would have won the auction, therefore, would have been in a very difficult and disadvantageous position in case they got into conflict with the local sheikh. Therefore, the Sheikhs remained the exclusive revenue farmer in their district and this did not change for some time. After the 1906 reorganization the revenues were as follows:

Table 3.4: Official tax burden of various Arab coastal Sheikhs

Name	Revenue amount in *tumans*
Khan of Dashti	Nil
Tamimi Sheikh	8,500
Nasuri Sheikh	7,000
Hamadi Sheikh	2,200
Obeydli Sheikh	1,600
Al Ali Sheikh	1,600
Marzuqi Sheikhs	1,000

Source: Lorimer, *Gazetteer*, vol. 2, p. 1790.

The rule of the Sheikhs was harsh and oppressive towards their subjects. Despite this, they enjoyed their full support to maintain their independence and oppose any encroachment by the central government. According to the Customs agent of Halleh, in Harami territory, 6 km from Asalu, who had visited the entire region, in 1922 the Harami Sheikh collected 10,000 *tumans*/month in taxes, but through extortion even 14,000 *tumans*. This he attributed to the fact that the subjects of each and every Shibkuh Sheikh were their workers (*kargar*), and the fruit of their year's work was all for the Sheikh; from all products imported for trade one-third was taken by the Sheikhs from their subjects not as taxes but as extortion. Therefore, nobody dared to import anything.[189] In this connection it is interesting to note when the fight about who would get Nakhl-e Taqi broke out between the Al Haram and Al Nasur, when given a choice by Daryabegi, the governor of the Gulf Ports, the local population expressed the wish to govern themselves and pay their taxes to him (see below). Despite their extortionate rule the Sheikhs were able to keep the loyalty of their subjects, in most cases, even in that of Nakhl-e Taqi, where Sheikh Hatem Al Nasur was able to induce the population to leave for Taheri. This was because "Local patriotism is strong among those who are subjects of the same chief, a bond which is here regarded as almost clanship."[190] This is borne out by the fact that the Nasuris had been almost exterminated on the Shibkuh coast by constant wars with the Al Haram and those of Dashti. By 1900, almost the only true Nasuris surviving were "the family of the Gabandi Sheikh, but a number of inhabitants of the Nasuri group of villages in Gabandi

---

188 Lorimer, *Gazetteer*, vol. 2, p. 1789.
189 Vothuqi, *Tahavvolat*, pp. 65-66.
190 Lorimer, *Gazetteer*, vol. 2, pp. 1779-84.

have assumed the name of Nasuri. Those who have done so are mostly Persian speaking Sunnis; few Shiites."[191] Furthermore, this feeling of loyalty was reinforced by the long time by which the Nasuri Sheikhs had been able to hang on to power in their ancestral lands. This feeling of the need to close ranks against outsiders did not only exist among the subjects of a particular Sheikh, but also among the Sheikhs themselves. Even those Sheikhs who normally would be feuding with each other would combine forces, as was the case against the intruding Tamimi Sheikh.[192]

The encroachment of the Tamimi Sheikh on the territory of the Nasuri Sheikh was not appreciated to put it mildly. The latter resented the usurpation of his traditional 'rights' and he joined forces with the Harami Sheikhs against the interloper. The chief of the Haramis was Mohammad b. Ahmad after the death of Sheikh Ahmad b. Seyf. He was his nephew and resided at Sarvbash in the Gavbandi valley. The Tamimi Sheikh and his son Mobarak were treacherously murdered in Fort Sarvbash by Sheikh Mohammad b. Ahmad b. Khalifeh Harami in 1907. As a result, there was no immediate successor for the Tamimi Sheikh.[193] This deed went unpunished, of course, as the control of the central government instead of increasing was decreasing. In fact, the entire Shibkuh coastal area was often in turmoil, due to feuding sheikhs, maritime violence, and efforts by the government to keep the unrest within bounds. The government was too weak to do more, and sometimes had to ask Great Britain for logistical and military support to enforce its decisions.

Feuding About Nakhl-e Taqi

A very long drawn out case was the conflict between the Al Haram and the Al Nasur about who had the right to Nakhl-e Taqi. In 1918, Nakhl-e Taqi, which had been held by the Al Nasur for many years, was returned to their enemy, the Al Haram. As a result of the feud with the Al Nasur, they destroyed people's houses in the village, at least so the Al Nasur maintained. Some 150 families had moved to Taheri, whose representatives in 1922 complained about their treatment to Yamin al-Mamalek, the visiting *kargozar*. Sheikh Hatem of Taheri, therefore, wanted to change the existing situation and urged that Nakhl-e Taqi be returned to the Al Nasur jurisdiction. He had complained about it to the government in Bushehr, which allegedly had promised to grant his demand, but nothing happened.[194] The Al Haram had, of course, a different account of what had happened. They maintained that the Nasuris knew very well that Nakhl-e Taqi was Harami land and therefore, had not claimed it before. The Harami Sheikh was not aware that people of Nakhl-e Taqi had fled due to oppression. He argued that when Sheikh Soleyman Nasuri, Sheikh Ebrahim Nasuri, and Sheikh Ali Akbar Khan Jami had held the government of Taheri the population had never claimed that Nakhl-e Taqi was Nasuri land. It has been Harami land until 1906, when Daryabegi, the governor of the Gulf Ports accompanied by Za'er Abdollah Khan and Musa Khan with the gun boat *Persepolis* came and expelled

---

191 Lorimer, *Gazetteer*, vol. 2, pp. 1783-84.
192 Lorimer, *Gazetteer*, vol. 2, pp. 1789-90.
193 Lorimer, *Gazetteer*, vol. 2, pp. 562, 1790; Archives Research Staff Ltd., *Political Diaries of the Persian Gulf 1907*, Archive Editions: Farnham Common, 1990, vol. 2, p. 114.
194 Vothuqi, *Tahavvolat*, pp. 43, 49-50.

Sheikh Ahmad Khan from the Al Haram district, who fled to Moqam.[195] The governor replaced him with Sheikh Saqr, the Tamimi Sheikh. Sheikh Ahmad Khan returned after one year and together with Sheikh Hasan Khan seized Qasr-e Kenar (in Gavbandi district), which was part of Al Haram territory, and settled there. Sheikh Saqr complained to Bushehr that Sheikh Ahmad had taken some Harami land. As a result, Za'er Abdollah Khan came with a canon and landed at Bidkhun, marched to Qasr-e Kenar, shelled and destroyed it. He took Sheikh Ahmad to Khiyar, a Harami village, but one that was under Sheikh Saqr, which Sheikh Ahmad refused. The latter then went to Gallehdar and from there he wanted to go to Bushehr to try to get the Al Haram lands back and out of the hands of the Tamimis. However, Sheikh Sagar allegedly paid the Jamis to prevent Sheikh Ahmad from doing so and they therefore, killed him.

When Sheikh Mohammad Ahmad Khalfan learned of Sheikh Ahmad's death he out of fear for his life and vengeance killed Sheikh Sagar. He believed that the Tamimis, Nasuris, and Gallehdaris were out to get him and, therefore, he fought them and regained some of the Al Haram lands. Asalu and Nakhl-e Taqi were then under Sheikh Ali Akbar Khan Gallehdari and remained so until 1916, when Sheikh Mohammad Ahmad Khalfan's complaints found a sympathetic ear in Bushehr. In that year, the governor of the Gulf Ports sent Za'er Abdollah Khan, Jamal Khan Dashti and other Dashti chiefs with the *Persepolis* and some government *grab*s to take Bidkhun, Asalu and Nakhl-e Taqi from Sheikh Ali Akbar Gallehdari; Sheikh Mohammad Ahmad Khalfan's force was joined by Sheikh Ahmad Hamadi of Moqam and with this force he besieged Asalu. Sheikh Mohammad Ahmad Khalfan from the landside and the Dashti force from the sea fired at the port. Immediately, Ali Akbar Khan Gallehdari, Sheikh Hatem Nasuri, Sheikh Mazkur Al Nasur with many Tamimis and Malekis and others opposed the government *grab*s. On the third night they counter-attacked; the cousin of Sheikh Mohammad Ahmad Khalfan was killed and the government boats left. They went to Hallah, where they landed their canon. Then with Sheikh Mohammad Ahmad Khalfan's and Sheikh Mohammad Hamadi's Arab force they besieged Naband and took its fort. After the conquest of Naband the government *grab*s returned to Bushehr and the troops dispersed. Asalu, Bidkhun and Nakhl-e Taqi thus remained in the hands of Sheikh Ali Akbar Gallehdari. Sheikh Mohammad Ahmad Khalfan successively complained in Bushehr that these were Al Haram lands and should not be in the hands of Gallehdaris.

Daryabegi sent a letter to the chiefs (*kadkhoda*s) of Asalu, Nakhl-e Taqi, and Bidkhun to vacate these places. Immediately Ali Akbar Khan Gallehdari sent his nephew Mohammad Taher Khan to Nakhl-e Taqi to reinforce the *kadkhoda*, who then did not vacate the place and replied he would oppose Daryabegi. The latter then asked British ships to cast anchor off Asalu and Nakhl-e Taqi; these fired at the forts, which then were taken and handed over to Sheikh Mohammad Ahmad Khalfan, who expelled the *kadkhoda*s. One of them, Mohammad Salem *kadkhoda* of Nakhl-e Taqi, wanted to stay, as he had faithfully served Sheikh Ahmad Al Haram, and promised to likewise serve Sheikh Mohammad Ahmad Khalfan under whatever conditions. Sheikh Mohammad Ahmad Khalfan accepted this

---

195 According to the Archives Research Staff Ltd., *Political Diaries 1904-06*, vol. 1, pp. 387, 400: on 24 June 1906 Daryabegi expelled Sheikh Ebrahim b. Mazkur of Asalu at the request of the Customs Department who called him "a smuggler and a bad character." Fearing punishment he fled to Bushehr where he sought sanctuary in the British Residency. At the end of June 1906 he left the Residency of his own volition.

request, because, as he said, he did not want to discomfort his subjects. In reaction, Sheikh Hatem Nasuri incited the people of Nakhl-e Taqi to all go to Daryabegi and tell him that they did not accept Sheikh Mohammad Ahmad Khalfan's *kadkoda* and wanted to separate Nakhl-e Taqi from the Al Haram district. The next day Sheikh Hatem and Hajji Mohammad *kadkhoda* went to Daryabegi to tell him that they did not accept the Harami chief. The latter then immediately also came aboard Daryabegi's ship. Daryabegi asked the representatives of the people of Nakhl-e Taqi whether they accepted Sheikh Hatem or Sheikh Mohammad Ahmad Khalfan as their chief? They replied that they wanted to manage their affairs (*zabeti*) themselves. Sheikh Hatem immediately scolded them, saying that they had misled him, and he then immediately left for Taheri. Daryabegi then decided to entrust the *zabeti* to neither of the two Sheikhs and, after consultation, appointed Hajj Mohammad as his own *kadkhoda*. In this function Hajj Mohammad allegedly robbed Al Haram property to the tune of 1,500 *tumans* to the detriment of the people of Asalu and Bidkhun. Sheikh Mohammad Ahmad Khalfan then wrote to Daryabegi, "this is the work of your *kadkhoda*." Daryabegi then came to Asalu where he asked Hajj Mohammad why he had stolen Al Haram property and given it to Gallehdar? Hajj Mohammad denied this, and said that they were false accusations. Daryabegi finally decided to dismiss Hajj Mohammad and to entrust the district to Sheikh Mohammad Khan. Two months later there was a small uprising in the Harami district and the Al Haram chief asked Daryabegi to come his assistance. Before Daryabegi's arrival, Hajj Mohammad harvested the dates of 300 trees of Sheikh Mohammad Ahmad Khalfan's property at the orders the Khan of Gallehdar. The dates were stored in Hajj Mohammad's house, who then wrote to Ali Akbar Khan Gallehdari asking him to send animals to transport the dates, but when these came Daryabegi also arrived. Hajj Mohammad then informed Ali Akbar Khan Gallehdari that he could not send the dates at that time, but after Daryabegi had left he would inform him. Hajj Mohammad loaded the dates in a boat, but then Sheikh Mohammad Ahmad Khalfan accused him of having stolen the dates. However, Hajj Mohammad claimed that he had bought the dates to ship them to other markets. Daryabegi was angry with Hajj Mohammad asking him how as his servant could he be giving a load of dates to Ali Akbar Khan Gallehdari? The more so, because he had promised not to get involved in any of this kind of activity or to assist the Gallehdari Khan. This time Daryabegi did not forgive him, but confiscated the dates, expelled him from Nakhl-e Taqi and gave it to Sheikh Mohammad Ahmad Khalfan, suppressed the 'uprising', took the fort, and handed it over to Sheikh Mohammad Ahmad Khan as well.

Furthermore, Sheikh Mohammad Ahmad Khalfan accused Sheikh Hatem of stealing taxes belonging to the Haramis. Sheikh Mazkur forbade to give any property or taxes to subjects of Al Haram there and kept those for himself, and this already for 3 years. During that period the land had been ravaged by locusts and drought and many people had left for Bahrain and thus, Sheikh Mohammad Ahmad Khalfan could not collect taxes from his subjects. In 1922 it had rained and he hoped that he might be able to pay taxes again. He would also greatly appreciate it when his wages were paid by those who had plundered the Harami lands and that his property be returned to so that the Haramis might be able to pay again.

After Sheikh Mohammad Ahmad Khalfan took control over Nakhl-e Taqi and the *kadkhoda* was expelled, the latter was induced by Sheikh Hatem to depart with his people from Nakhl-e Taqi and move to his territory and to demonstrate that "Sheikh Mohammad

Ahmad Khalfan is oppressing us and has turned us out of our houses." Sheikh Hatem used this as a means to get back Nakhl-e Taqi and its revenues. When the people had moved to Taheri, Sheikh Hatem told them that they had to declare that Nakhl-e Taqi was not Al Harami land, in which case he would exempt them from paying taxes and pay these himself. However, Hajj Mahommad refused to sign such testimony. After Hajj Mohammad and his people had moved to Taheri, at the instigation of Sheikh Hatem Jamavi his Jamavi adherents attacked Nakhl Taqi, Asalu and Bidkhun at night and in the morning drove all quadrupeds from these districts. Twenty days later Daryabegi came to Asalu, where he summoned both Sheikh Mohammad Ahmad Khalfan and Sheikh Hatem to his ship. Daryabegi then gave a written order to Sheikh Hatem and the *modir* of Asalu, Hajj Mirza Mehdi Khan Shirazi, whom he sent to Taheri, to reclaim all plundered property from each person, which had to be transferred to the *modir*, to be taken to Asalu. At Daryabegi's request eight prisoners were released who left by boat to Taheri. Allegedly, Sheikh Hatem did not hand over all animals and kept 50 sheep in Taheri.[196]

CONTINUED FEUDING AND DEFYING THE CENTRAL GOVERNMENT

After having his fiscal wings clipped somewhat in 1906, Sheikh Hasan b. Mazkur was able to reassert himself in the region; the fact that the Tamimis were leaderless helped, of course. Although Sheikh Hasan was a Sunni, his wife, who was a daughter of Sheikh Taher of Gallehdar, was a Shiite. However, his sons were raised as Sunnis, but his only daughter as a Shiite.[197] According to a local history, Sheikh Hasan b. Mazkur of Gavbandi was killed in 1916-17 by one of his closest retainers, and his son Mazkur became the last Khan of Gavbandi.[198] However, this information does not seem to be correct. To ensure that he had nothing to fear from the Ra'isha clan after he had taken back the rule over Gavbandi in 1886, Sheikh Hasan decided to kill Ra'is Ali and his immediate family. He invited him for an outing to Shivu and from there to Kalatu where two of his men killed Ra'is Ali. Sheikh Hasan had all other family members killed, except for a five-year old boy named Rostam. Almost two decades later he saw Rostam, who had become a strong lad, at a visit to the Dashti chief. He told him to forget the past and invited him into his inner circle against which he was warned. Rostam's mother and uncle urged him to kill his father's murderer, which he finally decided to do with the help of the Alagiha inhabitants of Borudel [?]. One night he entered Sheikh's Hasan residence and killed him; while trying to flee he was killed by the shots fired by the Sheikh's retainers.[199] This must have been after 1907 and before 1910, because Sheikh Hasan Nasuri was still alive in 1907.[200] Furthermore, the *Tarikh-e Jahangiriyeh* mentions that in 1910 Sheikh Mazkur, son of Sheikh Hasan b. Mazkur was Sheikh and *zabet* of Gavbandi, which was part of Bastak. Sheikh Mazkur b. Hasan asked the governor of Bastak to help him to take vengeance on the Hamadi and

---

196 Vothuqi, *Tahavvolat*, p. 67.
197 Lorimer, *Gazetteer*, vol. 2, p. 562.
198 Najmabadi, "The Arab Presence," p. 137.
199 Darya'i, *Goftarha*, pp. 27-36.
200 Archives Research Staff Ltd., *Political Diaries*, vol. 2, p.114.

Shibkuh [i.e. Charak] sheikhs.[201] Sheikh Mazkur was able to wrest some villages from the Hamadi sheikhs, which he returned after meeting with the governor of Bastak.[202]

Sheikh Mazkur's rule was challenged by Ra'is Soltan, a family member of Ra'is Ali, and his children. They intended to attack and kill Sheikh Mazkur and family members, but their plan was divulged to a follower of Sheikh Mazkur, and the plotters were killed or died shortly thereafter. A similar development took place in connection with the village of Dashti, where `Abdollah Sheikh Mazkur's *kadkhoda* was not liked by many. Warned that he might lose the allegiance of the people of Dashti Sheikh Mazkur dismissed Abdu. Sheikh Abdollah was in charge of Khirreh, on the border of Al Haram territory, which opponents of the Al Nasur, helped by some people of Khirreh, laid siege to the fort for 25 days. This action had been instigated by Sheikh Mohammad Ahmad Khalfan, the Harami chief of Kushkenar and Sarvbash. Sheikh Abdollah and his men were running out of supplies, but his brother sent some of his men led by Hajji Yusef Mohammadi to make the enemy raise the siege, in which he was successful. Hajji Yusef Mohammadi then attacked Sarvbash to get hold of or kill the Harami chief. However, after on both sides a few people died and were wounded he withdrew.[203]

The governor of Bastak also used his connections with the Shibkuh Arabs to keep his own house in order. By 1909, Mohammad Taqi Khan Sowlat al-Molk was so unpopular that the people of Bastak had invited his enemy, Gholam Hoseyn Khan, with his Warawi and Tarakameh adherents to expel him. In second half of September 1909 many armed men of the Tarakameh, Bikhehha, Warawi, Zanganeh, and Beyram under Hajji Gholam Hoseyn Warawi and Sayyed Hajji Baba Beyrami marched via Kal and Nistan and attacked Kuhan. Sowlat al-Molk, governor of Bastak sent *tofangchi*s to repel them, but they were not very successful, partly because their commander early on was killed. Feeling threatened in Bastak, Sowlat al-Molk moved part of the population of Bastak towards the coast. On 29 September 1910, Gholam Hoseyn Khan, one of Sayyed Abdol-Hoseyn's lieutenants, according to the British, took and sacked Bastak without any problem. He then left Bastak, leaving behind Mohammad Vali Khan, Sowlat al-Molk's son, as his deputy. Meanwhile, Sowlat al-Molk was able to assemble an armed force of Arabs of the Shibkuh coast in a short time. On 15 October 1910, he returned to Bastak and defeated his local opponents who surrendered. Through the intermediary of Sheikh Soltan Marzuqi and Sheikh Saleh Charaki they were pardoned and released and returned safely to their homes.[204]

Otherwise, with or without Bastaki involvement the various Arab chiefs became very active and aggressive at that time, and, as usual, old enemies were often on the opposing side. In the middle of October 1910 it was reported that the chiefs of the Warawi, Gavbandi, and Ishkanu districts, west of Mogam, had gathered a large force intending to raid Shibkuh and in particular to attack and plunder Lengeh. Gholam Hoseyn Khan of Warawi was near Bastak. The British Residency in Bushehr was informed, and as a result

---

201 Bastaki, *Tarikh-e Jahangiriyeh*, pp. 322-23; see also, Archives Research Staff Ltd., *Political Diaries*, vol. 4, p. 206 (Sheikh Mazkur, governor of Gavbandi).

202 Bastaki, *Tarikh-e Jahangiriyeh*, p. 324; Archives Research Staff Ltd., *Political Diaries*, vol. 4, p. 579 (re Bastak and Sheikh Saleh of Charak).

203 Darya'i, *Goftarha*, pp. 46-49.

204 Government of Great Britain, Persia No.1 (1911) *Further Correspondance respecting the Affairs of Persia.* London: HMSO, pp. 9-10; *Administration Report 1909*, p. 15. According to Bastaki, *Tarikh-e Jahangiriyeh*, pp. 319-20 the attack occurred after a period of drought.

3 / THE AL NASUR OF KANGAN, TAHERI AND GAVBANDI IN THE NINETEENTH CENTURY

HMS Fox arrived on 24 October 1910 on the roadstead of Lengeh. Captain Hunt sent Gholam Hoseyn Khan Warawi a strong message warning him not to come to Lengeh. On 25 October 1910 the 3,000 strong force of marauders were reported to be at two days' march from Jebel Turunjah. In October an Iranian force sent against them was said to have been defeated. On that same day the Warawis seized the passes to Shibkuh, despite having been opposed by the Sheikh of Mogam. As a result, they advanced to Bulaskar, 17 miles northwest of Charak. Sheikh Mazkur of Gavbandi brought a large force from Shivu and landed at Chiru, whose Sheikh also assisted the attackers. The deputy-governor of Lengeh felt that he had inadequate forces to defend the town, and on 27 October 1910 requested Captain Hunt of *HMS Fox* for help. The latter sent a force of 174 men from *HMS Fox* and *HMS Odin* and in consultation with the deputy-governor drew up a plan of defense.

HMS Odin, meanwhile, patrolled the Shibkuh coast having received information on 29 October that Sheikh Mazkur had embarked 800 men at Shivu to attack Lengeh. His troops had looted Jazza and Nakhilu on 29 and on 30 October his men landed and joined the Warawi force in an attack of Morbakh. On 31 October *HMS Odin* met with three dhows at Jazza belonging to Sheikh Mazkur with prisoners and loot plundered from Mogam district. While overtaking the dhows, Sheikh Mazkur's men fired at *HMS Odin* from ashore.[205] The dhows were captured and taken to Lengeh; two of them that belonged to Sheikh Mazkur's were burnt, the third one belonging to someone from Mogam, was returned to its Sheikh with all the plunder, which was valued at Rs. 8,000.

Daryabegi arrived at Lengeh from Bandar Abbas on 1 November and approved of the action taken by the deputy-governor and Captain Hunt. He then went to Charak mobilizing troops from the Sheikhs of Charak and Moghu and writing friendly letters to the Warawis asking them to withdraw. On 8 November he was at Rustami, 15 miles northeast of Charak, where he joined Mohammad Reza Khan, son of the chief of Bastak, who now had a total of 1,000 men. However, Daryabegi did not want to fight and punish the bandits, although the accompanying Sheikhs pressed him to do so. He toured the district, but only after he was sure that the Warawis would withdraw. He did not punish Sheikh Mazkur at all; the latter did not withdraw with the Warawis, but remained at Armaki, a few miles south from where Daryabegi was. The Sheikh of Mogam estimated the plunder taken by Sheikh Mazkur and the Warawis at five *lakh* of rupees, which the British considered an exaggeration[206] The force from Bastak was reinforced by reinforcements led by Sheikh Ahmad Marzuqi, Sheikh Saleh Charaki, Sheikh Abdollah Obeydli, Sheikh Soltan Hammadi, Sheikh Mohammad Rahma Bashiri. Daryabegi, the governor of the Gulf Ports, had brought field cannons and many Tangestani riflemen. Allegedly through the good offices of Satwat al-Mamalek governor of Bastak, the Warawis and their supporters made peace, apologized and withdrew. Bastaki does not mention the looting by the Marzuqi chief at all.[207] In September 1911, the chief of Taheri, whose jurisdiction also included Banak, Kangan, Tombak, Miyanlu, Akhtar and Nakhl-e Taqi, was the 30-year old Sheikh Hatem Khan, most likely Sheikh Hatem son of Hatem. He complained about the capture and burning of the two abovementioned dhows by the British navy just because

---

205 Because of these few shots, Hamidi, *Farhangnameh*, pp. 59-60, lauded and praised Sheikh Mazkur for being an ardent patriot, which he clearly was not.

206 *Administration* 1909-1910, pp. 22-25; Government of Great Britian, Persia No.1 (1911) *Further Correspondence*, p. 113.

207 Bastaki, *Tarikh-e Jahangiriyeh*, pp. 322-24.

they had a few rifles on board. According to Wilson, Sheikh Hatem Khan smuggled quite a lot of arms "and received a commission on all goods smuggled within ten miles or so of Taheri on either side."[208]

In early 1911, the Sheikhs of Mogam and Chiru fought about the repairs of a *berkeh* or water reservoir on the border of their districts. Sheikh Obeydli of Chiru asked the Sheikhs of Charak and Moghu to assist him in punishing those of Chiru.[209] In October 1911, the Sheikhs of Mogam and of Chiru were engaged in petty looting; the Sheikh of Moqam was assisted by a number of Warawis.[210] The Obeydli Sheikh of Chiru was building a fort at the border of the adjacent district of Kalat, whose Sheikh objected to this, and it was expected that fighting would ensue.[211] The Hamadi Sheikh of Mogam and the Obeydli Sheikh of Chiru settled their differences and allied to punish Saleh Sharif, head of a group of the Jat tribe, who had killed two suspected Obeydli spies during north of Humeiran. The two Sheikhs met at Bushehr and planned that on a fixed night the Obeydli chief would attack Saleh Sharif at Humeyran and that the Hamadi Sheikh on the same night would attack Kamalu, another chief of the Jat who was allied with Saleh Sharif, at Eshniz. The Obeydlis, out of greed, attacked one night earlier and captured 20 men, their wives and children. Kamalu was forewarned and marched with his followers and marched that night to the place where the Obeydlis were diving the plunder under a Sangar, leaving their prisoners on top. Kamalu by stealth reached the Sangar, freed Saleh Sharif and his men and jointly attacked the Obeydlis, who lost 10 men while the rest fled. The jats went to a secure place where they divided their plunder. Both parties felt insecure in their normal stamping ground and intended to go to Dashti, because they were not on good terms with their neighbors or with Ali Akbar Khan of Gallehdar.[212]

In the fall of 1911, the Warawis and Turakamis again were threatening the population of the Jahangiriyeh district supported by the Sheikhs of Gallehdar and Gavbandi, while Sheikh Abdollah Obeydli of Chiru, who had adopted a treacherous role during a similar October 1910 raid, was reported to be in sympathy with the enemy. Sheikh Ahmad Hamadi of Mogam, as before, loyally tried to check their advance into his territory, but due to treachery by Sheikh Obeydli of Chiru, assisted by 200 men, he was forced to defend himself.[213] This was not the end of their conflict, for in 1913, the Hamadi (Mugam) and Obeydli (Chiru) again commenced hostilities in the middle of the month over the border dividing their districts. The former were reported to have captured two villages.[214]

A similar event caused much ado in Lengeh in March 1912. In revenge for the capture of a large cargo of rifles belonging to the Warawi and Turakama tribes by *HMS Tamil* on 10 February 1912, the religious head, Aqa Mir Abu'l-Hasan Fali, called for an attack on the customs department and the British vice-consulate at Lengeh. To that end, he asked for support of Sayyed `Abdol-Hoseyn of Lar, who promptly declared a *jihad*

---

208 A. T. Wilson, *A Political Officer's Diary 1907-1914*. Oxford, 1942, p. 182. At an inderminated time, probably around this time, his *kadkhoda* Sheykh Seyf, probably a family member, had not paid all the revenues that were due and had been sent to Taheri. Vothuqi, *Tahavvolat*, pp. 35, 43.
209 FO 248/1025, News regarding Lingah for the period 8 to 14 August 1911; 1619
210 FO 248/1025, News regarding Lingah for the period 3 to 9 October 1911; 1629
211 FO 248/1025, News regarding Lingah for the period 17 to 23 October 1911; 1632
212 FO 248/1026, News regarding Lingah for the period 26 to 31 December 1911; 1645-46.
213 Archives Research Staff Ltd., *Political Diaries* 1910-11, vol. 4, p. 525.
214 Archives Research Staff Ltd., *Political Diaries* 1913-14, vol. 5, p. 230.

and promised to join forces with him. The threat of an attack looked serious on 7 March, when a force of 2,400 men were reported to be 60 miles from Lengeh. It was therefore, decided to strengthen the vice-consulate's guard. Since the local authorities had no force to oppose the attack, a British force from Jask of about 130 men was landed 12 March and remained on land until 19 April. The British vice-consul warned the Sheikhs of Chiru and Charak that if they allowed the raid to take place the British Navy would take punitive action against them. It was further intended to dynamite the fort of Chiru. The enemy was joined by the Sheikhs of Ishkanu, Gallehdar, and Gavbandi, and were some 5,000 strong at Ishkanu, where they waited for some time for Sayyed Abdol-Hoseyn Lari. The latter, it transpired later, was wary of the movements by the son of Qavam al-Molk, Nosrat al-Dowleh north of Lar. Because the Sayyed did not come and exaggerated rumors about the defensive steps taken at Lengeh, dissension grew in the ranks of the would-be attackers. The Sheikhs of Gallehdar and Gavbandi were the first to withdraw from the movement, which they were not really in sympathy with. Discontent increased, supplies were dwindling, and by the end of April 1912 the force was disbanded. Sayyed Abdol-Hoseyn tried to stoke the fire again one month later, but met with disinterest.[215]

Early in February 1913 a conflict broke out at Dovvan between the Al Ali and the Qavasem over fishing rights. Sheikh Khalfan b. Mosabbah Al Ali wounded two Qavasem men and imprisoned three of their leading men. Half of the village was under jurisdiction of Charak the other, occupied by Qavasem, under Lengeh. When the latter were released, they reported the case to the deputy-governor of Lengeh, demanding that Khan Bahador Aqa Badr, the British Agent in Lengeh, take up their case and protect them against the Al Ali. The deputy-governor promised to write Sheikh Khalfan, but the Qavasem told him "that his influence and intervention would be worse than useless." The deputy-governor finally appealed to Khan Bahador Aqa Badr, asking him to intervene. The latter replied that he was unable to do so without instructions from the Resident or the vice-consul. The deputy-governor then referred the matter to his chief in Bushire. In mid-February some 70 Qavasems left Dovvan for Moghu and Bostaneh.[216]

In 1915, there were surprisingly no inter-tribal conflicts on the Shibkuh coast. However Qavam al-Molk marched with a strong force into the Garmsir, because Sheikh Mazkur Khan, chief of Gavbandi had not paid his taxes for three consecutive years. Sheikh Mazkur Khan hearing this reinforced his defensive locations with *tofangchi*s and walls. As usual in case when a Shibkuh Sheikh was threatened by outside forces, Sheikh Mazkur received assistance from neighboring chiefs, in this case from Ali Akbar Khan *zabet* of Gallehdar, Sheikh Hatem of Taheri, and Sheikh Mohammad Ahmad Khan Al Haram. Qavam al-Molk who shied away from forcing his way through, asked Sowlat al-Molk, the governor of Bastak to mediate the conflict, because Sheikh Mazkur had blocked all roads and passes, which were under the command of his brother Sheikh Yusef Nasuri and Sheikh Seyf Nasuri, the Sheikh's uncle's son. They welcomed Sowlat al-Molk and Sheikh Mazkur paid one year's taxes and promised to pay his arrears and Qavam al-Molk returned

---

215 *Administration* Report 1912, pp. 36, 38; Government of Great Britain, Persia No. 5 (1912). *Further Correspondence respecting the Affairs of Persia*. London: HMSO, 1912, p. 108; Idem., Persia No. 1 (1913). *Further Correspondence*, p. 12.

216 *Administration* Report 1913, pp. 39-40 (Baqer Khan, chief of Ishkanu and his eldest son Hasan Ali Khan, were killed by six men hired by the brother of the late Sayyed Baba of Beyram, who was in constant fear of an attack by Baqer Khan. The latter was succeeded by his son Mirza Ali Khan).

to Shiraz. The amount received was much less than the cost of the military expedition, while Qavam al-Molk also lost face by backing down when opposed by local forces. As a result, Sheikh Mazkur Khan continued his defiant attitude towards the government and did not pay the promised amount.[217]

There also continued to be maritime or coastal violence. When in 1914 a British Indian vessel *Batal Zavar Prased* was stranded on the Shibkuh coast, it was plundered and its crew badly treated. The British Political Resident claimed 25,000 Rs from the Governor of the Gulf Ports, who told the deputy-governor of Bandar Abbas to negotiate with Sheikh Mazkur of Gavbandi, in whose jurisdiction the robbery had taken place. Since the latter had not paid his taxes to the government for many years, this was a rather futile suggestion as nobody expected anything positive to result from it. In fact, the case only was resolved in 1919, when Sheikh Mazkur promised to pay 10,000 Rs in two installments, and he indeed paid.[218] The situation of relative peace and quiet in Larestan continued in 1919, although in Bastak a dispute had arisen with those of Ashkanan due to a robbery of 14 camels belonging to Khan of Bastak by the Kharjai tribe, who were friendly with the Ashkenanis. The deputy-governor of Bastak retaliated by ordering attacks on Ashkanani caravans. Both chiefs finally appealed to Qavam al-Molk to settle their conflict. Elsewhere, the situation on the Shibkuh coast was about to enflame after those of Taheri had raided some of its villages. However, Daryabegi visited Kangan and returned the stolen animals to the owners.[219]

In 1916, little tribal trouble took place on the Shibkuh coast. The most serious incident was a conflict between Mohammad b. Rahman Bushri of Tavuneh and Sheikh Saleh of Charak, but timely arrival of Daryabegi averted the outbreak of fighting. In that same year, Daryabegi punished the sheikhs of the ports, who, in 1914, had aided the fugitives who had killed Aqa Badr, the British consular agent in Lengeh. Assisted by the British, he further installed a friendly Sheikh at Asalu, Mohammad Ahmad Khalfan, and drove Ali Akbar Khan from that port. The Sheikh of Chiru was expelled from Chiru and Henderabi for the same reason and in his stead Daryabegi appointed Sheikh Ebrahim Hammadi. This action included the bombardment of the port of Shivu, Sheikh Mazkur Khan's stronghold, which, according to the British, "had a most salutary effect throughout the Shibkuh coast."[220] Sheikh Mazkur Khan acted the innocent and in 1922 told the visiting *kargozar* that Daryabegi and the British bombarded Shivu during 17 days and that the shells destroyed many houses, while seven persons died. Moreover, the ships landed his enemies, the Hamadis at Shivu and Sheikh Mohammad Ahmad Khalfan at Basatin. Sheikh Mazkur claimed that he had no idea why his town was shelled, because he had no prior conflict with the British. However, as he admitted himself, Daryabegi sent him a note, which was brought by guards from Basatin, which to him looked as if it was in the handwriting of Sheikh Mohammad Ahmad Khalfan's clerk in Arabic, stating "I am charged by the government to attack you and thus be ready to fight," otherwise there was allegedly nothing in the note. Later, Sheikh Mazkur Khan sent one of his brothers,

---

217 Bastaki, *Tarikh-e Jahangiriyyeh*, pp. 326-227; *Administration* 1914, p. 15; *Administration* 1915, p. 13.
218 *Administration* Report 1914, pp. 15-16; *Administration* Report 1915, p. 15; *Administration* Report 1918, p. 13; *Administration* Report 1919, p. 13; Bastaki, *Tarikh-e Jahangiriyeh*, p. 345.
219 *Administration* Report 1920, pp. 12-13.
220 *Administration* 1916, pp. 14-15. Daryabegi and his ships also came to Moqam ,a Hammadi port, but no violence was used here. Vothuqi, *Tahavvolat*, p. 85.

Sheikh Abdollah, to Bushehr. From this visit it became allegedly clear that the bombardment had occurred because he was linked with (i) Ali Akbar Khan Gallehdari, the deposed chief of Asalu, (ii) the Qashqa'is, and (iii) allowing the passage through Shivu as well as of the protection of the Tangestani killers of Aqa Badr, all of which Sheikh Mazkur Khan denied being true. He further mused that the bombardment might have been due to the fact that before First World War he had refused presents such as a gold watch, binoculars, and a gun that Aqa Badr wanted to give him and other Sheikhs. To show how innocent he really had been Sheikh Mazkur Khan stressed the fact that although the *Persepolis* and the British ship had fired at his home, he had never fired at them.[221]

In 1917, barely one year after his appointment, Sheikh Ebrahim Hammadi was expelled from Chiru by Daryabegi, as punishment for his help to the killers of Aqa Badr. The British had considered the ouster of the Obeydli Sheikh from Chiru a blunder by Qavam al-Molk, who, however, instead of reinstating them, gave the port to Sowlat al-Molk of Bastak, which in effect was the same thing as giving it to the Obeydlis.[222] Sheikh Mazkur Khan continued his intrigues in Gavbandi, as a result of which in 1918, Sheikh Sayyir murdered his uncle, the Tamimi sheikh of Chah Mobarak and delivered the fort into the hands of Sheikh Abdollah b. Sheikh Hasan Nasuri, brother of Sheikh Mazkur Khan, against whom no action was taken by the government.[223] The Al Nasur were not happy with the loss of Nakhl-e Taqi to their Harami enemies in 1918, as discussed above. As a result, on 23 July 1919, 300 followers of Sheikh Hatem of Taheri raided the villages of Nakhl-e Taqi, Bidhakhan and took away some 1,000 goats and 170 donkeys and cattle. Soon thereafter Daryabegi went to Kangan and the animals were restored.[224] Sheikh Mohammad Ahmad Khalfan Al Haram of Asalu asked for a reduction of his taxes, because he always needed to keep *tofangchi*s at the ready because of Sheikh Hatem Khan and Sheikh Mazkur Khan Nasuri's enmity. In Qal'eh-ye Gharvizeh, in the Harami part of Gavbandi he kept 10 men. In the plain of Kushkenar he had a tower (*borj*) with four men to protect the people there, near it there were two other towers, each one with four men. In Qal`eh-ye Kushkenar itself he had 20 men as protection against Sheikh Mazkur. In Qal'eh-ye Sarvbash, his own residence, he had 40 men who were guarding day and night to protect him and his subjects around it. Despite all this vigilance, Sheikh Mazkur sent 20 men to plunder Harami territory during one month until they captured three of the marauders; these were imprisoned in Sarvbash, and were Kashkuli Qashqa'is.[225] In early 1920, there were fights between followers of Sheikh Mazkur and Sheikh Ebrahim Hammadi about the ownership of a village, but both sides agreed to settle their differences peacefully, for the moment.[226] Because, at the end of April 1922, Sheikh Mazkur's people stole 15 male and 30 female camels, which were taken to his district. The looters also killed two people. Sheikh Allaq Hammadi, chief of Mogam, complained to Sowlat al-Molk, who said that this was Qavam al-Molk's business. Sheikh `Allaq made it clear to Bushehr that he was willing to restore the village of Hashniz to Sheikh Mazkur, if that

---

221 Vothuqi, *Tahavvolat*, pp. 78, 80-81. For the local view of these events, see Sarya'i, *Goftaha*, pp. 51-56.
222 *Administration* 1917, p. 8.
223 *Administration* 1918, p. 12.
224 *Administration* 1919, p. 12.
225 Vothuqi, *Tahavvolat*, pp. 71-72.
226 *Administration* 1920, p. 14.

was what the government wanted, but on condition that Sheikh Mazkur would not later attack his district and restore the stolen property.[227]

The Final Chapter of the Arab Shibkuh Sheikhs

The above shows that there was never an idle moment on the Shibkuh coast; there was always an intrigue, a raid, a murder or something else going on. Furthermore, these violent and rebellious events since 1880 do not bear out those authors who argue that with the death of Sheikh Mazkur b. Jabbara the power and authority of the Arab Sheikhs of the Shibkuh coast had been broken. Locally in Gavbandi it was said that the power of the Arab sheikhs ended when Reza Shah took over the government of Iran. In particular, when some 2,000 soldiers were sent to Gavbandi ca. 1925 to arrest all sheikhs and bring them to Tehran.[228] This in my view is the more correct view, although the date is wrong as the cut with the past happened later and was a more long drawn-out process than just a simple event of the removal of one or more sheikhs.

Early in his reign Reza Shah made successful efforts to bring outlying regions, such as Arabistan that was held by Sheikh Khaz`al, under the full control of the central government. For the time being, he was less successful in the Persian Gulf littoral, for not only the Sheikhs of the Shibkuh coast remained a rather independent group of local chiefs, but so were the Khans of neighboring Dashtestan, Tangestan and Dashti.[229] In early 1928 there were reports of increased smuggling on the Shibkuh coast enabled, if not organized, by the local chiefs.[230] The military commander in Bushehr with 50 men went to Asalu with an armed dhow. The Tangestanis fired and killed the helmsman and the dhow returned to Bushehr. In reaction the military posted a few guards at Delvar and Asalu, but this had no significant impact on smuggling, and smuggled cigars and tea continued to enter Bushehr in large quantities. The Tangestani smugglers almost always escaped when sighted.[231] The Tangestanis also forced a group of soldiers to return, who came to arrest suspects of an attack in Bushehr. There also continued to be local disturbances between Angali and Shabankareh as well as between Asalu, Gallehdar, Kangan and Gavbandi, which unsettled the tribes.[232]

In reaction, in 1930 the central government began a disarmament drive of the tribesmen and peasants in Dashtestan, Tangestan, Dashti and the Shibkuh, a campaign that continued in subsequent years with some success.[233] In 1931, the commander of the Kerman regiment who was sent to the Shibkuh cost to establish full control over the area arrested 13 Arab Sheikhs and sent them to Tehran. It is further reported that the Khan of Bastak

---

227 Vothuqi, *Tahavvolat*, pp. 85-86, 88.
228 Najmabadi, "The Arab Presence," p. 138.
229 In 1926, Sheikh Mohammad b. Ahmad Khalfan of Asalu attacked Ali Akbar Khan of Gallehdar, while Sheikh Hatem of Kangan and Sheikh Mazkur of Gavbandi attacked the Sheikh of Asalu and took one of his strongholds. Archives Research Staff Ltd., *Political Diaries* 1922-27, vol. 7, p. 405.
230 For example, a boat belonging to Sheikh Mazkur of Gavbandi smuggling a cargo of rice, tea, and sugar was captured and taken to Lengeh. Archives Research Staff Ltd., *Political Diaries* 1922-27, vol. 7, pp. 327, 358-59, 484, 560 (Sheikh Mazkur handed over 500 rifles that he had taken from his subjects).
231 *Administration* Report 1928, p. 4.
232 *Administration* Report 1926, p. 4.
233 Sheikh Seyf Nasuri acted as guide for Col. Razmju and his troops to take and disarm the Al Haram. Taheri, *Az Morvarid*, p. 367.

assisted him in this operation. By the end of 1931 most Arab Sheikhs had been rounded up and sent to Tehran.[234] Sheikh Mazkur b. Hasan was among those arrested and on arrival in Tehran he was sent to prison where he died in 1931-32, allegedly of poisoned wine or water.[235] This arrest of the Sheikhs caused, of course, much uproar and unrest on the Shibkuh coast. Despite the stationing of 30 *Amniyeh* (gendarmerie) guards at Dayyir, Kangan and Taheri to maintain peace this did not happen.[236] The sons of Sheikh Hoseyn of Chahkutah rebelled in 1931 were arrested and sent to Tehran in June.[237] Moreover, the leading Sheikh of Teben, Sheikh Mohammed b. Ahmad Khalfan, who escaped arrest, mobilized the remaining Arabs and at the end of 1931 was still in rebellion, despite the fact that 1-2,000 troops had been sent against him. He visited Bahrain and Hasa and wanted to go to Riyad to seek support, but the Emir of Hasa did not allow him not to go beyond Hofuf. Sheikh Mohammed b. Ahmad Khalfan then returned to Teben and attacked an Iranian customs launch, killed an inspector and wounded an *Amniyeh* (gendarmerie) guard.[238]

In March 1934 a full regiment was sent to Shibkuh to disarm the followers of Sheikh Mohammad b. Ahmad Khalfan. The Sheikh tried to escape in his motor dhow to Bahrain, but he was sighted by the Iranian gunboat *Shahrokh*. He and his crew were arrested and taken to Shiraz to stand trial.[239] Despite the disarmament campaign smuggling continued unabated by the population of the coastal districts.[240] In the Shibkuh region, Sheikh Jaber, a nephew of Sheikh Mohammad b. Ahmad Khalfan continued his uncle's depredations and harassed the peasantry in that area. In April 1935 he was poisoned by another unnamed Arab chief, which ended this spree of banditry. Troubles caused by local chiefs in Tangestan and Dashti continued, however.[241] In November 1940, the sub-governorships of Ahram, Khormuj and Kangan were abolished to save cost. Their duties were thereafter carried out by subordinates under supervision of the governor of Bushehr. However, the new arrangement did not work well. Exactions by the officials only awakened the latent feeling of hostility among the tribes towards the central government authorities and there were serious classes between tribesmen and police and road guards. In December 1940, no less than 26 road guards were killed.[242] However, the government continued to make inroads on the traditional authority of the Sheikhs. In 1940, a land administration operation was ongoing in Bushehr, Borazjan and Rig. The inspectors assigned arbitrary values to the land, did not even respect their own valuations, and for a bribes lowered their assessment. New branches of the same office were to be opened in Deylam, Dayyir, Kangan and Taher.[243]

---

234 *Administration* Report 1931, p. 8; Archives Research Staff Ltd., *Political Diaries* 1930-31, vol. 9, pp 512, 534
235 Najmabadi, "The Arab Presence," p. 137.
236 Archives Research Staff Ltd., *Political Diaries* 1930-31, vol. 9, p. 566.
237 *Administration* Report 1932, p. 6.
238 *Administration* Report 1931, p. 8; Archives Research Staff Ltd., *Political Diaries* 1930-31, vol. 9, p. 534.
239 *Administration* Report 1934, p. 5.
240 *Administration* Report 1935, p. 3
241 *Administration* Report 1935, p. 7.
242 *Administration* Report 1940, p. 4.
243 *Administration* Report 1940, p. 3.

Sheikh Yaser b. Mazkur of Gavbandi neither succeeded his father in 1931 nor does he seem initially to have occupied an official function in the administration of Gavbandi.[244] However, after the abdication and exile of Reza Shah in 1941, his brother Sheikh Hareb Nasuri with Mobarak Ra'isi and 100 armed men made use of the confusion that existed at that time to attack and take Bandar-e Lengeh. By boat they sailed from Bastanu and when ashore at a place called Khurmlu. They were expecting that the soldiers were unprepared and leaderless, but they met with heavy resistance and had to return with empty hands.[245] Even then no complete break with the Nasuri past was made as other Nasuri chiefs continued to be appointed in the local administration. For example, Sheikh Yaser's second cousin, Sheikh Jabbara b. Hatem Nasuri was *bakhshdar* of Taheri, whose brother, Sheikh Soleyman Nasuri, was *bakhshdar* of Kangan in 1945. In February of that year they met the British consul in Bushehr and gave him reassuring reports concerning the safety and good crop prospects in their territory. Sheikh Soleyman built the Soleymaniyeh school and a public bath in Kangan.[246] By that time much of the control over the local administration had passed into the hands of the central bureaucracy as is clear when the British consul further reported in 1945 that Mr. Fahimi, the director of the economic department at Kangan, recently had sold stocks of sugar, tea, and cloth on the black market.[247] When Gavbandi became a separate district (*bakhsh*) in 1951, Sheikh Yaser b. Mazkur became its administrator or *bakhshdar*.[248] Thereafter, it seems that no more members of the Nasuri family were involved in the administration of their ancestral lands.[249]

---

244 He is credited to have built a road from Charak to Kalat, established a school (*Madraseh-ye Nasuri Gavbandi*) in Gavbandi, and set aside much land to fund charitable works such as the Friday mosque and a *Hoseynieh*, hence he had a good reputation. Darya'i, *Goftarha*, pp. 59, 61; Taheri, *Az Morvarid*, p. 370.

245 Darya'i, *Goftarha*, p. 60. There was also trouble in Gallehdar at that time, see Taheri, *Az Morvarid*, p. 368.

246 Archives Research Staff Ltd., *Political Diaries* 1944-45, vol. 16, p. 325; Idem, *Political Diaries*, 1946-47, vol. 17, pp. 181-82; Najmabadi, "The Arab Presence," p. 138; Taheri, *Az Morvarid*, p. 370. However, in 1942, Sheikh Soleyman of the Al Hamadi became *bakhshdar* of Kangan through bribery. It was also at that time that through contagion 3,000 people died in Kangan and its district. Archives Research Staff Ltd., *Political Diaries* 1942-43, vol. 15, pp. 36, 123. For a short biography of Sheikh Jabbara b. Hatem (1922-97), who wrote an unpublished [?] history of his family titled *Khandan-e Al Nasur*, as well as for a short bio of his brother Sheikh Soleyman b. Hatem (1885-1995), see Gholamzadeh, *Me`mari*, pp. 461, 463.

247 Archives Research Staff Ltd., *Political Diaries* 1944-45, vol. 16, p. 528. This process of the move of control over local authorities by the central administration had already started much earlier in ports such as Bushehr, Bandar Abbas and Lengeh, see Floor, *Bandar-e Lengeh*, Idem, *Bandar-e Abbas*; Idem, "Bushehr: Gateway to Southern Iran," in Larry Potter ed. *The Persian Gulf* [forthcoming] translated into Persian by Gholam Ali Tamhid as *Bushehr, darvazeh-ye tejarat-e Iran dar Khalij-e Fars*. Bushehr, 1390/2011.

248 Taheri, *Az Morvarid*, p. 370.

249 Except for Sheikh Abdol-Rasul Nasuri (1933-89), who was Sheikh of Nakhl-e Taqi, his birthplace, between 1950 and 1970. Gholamzadeh, *Me`mari*, p. 463. It is unlikely that he is the same Abdol-Rasul about it is reported that in 1943 the government sent Sheikh Jabbara Nasuri to Kangan "to take security for the future good behavior" of his brother Sheikh Abdol-Rasul of Asalu, who was implicated in a murder. Archives Research Staff Ltd., *Political Diaries* 1942-43, vol. 15, p. 399.

Wall decoration and column plinth of the Taheri residence

CHAPTER FOUR

The Extent of Al Nasur territory

The Al Nasur group members mostly lived in Taheri, Kangan, and Gavbandi by the mid-nineteenth century. By the early 1800s it was Kangan that was the seat of the Al Nasur chief. However, at various times the area over which the Al Nasur chief exercised control was much larger. In 1756, the Al Nasur controlled the Taheri, Kangan and Shilaw part of the littoral, and also possibly Gavbandi, if we may believe oral tradition.[1] In 1818, however, Captain Taylor submitted that the Al Nasur chief's territory only extended "to a small village, at a short distance to the west ward of it."[2] The area of the district (*boluk*) of Kangan proper stretched 13 *farsakh* from Nakhl-e Taqi to the village of Nik and its width was half a *farsakh*. In the east and north it was bounded by Gallehdari and to west and south by the sea. Kangan was situated at a distance of 60 *farsakh* or some 360 km south of Shiraz.[3]

It is not clear why the Al Nasur district allegedly had shrunk so much in size, unless Taylor was mistaken or unaware of the extent of the Al Nasur territory, which seems likely. However, by the 1830s the Al Nasur were in a different situation. By that time "The whole country along the coast from Cape Bardistan to Aseloo is under the place [i.e. Kangan].[4] In about 1844 Gavbandi, a Larestan district, came to the Al Nasur chief, if he did not have it earlier already.[5] After the sack of Kangan in 1858, Sheikh Mazkur, when in exile, was Sheikh of Sho`eyb for a while. By the 1870s Sheikh Mazkur b. Jabbara was governor of Banak, Kangan, Tombak, Ayenat, Akhtar, Taheri (under his brother Sheikh Hatem), Barak, Haonah,[6] Nakhl-e Taqi, Asalu, Beyzeh Khan (Bed Khan), Nakhl-e Hashel,

---

1 One may draw some support for this oral tradition by the fact that Sheikh Jabbara supported Sheikh Ahmad Madani's rebellion in 1731 (see chapter two), which would have been facilitated by the fact of the former being in charge of Gavbandi.
2 Taylor, "Extract," pp. 20.
3 Fasa'i, *Farsnameh*, vol. 2, 1462. Fasa'i, vol. 1, p. 115 adds, that in the early Moslem period the *boluk-e* Kangan was called Siraf.
4 Brucks, "Memoir," pp. 590; 3/4 *farsakh* from coast to mountains, and at some places half *farsakh*. Three sides are toward the land. Kazeruni, *Tarikh*, p. 73.
5 Fasa'i, *Farsnameh*, vol. 2, p. 1463.
6 This should be Ras al-Shajar, see Lorimer, *Gazetteer*, vol. 2, p. 1792.

Ras Asfan, Bandar Kalat, Shiyu, Basatin, Mogam (Al Mukham), Nakhilu, Ras Zalee,[7] and the islands of Sheikh Sho`eyb and Henderabi. It is of interest to note that Sheikh Mazkur controlled the district of Asalu, which was previously held by the Al Haram as well as Nakhilu, although a local chief, Sheikh Hatem was his representative as was his brother, also named Sheikh Hatem, in Taheri.[8] However, with the fall and death of Sheikh Mazkur in 1882, the Al Nasur only held onto Gavbandi, although they still had much influence in Kangan and Taheri. Kangan was part of the governor of the Gulf Ports' jurisdiction as of 1888.[9] Therefore, the Al Nasur were able to get control over these two ports again in 1902-1903, but they were expelled from there in 1904.[10] Even in Gavbandi the Al Nasur lost control over those parts that were inhabited by those who claimed to belong to other groups than the Al Nasur in 1906. In 1912, the Kangan district was still described as being 78 km long and 3 km wide stretching from Nakhl-e Taqi till Beng. To the north and east bounded by Gallehdar, and south and west by sea.[11] As of 1940, like other coastal chiefs, the Al Nasur lost their hold over Gavbandi, which became part of a larger district administrated by an official appointed from Tehran.

The Kangan-Taheri District

Although the Al Nasur Sheikhs at times controlled a territory that was larger than their traditional home base it was two districts: Kangan/Taheri and Gavbandi that constituted the basis of their power. In this section I, therefore, discuss the lay of the land in each of these two districts so as to have an idea about their size and importance, or lack thereof. According to Fasa'i, writing in 1882, the district of Kangan had 12 villages, to wit: Akhtar, Parak, Taheri, Banak, Tonbak, Chah-Kur, Sabakheh, Nakhl-e Taqi, Gudeh, and Nakhl-e Ghanem [Qayem] plus Bandar-e Taheri[12] The government of Iran estimated the population of the entire district at 12,000 in 1911. This number dropped to 8,000 in 1940, due to demand for labor at the head of the Persian Gulf.[13] In what follows I describe some of these villages about which information is available.

Kangan

The port of Kangan is the northernmost of the Shibkuh ports, "and the only one lying north of the region in which the main maritime range fall directly into the sea. These

---

7 Perhaps Ras al-Chiru, which is quite near to Henderabi.
8 Saldanha, *Précis*, vol. 7/2, p. 3; also *Administration Report* 1875-76, pp. 16, 20; In 1866, according to Colville, "Land Journey, p. 38, Sheikh Mazkur ruled from "Bussaf to the district of Hameroon."
9 Government of India, *Military Report on Persia*. 4 vols. Simla, n.p., 1924, vol. 4, part 2 (Fars, Gulf Ports, Yazd and Laristan), p. 52.
10 "It is now governed on behalf of the Khan of Dashti who holds it in farm." Adamec, *Historical Gazetteer*, vol. 3, p. 387; "It was considered at that time part of the Vilayat-e Dashti." Anonymous, "Les Reformes Administratives," *RMM* 23/1913, pp. 73-74; copied in Mas`ud Keyhan, *Jografiya-ye mofassal-e Iran*, 3 vols. Tehran, 1311/1932, vol. 2, p. 480.
11 Anonymous, "Les Reformes Administratives," pp. 73-74.
12 Fasa'i, *Farsnameh*, vol. 2, pp. 1462-1634; Anonymous, "Les Reformes Administratives," pp. 73-74; copied in Keyhan, vol. 2, p. 480.
13 Anonymous, "Les Reformes Administratives," p. 74; Lindberg, *Voyage*, p. 73.

high hills first strike the coast about 5 miles west of Kangan."[14] It is situated on the eastern shore of a deep bay near Cape Bardestan. It had an excellent roadstead with good anchorage, and was well sheltered from north-westerly winds (the *Shomal*), although anchorage at Dayyir was better. This rival port, which was part of Dashti, is situated at the opposite western side of the bay, 14 km to the west. Kangan was about 32 km northwest of the next considerable Shibkuh port, that of Taheri and exactly opposite Bahrain, from which it is distant about 220 km.[15] In the 1750s its anchorage was described as "You may anchor here at what Depth you may please, and it is four fathoms about a Quarter of a Mile distant from the Shore."[16] Kangan's most outstanding landmark was the rugged peak known variously as the Sugarloaf or conical hill or as Barnhill or Jebel Serai, "a remarkable piece of land, (which derived is name from its resemblance to an old decayed thatched building, and which is situated over the town of Congoon)."[17]

As so many other settlements along the Shibkuh coast the available space from coast to mountain was rather narrow. "In some places one day's, in others two days' journey inland."[18] In the case of Kangan itself it is not more than one km and all around it are mountains. The land in between is stony with non-arable wadis. Apart from date palms there were no trees. From April to October the weather was hot and very humid, like everywhere along the littoral. The rainy season was from December to March, and water came down from mountain that mostly ran into the sea. Thereafter it did not rain and there was no water at all, although the plain was split by heavy run-off gullies. Drinking water was from wells and was somewhat brackish. There were also water cisterns, which were badly built. Sweet water there was very good and pleasant, such as in Taheri and Tombak where they had cisterns that are open on top to let rainwater in.[19] By 1900, there was good water in three wells, that were 4 to 5 fathoms deep. There was also a hot spring that was resorted to on account of its curative properties.[20] In 1940, the drink water situation had not changed. The town still relied on its many wells with brackish water and four that had drinking water. There also was a water cistern that was not used any more. Unlike other Shibkuh ports, such as Asalu, no Guinea worms were present in the water, but malaria was rampant. There was no doctor in Kangan.[21]

Population

Around 1810, according to Kinneir, "The port of Congoon contains six or seven thousand inhabitants.[22] Some 20 years later it had 500 households, or some 3,000 inhabitants.[23]

---

14 Lorimer, *Gazetteer*, vol. 2, p. 972.

15 Brucks, "Memoir," pp. 590-91; John MacDonald Kinneir, *A geographical memoir of the Perdian empire*. London: J. Murray, 1813, p. 81; Curzon, *Persia*, vol. 2, p. 406; Adamec, *Historical Gazetteer*, vol. 3, p. 387.

16 Plaisted, *A Journal*, pp. 17-18.

17 Morier, *Journey*, p. 7; R.B. M. Binning, *A Journal of Two Years' Travel in Persia, Ceylon, etc.* 2 vols. London: Wm. H. Allen & Co., 1857., vol. 1, p. 137; Brucks, "Memoir," p. 591.

18 Taylor, "Extract," p. 20.

19 Fasa'i, *Farsnameh*, vol. 2, p. 1462 (according to whom the well was at 100 paces from the shore and had sweet water); Anonymous, *Do safarnameh*, pp. 100-02.

20 Adamec, *Historical Gazetteer*, vol. 3, p. 387.

21 Lindberg, *Voyage*, p. 76.

22 Kinneir, *A geographical memoir*, p. 81.

23 Anonymous, *Do safarnameh*, p. 100.

Around 1840, when Kangan was still a sizable port with a population living in an estimated 3,000 houses, of which 1,500 were from lime and rock and the rest mud and rock and date timber.[24] An Iranian bureaucrat visiting Kangan in 1837 gave as his opinion about its people that they were totally unreliable and opportunistic, i.e. people who followed the rule of the *ahl-e Saqr*.[25] In the 1860s, i.e., after the sack of the port in 1862, it was reported that "Bunder Congoon was once well inhabited."[26] The drop in population was due to the subsequent sacks of the town as well as its transfer to the jurisdiction of the Khan of Dashti in the 1880s, who favored the development of his rival port of Dayyir. As a result, "The place [i.e. Kangan], at the present time (1906) partially abandoned, normally consists of some 300 Arabs of mixed tribes; about two-thirds of the population are Sunnis and the remainder Shias." After a short Al Nasur interregnum (1903-04) some inhabitants left for Fao and other places.[27] In 1912, the government of Iran, erroneously, estimated the population of the district of Kangan at 12,000 and of the port itself at 8,000 inhabitants. As this report was but a translation of Fasa'i entry in his *Farsnameh*, these figures do not reflect the situation of Kangan at that time.[28] In the nineteenth century, some 20 Jewish families or 120 persons lived in Kangan.[29] Around 1914, the town had a population of 300, including 50 Jews and Arabs, according to Vadala. This population number is at odds with that given by the chief (*kadkhoda*) of Kangan in 1922. Then he said there were 1,200 people, of which two-third were Sunnis, including 10 Jewish families.[30] It is possible that the increase in population was due to the fact that in 1911, Sheikh Ahmad Dashti lost control over Kangan and was replaced by Sheikh Hatem Khan Al Nasur (see above).[31] By 1940, Kangan was the most important and most populous port s.w. of Bushehr. The town boasted of 1,000 inhabitants and 8,000 for the entire district. The bazaar seemed to be bigger than in Dayyir, and there were no less than five mosques as well as an old mosque in ruins. The new additions to the town were the government building, which had sleeping arrangements for traveling officials, as well as an elementary school, the *Dabestan-e Onsuri* with a hundred or so boys and a few girls.[32]

Table 4.1: Estimated population size of Kangan (1756-1940)

Year	Population size	Observations	Source
1756	5,000*	Incl. Jews, Banians	Floor, *The Rise*, p. 29
1800	7,000	-	Kinneir, *Geographical memoir*, p. 81
1809	10,000	-	Morier, *Journey*, p. 8

---

24 Kazeruni, *Tarikh*, p. 73.
25 Anonymous, *Do safarnameh*, p. 100, referring to Surah al-Nisa', ayah 56.
26 Anonymous, "Brief Account," p. 185.
27 Adamec, *Historical Gazetteer*, vol. 3, p. 387; Lorimer, *Gazetteer*, vol. 2, p. 972; Vothuqi, *Tahavollat*, p. 37.
28 Anonymous, "Les Reformes Administratives," pp. 73-74.
29 David Yeroushalmi, *The Jews of Iran in the Nineteenth Century: Aspects of History, Community*, Leiden: Brill, 2009, p. 74.
30 R. Vadala, *Le Golfe Persique* translated into Persia by Shafi' Javadi as *Khalij-e Fars dar `asr-e este`mar*. Tehran, 2537, p. 133; Vothuqi, *Tahavvolat*, p. 37.
31 Vothuqi 1381, pp. 35-36. Sheikh Hatem b. Hatem died in Kangan in 1376/1956. Hamidi, *Farhangnameh*, p. 58.
32 Lindberg, *Voyage*, p. 73.

Year	Population size	Observations	Source
1820	6,000	-	Fraser, "Notes", p. 412
1836	1,400	-	Brucks, "Memoir," p. 591
1837	15,000	3,000 houses	Kazeruni, *Tarikh*, p, 73.
Ca. 1840	3,000	500 households	Anonymous, *Do safarnameh*, p. 100
1906	300	-	Adamec, *Hist. Gazetteer*, vol. 3, p. 387
1911	8,000	Highly unlikely	Anonymous, 1913, p. 74
1914	300		Vadala, *Khalij-e Fars*, p. 133
1922	1,200	600 households	Vothuqi, *Tahavvolat*, p. 35
1940	1,000		Lindberg, *Voyage*, p. 73

* 1,000 men, assuming a family size of five-six persons.

Given the attacks that Kangan was regularly subjected to it is no surprise that in 1840 or thereabouts the port had a wall with 25 towers on a gate to the east and one to the south.[33] Right in the middle of the town stood a square fort. Curzon's statement that "Kangun was once a trading port of renown, having been a Portuguese settlement, and still contains the ruins of the factory built by that people" is entirely wrong.[34] It is well-known that whenever foreign travelers saw a fort in any of the Persian Gulf ports they almost invariably ascribed it to the Portuguese, for which only evidence to the contrary exists.[35] Ahmad Eqtedari who visited the various Gulf ports, including Kangan, rightly made the point that the fort in Kangan was of recent date.[36] In 1940, there still was old ruined fort, which is flanked on side by a square tower and the other by a round tower.[37] Apart from the personal arms of its inhabitants, there also were 7 good iron pieces of 8- and 12- and 18-pounds in the late 1830s.[38] In 1922, Kangan could mobilize 200 *tofangchi*s, while 20 of them were paid 4-10 *tuman*s by Sheikh Hatem to guard the town. The latter was locally represented by a *kadkhoda*, who, in 1922 was Hajji Ahmad. Prior to that year it had been his son Hasan.[39] The best building in town was the fort that had been built and was owned by Sheikh Hatem.[40] In 1940, Kangan still had an old ruined fort, which was flanked on side by a square tower and on the other by a round tower.[41] In 1837, half of the 3,000 houses were constructed from lime and stone and the other half from mud, stone and date palm wood.[42]

---

33 Kazeruni, *Tarikh*, p. 73.

34 Curzon, *Persia*, vol. 2, p. 406. This piece of fiction also found its way into the Gazetteer. Adamec, *Historical Gazetteer*, vol. 3, p. 387; Lorimer, *Gazetteer*, vol. 2, p. 972; and US Government, *Persian Gulf Pilot*, p. 252.

35 See the discussion on this topic in Floor, *Political Economy*, p. 599.

36 Ahmad Eqtedari, *Athar-e Shahrha-ye Bastani*. Tehran: Anjoman-e Athar-e Melli, 1348/1969, p. 323. For a photo, plan and description of the Qal`eh-ye Kangan, see Gholamzadeh, *Me`mari*, pp. 408-11, who gives the end of the 19th century as the construction date.

37 Lindberg, *Voyage*, p. 74.

38 Anonymous, *Do safarnameh*, p. 100.

39 Vothuqi, *Tahavvolat*, p. 35.

40 Vothuqi, *Tahavvolat*, pp. 35-36. Sheikh Hatem died in Kangan in 1376/1956. Hamidi, *Farhangnameh*, p. 58.

41 Lindberg, *Voyage*, pp. 73-74.

42 Kazeruni, *Tarikh*, p. 73.

Kangan Fort

In about 1840, the road between Bardestan and Kangan was flat and even over a distance of two *farsang*.⁴³ In 1932, Kangan was connected to Bushehr by a modern road, when in that year relief work road construction work started on a road from Bushire to Lengeh, which road extended as far as Kangan by the end of that year.⁴⁴ According to Lindberg, in 1940 Kangan in winter a creek (*khur*) with swamps around and much water was an obstacle between Dayyir and Kangan.⁴⁵ Nearby, there was a small sweet water river, where in 1940 stood small white cottages that were built by wealthy inhabitants of Kangan to find relief during the hot season.⁴⁶

Economic activity

Like the other small ports on the Iranian littoral the people of the district of Kangan were gainfully employed as cultivators, fishermen, pearl divers, sailors, and traders; in bad times they also engaged in maritime violence. These various occupations are a reflection of the resources available to Kangan.

---

43 Anonymous, *Do safarnameh*, p. 100.
44 *Administration* Report 1932, pp. 4, 6.
45 Lindberg, *Voyage*, pp. 70-71.
46 Lindberg, *Voyage*, p. 73.

Kangan was surrounded by many date groves and grain cultivation.[47] Together with trade and cattle Kangan's most important resource were its date groves.[48] Although the space between the coastline and the mountains was only some 3 km this area was covered with date-groves, over a distance of some 2.5 *farsakh*, i.e. between *Qal`eh-ye Derak* [Dereng?] to the north until another fort to the south of the port. From the mountains to the east ran a stream and below it was a mill used by the inhabitants. Its water was also used to irrigate the date-groves and gardens.[49] Around 1900, Kangan had as many as 2,000 palms.[50]

Palm trees were not the only trees in the district, because its gardens were filled with *konar* or jujube trees, while there also were many fig gardens.[51] According to Fasa'i, writing in the 1880s, Kangan's agriculture consisted of date groves with rather small palms, which were all rain-fed (*deymi*), as well as the cultivation of pulses and vegetables such as onions and purslane (*khorfat*) with the help of *ab-e gavchah*.[52] This was an ancient technique that was already applied 800 years earlier if not prior to that time in the Irahestan district, including the interior, according to Ibn Balkhi. "Then during the winter these trenches are filled by the rain with water, [which sinks in] and so all the year round the palms gets moisture. The dates are of rare excellence."[53] Perhaps the small river mentioned in the 1840s had dried up, or the system had been destroyed during one of the many wars with Dashti. In the beginning of the twentieth century the system of agriculture had not changed much, where dates, of which there were 2,000 palms, and grain still dominated.[54]

In addition Kangan had supplies of indifferent cattle and excellent water.[55] In 1900, or thereabouts, Kangan had 5 horses, 200 camels, 100 donkeys, 200 cattle, and 2,000 sheep and goats.[56] For those who wanted to have some exercise there also were pheasants that were hunted.[57] Fish could also be had in this district because many of its inhabitants made their living with fishing in small vessels. In addition, Kangan supplied firewood and charcoal, both scarce items in the Persian Gulf.[58]

However, in the 1830s Sheikh Jabbara b. Mohammad Hatem pointed out that his people made their living at sea not on land, which brought no benefit, and this held true for all coastal Arabs. The dates only sufficed for a few months, the rest were bought in Basra. Kangan's grain local grain production sufficed for only one week's consumption. Therefore, its grain was actually transported by traders from inland, who traded that with visiting Arabs and inhabitants here.[59]

Consequently, a great part of its population were sailors, who sailed to India and Yemen trading in their *baghala*s, *batil*s, and *baqarah*s. Many of its inhabitants didn't trade but

---

47 Anonymous, *Do safarnameh*, p. 100.
48 Taylor, "Extract," p. 19.
49 Kazeruni, *Tarikh*, pp. 73-74.
50 Lorimer, *Gazetteer*, vol. 2, p. 972.
51 Kazeruni, *Tarikh*, p. 74.
52 Fasa'i, *Farsnameh*, vol. 2, pp. 1462, 1526; Anonymous, *Do safarnameh*, pp. 103-04.
53 Ibn Balkhi, *Description*, pp. 48-49.
54 Anonymous, "Les Reformes Administratives," pp. 73-74; copied in Keyhan, vol. 2, p. 480; Adamec, *Historical Gazetteer*, vol. 3, p. 387.
55 Brucks, "Memoir," p. 591.
56 Lorimer, *Gazetteer*, vol. 2, p. 972; Adamec, *Historical Gazetteer*, vol. 3, p. 387.
57 Fasa'i, *Farsnameh*, vol. 2, 1462.
58 Morier, *Journey*, p. 8; Kinneir, *A geographical memoir*, pp. 81-82.
59 Anonymous, *Do safarnameh*, p. 101.

were lease-holders (*kerayeh-kesh*) or were owners, and there was prosperity in the town, where one also saw people from all parts (*motafareqeh*).[60] In about 1840, there were about 20 big *baghala*s at Kangan that were owned by its chief and inhabitants.[61] In the 1850s, "several of the finest Buggalows in the Gulf belong to this port and they carry on a very extensive trade, principally as carriers to Bombay and the Malabar Coast, and to most of the ports in the Persian Gulf and Red Sea."[62] The Kangani vessels were dismasted for the season in the gut of the small woody island of Malgaram.[63]

Kangan must have suffered considerably from the many attacks it had to suffer from Dashti (see above) as well as the fact that it was sacked several times by the same tribe, the last time in 1867. Consequently, according to Colvill in 1866, the prosperity of Dayyir dates from the destruction of Kangan in 1858 by Jamil or Jamal Khan of Dashti.[64] There were many pearl divers at Kangan, for there were pearl banks at Mahalu or Miyalu, where pearls continued to be caught. However, only by those who had permission to do so, because no stranger dared engage in pearl diving in the Sheikh's territorial waters. Despite this activity, there was no pearl trade anymore, like in the seventeenth and part of the eighteenth century, when the pearl trade was important to Kangan. In the 1750s it was reported that Kangan had "a tolerable Trade, for most of the Pearl which is fished up at Bareen on the Arabian Side is brought hither to be sold, and there are likewise many fine Horses exported from hence to be carried to India."[65] However, in the nineteenth century Kangan had neither a pearl nor a horse trade.[66] The structure of economic activity had not changed much by 1900, when people were still fishermen, pearl-divers, and sailors. The town had 8 *sambuk*s that sailed to Qatar, Bahrain, Qatif, Basrah, and various Iranian ports, also a dozen small *baqarah*s of the kind called `amilah which were used for fishing.[67] In 1922, the sale of fish and foodstuff yielded about 1,000 *tuman*s per year. There also was a gypsum mine that served local demand, while there also was production of earthenware vessels and pots.[68]

Table 4.2: Ships owned by inhabitants of Kangan

Year/Vessel type	Coastal vessel	Fishing boats	Tons	Crew	All vessels
1875	12	11	265	167	23
1900	8	10-12	-	-	18-20
1914	-	-	-	-	15

Source: *Administration* 1875-76, p. 42; Lorimer, *Gazetteer*, vol. p. 972; Vadala, *Khalij*, pp. 108, 133

Around 1840, Kangan boasted of a bazaar in which many craftsmen and traders were to be found as well as four caravanserais and traders were living in them.[69] Circa 1900,

---

60 Kazeruni, *Tarikh*, p. 73
61 Anonymous, *Do safarnameh*, p. 100.
62 Brucks, "Memoir," p. 591.
63 Brucks, "Memoir," p. 589 (Mulgurram).
64 Colville, "Land Journey," p. 37.
65 Plaisted, *A Journal*, pp. 17-18.
66 Morier, *Journey*, p. 55; Vadala, *Khalij-e Fars*, p. 133.
67 Adamec, *Historical Gazetteer*, vol. 3, p. 387; Lorimer, *Gazetteer*, vol 2, p. 972.
68 Vothuqi, *Tahavvolat*, p. 36.
69 Kazeruni, *Tarikh*, p. 73.

the number of the shops was about 20.[70] The 10 Jewish families of Kangan worked as drapers (*bazzazi*), pedlers, and goldsmiths.[71]

Table 4.3: Exports from Bushehr to Kangan 1915-16 (in tons)

Year	Loaf sugar	Crystal sugar	Piece-goods	Yarns	Rice	Spices	Kerosene	Tea	Miscellaneous	Total
1915-16	-	13	1	-	1	1	2	-	-	18
1916-17	-	28	2	-	9	2	3	-	1	41

Source: Report 1915-16. p. 7; Report 1916-17, p. 8.

Kangan was the port of Jam and Riz in the interior, 10 to 20 miles distant northwards. As a result, there always was a small mercantile community in Kangan that consisted of Arabs, Banyans and Jews, although the Banyans disappeared in the 19th century. Most visiting traders were from Bahrain, Qatif and Lahsa, who brought fabrics such as bath-cloths (*shal-e longi*) and other Arab goods trading those for grain. Part of the local agricultural production as well as that which traders brought from the hinterland (such as grain and tobacco) was exported. In short, the district of Kangan exported the following goods: grains, dates, animals, earthenware vessels, firewood, and charcoal. Its imports were: sugar, tea, rice, and piece-goods.[72] Kangan was some 360 km from Shiraz, with which it was connected via a route that went to Firuzabad, a route that had been in use since ancient times (see Table 4.4).[73]

Table 4.4: Route between Kangan and Firuzabad

From	To	Distance in *farsakh*	Observations
Firuzabad	Rouechkeft	5	Salt river crossing
Rouechkeft	Dehran	4	
Dehran	Moudecht [Miyandasht]	6	
Moudecht	Desgua [Dezgah]	3	Salt river crossing; Mand
Dezgua	Rizeh [Riz]	7	
Rizeh	Tenghi Darek [Pas-e Durak]	4	
Tenghi Darek	Bender-Kengoun	3	Total 32 *farsakh*

Source: Dupré, *Voyage*, vol. 2, p. 492; Adamec, *Historical Gazetteer*, vol. 3, pp. 585, 620

---

70 Adamec, *Historical Gazetteer*, vol. 3, p. 387.
71 Vothuqi, *Tahavvolat*, p. 37.
72 Adamec, *Historical Gazetteer*, vol. 3, p. 387; Kazeruni, *Tarikh*, p. 73; Anonymous, *Do safarnameh*, p. 100.
73 For a discussion of the old route, see Lindberg, *Voyage*, pp. 273-75. It was said that, in some of the passes, ropes are required in ascending the most difficult parts; without ropes they are inaccessible." US Government, *Persian Gulf Pilot*, Washington DC, 1920, p. 252.

Taxation

The hereditary Sheikh of Kangan was the exclusive tax farmer of his own district. The above-mentioned economic activities were, therefore, taxed by the Nasuri Sheikhs who paid their annual tribute and other fees to the government of Fars or Bastak, in the case of Gavbandi. Initially, Kangan's tax burden seems to have been light. Sheikh Jabbara b. Mohammad Hatem swore in the late 1830s, that under the two previous shahs 700 *tuman*s in cash as *pishkesh* was given and absolutely nothing as *maliyat*![74] However, in 1812, the district of Kangan paid 1,000 Tomans yearly to the government of Iran.[75] One hundred years later this amount had reached 2,186 *tuman*s.[76]

One of the sources of revenue out which the Sheikhs of Kangan paid the central government was the cultivation of dates. Around 1840, Sheikh Jabbara collected 100 dinar per date tree (*asleh*), or as they were called locally one *bayaz*, i.e. old money of 100 dinar, which equaled 200 current dinars (*dinar-e rayej-e soltani*) in Kangan. The Sheikh also collected one-fifth (*khoms*) of the production to which end he sent somebody to collect it.[77] According to Siddiq, under the Nasuris the people had to pay 10% on all agricultural production and animals and pearl fishing, which, in Gavbandi, the Ra'isi family had to collect.[78] However, the term 'oshr, literally, one-tenth, was often used indicate to simply indicate an unspecified tax rate that often was more than 10%.[79] In 1905, when Kangan was under the Khan of Dashti, it pays 1,800 *tuman*s, including the amounts paid by the villages of Banak and Kangan (300), Alanat (650) and Akhtar (400), which were all sublet by the Dashti chief to his cousin Ahmad for 1,500 *tuman*s.[80] In the early twentieth century, Kangan paid 1,000 *tuman*s in taxes as follows: per cow-12 *qran*; wheat, dates- per *buneh* 1 *qran* in 4 installments, and per installment 50 *tuman*s, or per year 200 *tuman*s was collected from these revenue sources. Later, in 1922, Sheikh Hatem collected 1,322 *tuman*s per year, which he paid to the Tax office. The first two years when Soleyman Mirza was head of the Tax office he was paid 600 *tuman*s wages from the customs revenues; there after until the British left Bushehr in 1918, he annually paid 600 *tuman*s as customs. In 1911, when Ahmad Khan Dashti held Kangan, at the orders of Movaqqar al-Dowleh, Sheikh Hatem was sent with the *Persepolis* and *Mozaffar*, expelled Ahmad Khan and he took control of the town. Since then until 1922 he claimed that he had paid his taxes regularly. As of 1918, Sheikh Mohammad Ahmad Khalfan held Nakhl-e Taqi, which meant a reduction of 300 *tuman*s of Sheikh Hatem's revenues. At that time, he only collected 0.5 *qran* per date tree and 15 *qran*s as head tax and nothing else. According to the chief of Customs the annual customs revenues were varying, but in 1921 were 1,130 *tuman*s and in 1922 30 *tuman*s higher. Sheikh Hatem owned the Customs building, which he rented for 5 *tuman*s per month. The Jewish population (ca. 50) paid a poll-tax of 30 *tuman*s per year.[81] The Sheikh, of course, also collected taxes from the other towns ands villages in his district (see below).

---

74 Anonymous, *Do safarnameh*, p. 100.
75 Taylor, "Extract," p. 20.
76 Anonymous, "Les Reformes Administratives," pp. 73-74.
77 Kazeruni, *Tarikh*, pp. 74-75.
78 Najmabadi, "The Arab Presence," p. 138; it is not entirely clear whether this rate and its collection method applied to the entire district or, given the involvement of the Ra'isi family, to Gavbandi.
79 Willem Floor, *A Fiscal History of Iran in the Safavid and Qajar Period*. New York: Bibliotheca Persica, 1999.
80 Adamec, *Historical Gazetteer*, vol. 3, p. 676.
81 Vothuqi, *Tahavvolat*, pp. 35-37, 44.

4 / THE EXTENT OF AL NASUR TERRITORY

Akhtar is situated at 12 km west of Taheri. In Akhtar wheat and barley were cultivated as well as onions. Akhtar also produced good water melons and bad sweet melons. Agriculture was arduous work in Akhtar, as well as in other parts of Kangan district, where the entire land was covered with stones and to cultivate the peasants had to remove the stones. To water their crops, in particular onions, they made use of a water-wheel (*dulab*).[82] Around 1900, Akhtar had 30 houses and a population of 70. Its population were mostly Sunnis, who cultivated wheat, barley, and dates (1,000 palms) and were sailors and fishermen. The people also kept a number of animals: 100 camels, 60 donkeys, 200 cattle, as well as 2,000 sheep and goats. The village was farmed at 400 *tumans*.[83] In 1922, it had 50 households or 150 inhabitants, of which 30 were also *tofangchi*s.[84]

Table 4.5: Ships owned by inhabitants of Akhtar

Year/Vessel type	Coastal vessel	Fishing boats	Tons	Crew	All vessels
1900	Several	6 *baqarah*s	-	-	8-10
1914	-	-	-	-	4
1922	-	-	-	-	2

Source: Adamec, *Historical Gazetteer*, vol. 3, 680; Vadala, *Khalij*, pp. 108, 133; Vothuqi, *Tahavvolat*, p. 46.

Parak Fort

---

82 Kazeruni, *Tarikh*, pp. 75-76.
83 Adamec, *Historical Gazetteer*, vol. 3, p. 680; Vadala, *Khalij-e Fars*, p. 108, 133.
84 Vothuqi, *Tahavvolat*, p. 45.

Banak was a small dependency, and is the northernmost of the Shibkuh ports on the Iranian coast. Around 1900, it had 20 stone houses, and a decade later a population of 190 people, who were cultivators and sailors. Banak was administered from Kangan, but after 1844 it was most of the time under the control of the Dashti chief. People cultivated wheat, barley, and dates; it had 800 date palms. There also was some animal husbandry with 50 camels, 100 donkeys, 100 cattle, 3,000 sheep and goats. Its water supply came from cisterns and wells, which were 12 fathoms deep.[85] As other ports it a small number of vessels, both for trading and fishing.

Table 4.6: Ships owned by inhabitants of Banak

Year/Vessel type	Coastal vessel	Fishing boats	Tons	Crew	All vessels
1875	2	8	91	39	10
1914	-	-	-	-	5
1922	-	-	-	-	2

Source: *Administration* 1875-76, p. 42; Vadala, *Khalij*, pp. 108, 133; Vothuqi, *Tahavvolat*, p. 46.

Barak or rather Parak was a small town 5 km SSE of Taheri with 200 inhabitants of the Nasur tribe.[86] It had a fort, a square tower, and a date grove.[87] In 1922, it had 30 households or 80-90 inhabitants, of which 30 were *tofangchi*s. South of Parak there were 15 households of nearby Miyanlu who also were armed and did not pay taxes.[88]

Miyanlu (also Mahalu, Mayalu) was a small village, dominated by the 4,660 feet high Jabal Siri some 7 km in land. In the 1830s it had about 100 inhabitants of the Qavasem (Joasmee) tribe. Around 1900, it had 150 inhabitants, who made a living from their pearl banks, trading, and from some cultivation of wheat, barley and onions. The village had a few boats, for pearling, fishing and trading. It mostly exported animals, grain and onions.[89] In 1922 it had 30 households or 120 inhabitants of which 30 were *tofangchi*s.[90]

Table 4.7: Ships owned by inhabitants of Miyanlu

Year/Vessel type	Coastal vessel	Fishing boats	Tons	Crew	All vessels
1875	2	6	70	48	8
1914	-	-	-	-	5
1922	-	-	-	-	3

Source: *Administration* 1875-76, p. 42; Vadala, *Khalij*, pp. 108, 133; Vothuqi, *Tahavvolat*, p. 46.

---

85 Adamec, *Historical Gazetteer*, vol. 3, p. 679; Vadala, *Khalij-e Fars*, p. 108, 133.
86 Brucks, "Memoir," p. 592.
87 US Government, *Persian Gulf Pilot*, p. 250.
88 Vothuqi, *Tahavvolat*, pp. 45-46. For a photo and a short description of Qal`eh-ye Parak, see Gholamzadeh, *Me`mari*, p. 382.
89 Kazeruni, *Tarikh*, p. 75; Brucks, "Memoir," p. 591; Adamec, *Historical Gazetteer*, vol. 3, p. 387; Vadala, *Khalij-e Fars*, p. 108, 133.
90 Vothuqi, *Tahavvolat*, p. 45.

Nakhl-e Ghanem [Qayem] was a small village subject to the Sheikh of Kangan; in 1835 it had 150 people of the Bani Malah tribe. There were several small villages around it at a short distance of the bay, which also were subject to Kangan and housed altogether 900-1,000 men of the Bani Malek and Bani Tamim tribes.[91]

Nakhl-e Taqi is situated at 20 miles s.w. of Taheri. When the Al Nasur settled there they allegedly renamed it al-Na`imah.[92] In the 1830s, it was "a small village with a Ghuree [headman] dependent on Aseeloo. It had 70 inhabitants who were of the Nussoor tribe.[93] Its most important landmark was Sir-e Yalfal, some 10 km inland from Nakhl-e Taqi; its height was some 1,620 m. Around 1900, its 900 inhabitants lived in 80 huts. In 1922, the village had 200 families. The village had a fort and a tower. One quarter were Shiites, while the rest were Sunnis. In summer the population was engaged in pearl diving, trading and fishing; cultivating and growing dates occupied them when they were back home. Its major exports were wheat, barley, firewood, and charcoal.[94] After it had been for many years in the hands of the Al Nasur, in 1918, the government returned this village to the Al Haram (see above). By 1940, the village's situation had not much changed. Pearling is not mentioned, but fishing and trading are as people's occupation. Lindberg noted that all around the village onions were cultivated, which were exported to Bahrain, Muscat, and Arabia, while there also was wheat and date cultivation. Its water came from slightly brackish wells.[95]

Table 4.8: Ships owned by inhabitants of Nakhl-e Taqi

Year/Vessel type	Coastal vessels	Fishing boats	Tons	Crew	All vessels
1900	5 *bum*	14 *baqarah*	-	-	19
1914	40	-	-	-	40
1922	-	-	-	-	4

Source: Adamec, *Historical Gazetteer*, vol. 3, 680; Vadala, *Khalij*, pp. 108, 133; Vothuqi, *Tahavvolat*, p. 46.

Taheri

Taheri was a large village situated in a small open bay, formed by two low points some 3 km apart, with excellent shelter in a north-wester, and good in a south-easter. This meant that vessels could be brought quite close inshore, instead of, as was usually the case in the Persian Gulf, having to lie a long way out. The bay deepens regularly from the coast to 8 fathoms and 800 m offshore. In the early Middle Ages, Taheri had been a major commercial center and was known as Siraf. However, it lost this function to Kish and it became an unimportant fishing village. From the remaining ruins it was clear to visitors that once it had been a large and flourishing town. When the Al Nasur settled down in Siraf they

---

91 Brucks, "Memoir," p. 593 (Nakle Haghel).
92 Kazeruni, "Al Nasur," p. 55.
93 Brucks, "Memoir," p. 592.
94 Adamec, *Historical Gazetteer*, vol. 3, p. 680; Lorimer, *Gazetteer*, vol. 2, p. 1780; Vadala, *Khalij-e Fars*, p. 108, 133; Vothuqi, *Tahavvolat*, p. 49; US Government, *Persian Gulf Pilot*, p. 250. For a description and photo of the Qal`eh-ye Nakhl-e Taqi, built by Sheikh Hatem b. Hatem and Sheikh Abdol-Rasul Nasuri, see Gholamzadeh, *Me`mari*, p. 412.
95 Lindberg, *Voyage*, p. 93.

renamed it Taheri. In the early nineteenth century, Taheri was one of the so-called *Thalitha* or Three Ports, which from Bushehr to the south, included: Kangan, Taheri, and Asalu. Taheri like Kangan was part of the governor of the Gulf Ports' jurisdiction as of 1888.[96]

It would seem that Taheri was independent of Kangan during much of the eighteenth century. However, by around the 1800s Taheri had lost its pre-eminence, if that what it had been, and became a dependency of Kangan. According to an anonymous Persian source written in 1865, "Some 100 years ago Bunder Taurie was in a better condition. It then contained about 100 merchants and some good buildings; these are now in ruins."[97] This decline may have been due to the Omani attacks on Taheri in the 1730s, losses suffered after the naval mutiny against Nader Shah in 1741 and following years, the loss of Bahrain to Bushehr and Rig in 1751. A fact is that in the nineteenth century Taheri is only mentioned as a dependency of Kangan.[98]

The village was partly built on the shore and partly on the side of the coast range. In 1835, Taheri had a population of 350 Arabs of the Nasur tribe and few supplies were available.[99] In 1865, Taheri, which was the residence of Sheikh Hatem (Khatham), the younger brother of Sheikh Mazkur, had a population of 300 families, and was somewhat dilapidated.[100] Around 1900, it had 150 stone houses; its inhabitants were mainly Arabs and some Iranian Shiites. It had a population of 700, including 200 Jews.[101] In 1922, Taheri had 100 households or 250-60 inhabitants. The population was one-third Shiite, but there was no history of enmity between the Shiites and Sunnis. Sheikh Hatem Khan claimed that his forebears had always maintained good relations and had helped the Shiites. As they had no means he himself had built a Hoseyniyeh for them and for the mourning ceremonies in the months of Moharram and Safar he and the people of Taheri provided them with financial assistance. There were only 8 Jews left in Taheri in 1922, who were peddlers.[102] There were two white mosques in the middle of Taheri at some 100 meter apart; to the west of it there were the ruins of a mosque.[103]

The most attractive building in town was the fortlike mansion that Sheikh Jabbara had built at the beginning of the nineteenth century. The walls on the inside had been embellished with mural sculptures of scenes from the *Shahnameh*. The relief or rather a series of reliefs are done in plaster mould (*gach-bari*) and constitute the main back part of the portico or *ivan* of the fort's outer courtyard. The reliefs, made by Ostad Ali Asghar Shirazi, consist in two categories. One is a series of reliefs displaying trees, branches with leaves, angels, birds, parrots, and peacocks. The other constitutes in a set of 18 frames of the best stories of the *Shahnameh*, and depict: (1) Keykhosrow and Keyka'us; (2) Rostam kills the Div-e Safid; (3) Soltan Mahmud Ghaznavi and his courtiers; (4) Ferdowsi and other contemporary poets, `Asjadi, Farrokhi, and `Onsori; (5) Anushirvan the Just's court;

---

96 *Military Report Fars*, p. 52; Hamidi, *Farhangnameh*, p. 55; Anonymous, "Les Reformes Administratives," pp. 73-74; Arthur W. Stiffe, "Ancient Trading Centres of the Persian Gulf. I. Siraf", *Geographical Journal* VI (1895), pp.166-73; David Whitehouse, *Excavations at Siraf* (with Persian translation as *Kaveshha-ye bastanshenasi dar Bandar Siraf* by GholamReza Ma`sumi), Bushehr: Shoru`, 1384/2005.
97 Anonymous, "Brief Account," p. 185.
98 Anonymous, *Do safarnameh* 1368, p. 104; Taylor, "Extract," p. 19.
99 Brucks, "Memoir," p. 590.
100 Colville, "Land Journey," p. 38.
101 *Military Report Fars*, p. 53; Vadala, *Khalij-e Fars*, p. 133 ; Adamec, *Historical Gazetteer*, vol. 3, p. 680.
102 Vothuqi, *Tahavvolat*, pp. 45-47, 50; US Government, *Persian Gulf Pilot*, p. 251 (200-300 people).
103 US Government, *Persian Gulf Pilot*, p. 251.

Mural decoration of scene from the *Shahnameh*, and doorway of the Sheikh's Taheri residence

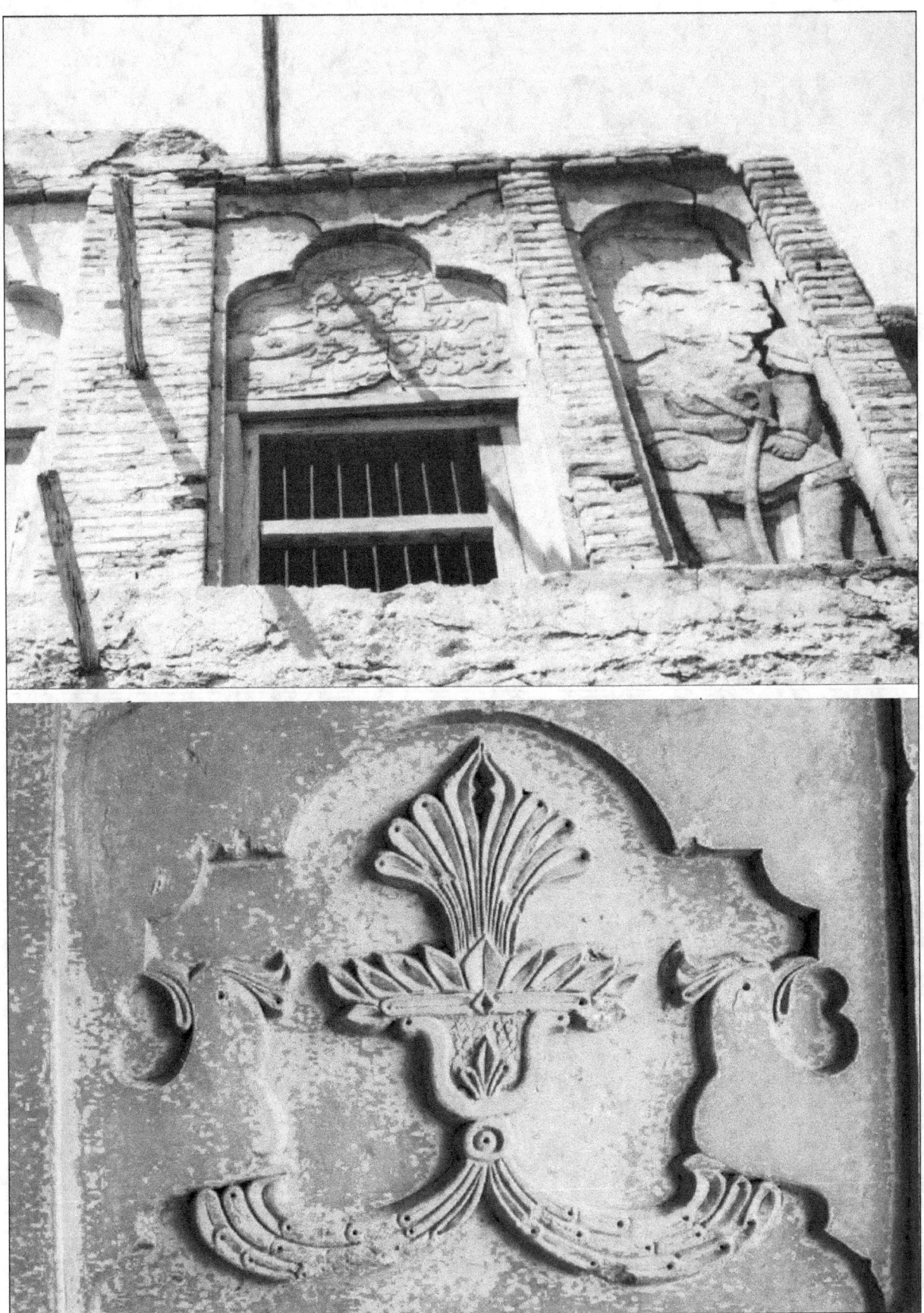

Mural decorations of the Sheikh's Taheri residence

(6) Akvan, the Div throws Rostam into the ocean; (7) Siyavosh passes through fire into safety; (8) Rostam kills the white elephant; (9) Siyavosh hunting; (10) Gudarz and Giv; (11) Keykhosrow's court; (12) Rostam and Zal; (13) Rostam gets Bizhan out of the pit; (14) Bahman, Esfandiyar's son, throws a rock from the mountain and Rostam kicks it aside; (15) Sohrab in search of his father; (16) Sohrab is killed by his father Rostam; (17) Rostam shoots an arrow into Esfandiyar's eye; and (18) Shaghad, Rostam's brother, tricks Rostam and his horse Rakhsh into a pit, but Rostam nails Shaghad to a tree with one arrow. Furthermore, the portico has stone sculptured pillars.[104] Unfortunately, these reliefs were destroyed by vandals in 1979, believing that in doing so they would do the Lord's work and hasten the advent of the Mahdi.[105]

Apart from stone houses, "many parts of the rock have been excavated for residences in the hot season. The pass in the hill is fortified in a manner beyond the abilities of the natives, at least now."[106] In 1818, there ran a mud wall, as far up to the hills "as is supposed passable for troops, with six bastions at distances near the foot of it."[107] Around 1840, there were two forts on two hills on either side of fort.[108] "The only routes into the interior are by 2 passes, by blocking which an enemy could be confined to the narrow strip of the sea coast."[109] The fort, like in any other port, was no luxury as these places were surrounded by groups of people that considered them either to be enemies or prey. Therefore, each port and village had a number of *tofangchis* to be on the alert for attacks. In 1922, Taheri itself had no *tofangchis* of its own, apart from Sheikh Hatem Khan's 50 servants, which he paid for himself. These remained in town, while 100 Baluchis stayed in the mountains and did guard duty only. This was really necessary given raids by neighboring groups. The Jewish population of Taheri, who made their living peddling all kinds of wares in 1922 had been without income for more than one year, because they could not travel anymore. The reason were those of Jam, who plundered them and, for example, goods that they wanted to take to Akhtar and Tombak were stolen from them. Sheikh Hatem said that from the moment that he became governor he had given those of Jam such a beating that they were not able to take even one skin from his people. However, in 1921 a Qashqa'i chief had summoned him to Jam and told him not to molest those of Jam anymore, and if he did then the tribal chief would hold Sheikh Taher responsible. As a result, Sheikh Taher claimed that those of Jam had been raiding, plundering and killing

---

104 Gholamreza Ma`sumi, *Siraf – Bandar-e Taheri*. Tehran: Anjoman-e Athar-e Melli, 1352/1973, pp. 321-25. The book further contains pictures of all the reliefs as well as drawings of them, while as to the *Shahnameh* scenes were possible miniatures representing the same scenes as on the reliefs also have been published in Ibid., pp. 326-622. See also for a photo of scene (3), Eqtedari, Ahmad. *Athar-e Shahrha-ye Bastani-ye Savahel va Jaza'er-e Khalij-e Fars va Darya-ye `Oman*. Tehran: Anjoman-e Athar-e Melli, 1348/1969, p. 436, figs. on pp. 344-49; Vothuqi, *Tahavvolat*, p. 36; Hamidi, *Farhangnameh*, p. 57. For those knowing Persian the entire story of each scene is related in Ma`sumi's book. Those not knowing Persian may consult the *Stories from the Shahnameh* in 3 vols. published by Mage Publishers, where these stories are retold in excellent prose and embellished with beautiful illustrations. Although Sheikh Jabbara is credited with the construction of the fort-mansion he was not in Taheri in the early 1800s, but rather his cousin Sheikh `Allaq, who may have built it at his orders. For a photo, plans and description of the Qal`eh-ye Sheikh or Qal`eh-ye Nasuri, see Gholamzadeh, *Me`mari*, pp. 386-406.
105 When I visited Taheri in 2005 I was able to see this mansion and the damaged art work, and the local people apprised me of the cause of the destruction of the murals.
106 Brucks, "Memoir," p. 590.
107 Taylor, "Extract," p. 19.
108 Anonymous, *Do safarnameh*, p. 104.
109 Government of India, *Military Report Fars*, pp. 52-53.

since one year and four months. With considerable exaggeration, Sheikh Hatem claimed so far those of Jam had killed 50 people and plundered people's possessions, allegedly to the tune of 100,000 *tuman*s, which is clearly an inflated made up amount. He had written to the governor of Bushehr, who had not replied. He then had written to the Qashqa'i chief who replied that he would come and fine the looters of Jam to the last dinar and take vengeance on the killers, but he had not come.[110]

Taheri was a village with date groves and cattle, while its people also lived off fishing in small vessels. The village had some cisterns high up that were open on top to let rainwater in with excellent water. It also had water from wells 3 fathoms deep. Around 1900, it had a few horses, 25 cattle, 300 sheep and goats.[111]

Taheri had trade relations with Bahrain (rice, textiles), Bushehr (sugar), Basra and Mohammareh (dates). Its exports were: onions (Basra; Mohammarah), firewood and charcoal (Bushehr, Bahrain), animals from its hinterland for Bahrain, as well as some wheat, barley, lime, stones, and salt fish from the surrounding villages. In the mid-nineteenth century tobacco from Gallehdar was an important export article. Sometimes, there was export of animals from Gallehdar and Dashti, when relations were good, as they were in 1922, or from Jim and Gallehdar (but in 1922 relations were bad), which animals were exported to Bushehr and Bahrain.[112] From Taheri there was a good road via the Gallehdar district and the village of Jaharan to Shiraz, an 8 to 9-days journey.[113]

Table 4.9: Export from Bushehr to Taheri 1915-16 (in tons)

Year	Loaf sugar	Crystal sugar	Piece-goods	Yarns	Rice	Spices	Kerosene	Tea	Miscellaneous	Total
1915-16	18	47	9	-	6	4	3	6	2	94
1916-17	3	95	8	1	28	1	3	-	1	140

Source: Report 1915-16. p. 7; Report 1917-17, p. 8

In 1905, Taheri paid 1,900 *tuman*s in taxes, which were composed as follows: Bagh-e Sheikh and Taheri (1,600) and Banak plus Ras al-Shajar (300).[114] Customs revenues in 1922 were estimated at 400-600 *tuman*s per month, but expenses were 400 *tuman*s. The area was unsafe, which negatively impacted on Customs revenues and also travel to nearby ports such as Dayyir. There also was much smuggling.[115]

For its various maritime activities (fishing, trading, pearling) the village needed ships. In 1835, it had "several trading boats of varying size,"[116] usually about 20 (See Table 4.9). In the early twentieth century its people had 14 sailing boats, mainly *bum*s of 15-20 tons

---

110 Vothuqi, *Tahavvolat*, pp. 45, 50-52. The inhabitants of Gallehdar and Jam were Persian speakers and didn't understand a word of Arabic, according to Colville, "Land Journey," p. 38.

111 Fasa'i, *Farsnameh*, vol. 2, 1462 (according to whom the well was at 100 paces from the shore and had sweet water); Anonymous, *Do safarnameh*, pp. 100-02; Taylor, "Extract," p. 19; *Military Report Fars*, p. 53.

112 Vothuqi, *Tahavvolat*, p. 45; Colville, "Land Journey," p. 38; Adamec, *Historical Gazetteer*, vol. 3, p. 387; Vadala, *Khalij-e Fars*, pp. 108, 133; Government of India, *Military Report Fars*, p. 52.

113 Colville, "Land Journey," p. 38.

114 Adamec *Historical Gazetteer*, vol. 3, p. 676.

115 Vothuqi, *Tahavvolat*, pp. 48-49.

116 Brucks, "Memoir," p. 592.

Tombak Fort

average and about six trading *sambuk*s.[117] Also important for trade was a post office. In 1907 there was one with the Customs office and there was a regular in- and outgoing mail. Thereafter, letters were sent by sailing boat to Bushehr.[118]

Table 4.10: Ships owned by inhabitants of Taheri

Year/Vessel type	Coastal vessel	Fishing boats	Tons	Crew	All vessels
1875	11	6	309	145	17
1914	-	-	-	-	20
1922	-	-	-	-	20

Source: *Administration* 1875-76, p. 42; Vadala, *Khalij*, pp. 108, 133;; Vothuqi, *Tahavvolat*, p. 53.

Modern times did not pass by Taheri, because about 1920 a school was established that in 1922 had 20 students, where Persian, Arabic and English were taught. However, there

---

117 Government of India, *Military Report Fars*, pp. 52-53.
118 Vothuqi, *Tahavvolat*, p. 47.

was apparently a teachers problem, because in 1922 Sheikh Hatem Khan was willing to pay 150 *tuman*s per year to attract an English or Persian teacher to the school.[119]

Tombak or Bandar Tanbak or `Aniyat as the Arabs called it is at 19 km s.e. of Kangan. To the north of it is the village of Sanjeh. It was a small town where in the mid-1830s about 500 men of the Bootambee Tribe lived. It had a tolerably good anchorage in 10 fathoms in a north-wester. Its inhabitants owned several trading boats.[120] According the American *Persian Gulf Pilot*, `Aniyat and Tombak were two villages situated at 2 km from each other. `Ayinat had a small square tower, and at either end a date grove, and at its western end a large square house. Tombak to the north of it had 100 inhabitants and several square towers among the houses and one round tower on the western side that stood out. There were many trees inside the village, which was surrounded by date groves.[121]

It also had good sweet water stored in cisterns that were open on top to let rainwater in.[122] In 1837, agriculture was not doing well in Tombak due to lack of rain.[123] North of Bandar Tombak in the village of Sanjeh the people raised cattle and sheep.[124] In about 1900, Tombak had 225 stones houses and a population of 400. The people were Shafi`i Sunnis, except for 20 Jews living in the town. However, by 1922, there were no more Jews in Tombak. The people were engaged in cultivating dates and grain (each village in its environs had a date grove), fishing and traded with various Gulf ports, Oman, and Basra. Its major exports were grains, dates, animals, firewood, charcoal. It was farmed for 650 *tuman*s, while there was a Customs post.[125] In 1922, the long time *kadkhoda* or assistant (*pakar*) of Sheikh Hatem was Hasan. At that time the village had 200 households or about 1,000 inhabitants. To protect the village some 50 men had guns, but some 150 might be armed, if guns would have been available.[126] In 1840, or thereabouts, Sheikh Jabbara b. Mohammad Hatem collected from the Tombak area 200 *bayaz* dinars or equal to 400 current dinars in Shiraz, in addition to one-fifth of the harvest.[127] In 1922, taxes were collected on dates and as head-tax. Per tree 0.5 *qran* was collected and the head-tax was 15 *qran*s per person/year. Nothing was collected from other cultivation, which was limited to wheat and onions, or from keeping cows. Part of the onions as well as firewood was exported to Bahrain and Bushehr, but to Basra only onions. Wheat for people's own consumption was imported. In good years the people of Tombak also exported animals to Bahrain. From these markets they imported sugar, rice, and textiles. There were neither traders nor craftsmen in the village. If the fish catch was good the fish surplus (catch minus local consumption) was exported to Bushehr and Bahrain. Total annual revenues amounted to 300 *tuman*s that were collected by Sheikh Hatem, who also owned the Customs building that he rented out for 5 *tuman*s/month. There were three *tofangchi*s with the Customs official, who collected 1,200 *tuman*s in customs, of which after deduction of

---

119 Vothuqi, *Tahavvolat*, p. 46.
120 Brucks, "Memoir," p. 591; Kazeruni, *Tarikh*, p. 75.
121 US Government, *Persian Gulf Pilot*, pp. 251-52. For a photo and short description of the Qal`eh-ye Tombak, built in the 1940s or thereabouts, see Gholamzadeh, Me`mari, pp. 383-84.
122 Anonymous, *Do safarnameh*, p. 102.
123 Kazeruni, *Tarikh*, p. 75.
124 Kazeruni, *Tarikh*, p. 75.
125 Adamec, *Historical Gazetteer*, vol. 3, p. 679; Vadala, *Khalij-e Fars*, pp. 108, 133; Vothuqi, *Tahavvolat*, p. 39.
126 Vothuqi, *Tahavvolat*, pp. 38-39.
127 Kazeruni, *Tarikh*, pp. 74-75.

expenses they transferred 600 to 700 *tuman*s to Bushehr. The *kadkhoda* complained about the insecurity in the village's hinterland and therefore, his unpaid *tofangchi*s had always to be on their guard. As a result they could not have their animals graze there.[128] In 1940, Tombak had 800 inhabitants, who were mostly fishermen.[129]

Table 4.11: Ships owned by inhabitants of Tombak

Year/Vessel type	Coastal vessel	Fishing boats	Tons	Crew	All vessels
1875	5	7	129	81	12
1900	12	6	-	-	18
1914	-	-	-	-	400 [?]
1922	-	-	-	-	15

Source: *Administration* 1875-76, p. 42; Adamec, *Historical Gazetteer*, vol. 3, 679; Vadala, *Khalij*, pp. 108, 133; Vothuqi, *Tahavvolat*, p. 39

The Gavbandi District

Gavbandi

Only Siddiq, a local historian, mentions that Gavbandi (locally pronounced as Gaobandi and today called Parsiyan) was part of the Al Nasur lands, because Fasa'i explicitly states that only under Sheikh Hasan b. Jabbara that district came under the Nasuri sheikhs. Its status was also different from Kangan and Taheri in that it was not a port, and that like most of the Shibkuh coast districts it was a dependency of the governor of Bastak. Until the Nasuri Sheikh became *zabet* of Gavbandi, according to the *Tarikh-e Jahangiriyeh*, the Nasuri part appeared to have been managed by Mohammad Saleh Ra'isi and the chiefs of Fumestan, but the so-called Dehestan-e Harami was under the Sheikhs of the Bani Tamim, Bani Maleki and Al Haram.[130] Until 1906, Sheikh Hasan b. Mazkur's district included: on the coast Dastur, Kharabeh, Bustanu, Buragheh, Ziyarat, Kalatu, Shivu, Saifal Shaikh and the Harami, Maliki, Nasuri, Tamimi villages of the Gavbandi valley and the villages of Darveh Asuh valley.[131]

Gavbandi is a valley in the Shibkuh district, parallel to the coast, situated at an average distance throughout of about 16 km, reaching the sea at Naband. The length of the valley is ca. 75 km. The center point in the valley was Chah Mubarak. There were Harami, Maliki, Tamimi and Nasuri villages. In about 1900, these were as follows:[132]

---

128 Vothuqi, *Tahavvolat*, pp. 38-41 (the *tofangchi*s had a wage of 9 *tumans* each).

129 Lindberg, *Voyage*, p. 78.

130 Gavbandi, Fumestan, and Asaluyeh were part of Bastak, see Bastaki, *Tarikh-e Jahangiriyeh*, p. 132, 152, 219, 282 is sometimes also used as a synonym for Gavbandi, see, e.g., *Encyclopedia Britannica* vol. 10, 1911, p. 190. It is also the name of a village in Gavbandi district (see table 4.10).

131 Lorimer, *Gazetteer*, vol. 2, p. 562. In 1892, the governorship of Gavbandi seems to have been in the hands of Rostam Khan, son of Fath Ali Khan, governor of Lar. Why and for how long he held sway there I have not been able to find out, see FO 248/567 Maughu bin Meyia to Lengeh Agent, 8 October 1892/16 Rabi` I 1310.

132 For the situation in 1875, see *Administration Report* 1875-76, p. 21 (32 villages plus the district of Kooskunar).

Table 4.12: List of the villages of Gavbandi District by ethnic group affiliation, ca. 1900

Name	Houses	Camels	Donkeys	Cattle	Sheep	Horses	Palms	Cisterns	Wells
			Nasuri	Villages					
Ahsham	150	40	150	100	3000	-	2000	2	-
Amuni	50	12	20	80	1200	-	700	-	-
Bambari	20	4	10	30	200	-	1500		-
Bardul	50	-	30	60	20	-	3000		water mil
Dailam	20	6	20	40	-	-	500	-	-
Dashti	200	70	200	320	2000	-	1000	-	-
Dukun	90	20	30	150	2000	-	2000	-	-
Fumistan	70	-	30	100	300	-	500	-	Springs
Gabandi	300	30	200	400	2500	15	11000	8	wells
Garit	30	7	90	45	200	-	1000	-	-
Khalaf	20	20	30	30	1500	-	1500	Water fr.	Gabandi
Kunar Bahar	35	30	40	70	2000	-	1000	Water fr.	Gabandi
Milaki	40	5	15	30	1500	-	800	-	-
Muqbil	20	3	15	15	70	-	300	-	-
Sitiu	60	30	20	45	1500	-	800	-	-
Surkhuha	30	12	40	35	400	-	1000	-	-
			Harami	Villages					
Askar[Bu]	80	4	4	90	600	-	1300	-	10
Bazbaz	50	-	30	70	1500	-	3000	2 sprs.	3
Den Now	70	3	50	45	800	-	3000	-	Many
Ghoweyzireh	50	6	-	40	500	-	700	-	8
Kashkonar	425	60	500	900	5000	-	16000	5 reserv	Many
Khiyaru	120	10	60	100	1600	-	4000	-	14
Khond	260	15	130	280	3000	-	15000	2sprs.	30
Sarvbash	110	6	40	-	500	-	3500	3 reserv	25
Tang Sharzeh	10	-	15	35	500	-	2500	3 sprs.	-
Tombu	70	3	25	40	800	-	1600	-	14
Tombu Gharbi	40	2	25	150	2500	-	2500	-	12
			Maleki	Villages					
Akabir	60	5	15	40	300	-	2500	-	18
Banud	80	10	90	100	1500	-	7000	-	18
Basaten	100	7	40	60	800	-	6000	-	8
Favares	70	5	30	40	300	-	2300	-	15
Kharch	100	10	100	130	800	-	10000	-	22

Name	Houses	Camels	Donkeys	Cattle	Sheep	Horses	Palms	Cisterns	Wells
Kunehkeymeh	70	5	25	40	800	-	5000	-	12
Safiyeh	70	15	30	65	600	-	5000	1 reserv	6
Savahel	50	3	25	45	350	-	500	-	4
Zubar	90	15	70	75	300	-	5000	1 reserv	8
			Tamimi	Villages					
Ayn al-Sawdeh	20	-	-	-	500	-	1000	3 sprs	-
Bondu	80	-	20	80	1000	-	500	-	7
Bostanu	110	10	70	100	2000	-	4500	-	12
Chah Mobarak	230	20	160	250	1500	8	12000	4 reserv	20
Jalalat	50	-	15	40	-	-	1300	-	3
Morva'eh	40	-	25	45	500	-	600	-	5
Sahmu	90	6	50	100	800	-	3000	-	7
Sahmu Sharqi	70	5	40	-	600	-	3500	-	5

Source: Adamec, *Historical Gazetteeer*, vol. 3, pp. 259-62.

The people of Gavbandi, numbering about 19,500 based on the number of houses around 1900, were of mixed origin, speaking both Persian and Arabic, and were mostly Shafi`i Sunnis. There also were Shiites and only 4 Jews in Gavbandi in 1922. The Nasuri villagers were not really Nasuris only the family of their chief and a few others belonged to that tribal group. Wheat, barley, maize, rice, flax and tobacco were cultivated, mostly rain-fed, but in some places crops were irrigated. Date palms were everywhere and some villages cultivated limes, pomegranates and vines. Most of its inhabitants were cultivators, while some were pearl divers who went to the other side of the Gulf during the pearling season.[133] In Gavbandi, Kash Konar (Khooch Khonar) was the largest village with 100 families; it was a flax producing area. What was not consumed locally was supplied to the surrounding villages as material for their nets.[134] In 1905 or so the population in the valley was distributed as follows:

Table 4.13: Population distribution in Gavbandi by political affiliation (ca.1900)

Political affiliation	Number of people
Harami villages	6,400
Maleki villages	3,700
Nasuri villages	5,900
Tamimi villages	3,500
Total	19,500

Source: Lorimer, *Gazetteer*, vol. 2, p. 562.

---

133 Adamec, *Historical Gazetteer*, vol. 3, p. 262; Vothuqi, *Tahavvolat*, p. 76.
134 Colville, "Land Journey," p. 38.

Gallery of the Gavbandi fort

Due to political troubles, i.e. fights between the various Sheikhs, many people left the valley and emigrated to Bahrain, Kuwait and Fao and in most villages there were empty houses around 1900.[135] Until 1906, Sheikh Mazkur held sway over the whole valley of Gavbandi, but in that year the valley was divided in three areas. Sheikh Mazkur's revenues that had been 12,000 *tuman*s per year, were reduced to 7,000 *tuman*s for the district that included the Nasuri villages in the valley, Shivu, the villages of Darveh Asuh and some other places on the Shibkuh coast (see above). In 1906 the Tamimi villages were split off and given to Tamimi Sheikh, Saqr b. Mobarak of Chah Mobarak. The latter was henceforth responsible to pay 5,000 *tuman*s to the governor of Bastak for the Maleki and Tamimi villages and 3,500 *tuman*s to Imperial customs for the Harami villages in Gavband and on the Shibkuh coast. Sheikh Saqr was killed in March 1907 and there was no immediate successor.[136] The new Sheikh probably remained in office until 1918, when he was murdered by his nephew, who handed the Tamimi district to Sheikh Mazkur Nasuri,

---

135 Lorimer, *Gazetteer*, vol. 2, p. 562.
136 Lorimer, *Gazetteer*, vol. 2, pp. 562, 1787.

who seemed to have transferred the district again to a Tamimi Sheikh, as is clear from the extent of his jurisdiction in 1922.[137]

In 1918, Sheikh Mazkur lost the government over Akbari and Farsi, which Qavam al-Molk, governor of Lar, gave to Sheikh Mohammad Ahmad Khalfan Al Haram, the Al Nasur enemy; this represented a loss in revenue of 500 *tuman*s.[138] In 1922, Sheikh Mazkur Khan Nasuri governed the following 3 districts and their villages: (i) Hashaniz, Beh Deh, Ketardun, Ahsham, Bardul, Fumsan, Milaki, Amani, Berkeh-ye Dokun, Bandul, Sahmon `oliya and Sofeleh Savahel; (ii) Chah Mobarak, Bastanubari, `Askari Nakhl Hasheh, Basatin, Safid, Zebar, Banud, Kenar-e Kheymeh; (iii) Seh telleh, Dashti, Bambaris, Kenar-e nehar, Bord Khalaf, Bagh-e Moqbel At the coast: Makhdun, Shivu, Ziyarat, Bostanu. Taxes were 6,000 *tuman*s/year together with the Tamimi and Maleki villages, which had a separate *zabet*, but the Maleki villages by 1922 were again under Sheikh Mazkur. Gavbandi paid 3,000 *tuman*s and the Maleki villages 1,500, of which 500 *tuman*s was on account of Akbari and Farsi, which had been given to Shaikh Mohammad Ahmad Khalfan. The Tamimis paid 1,500 *tuman*s, which was them an independent *kalantari*. Taxes were collected per palm (*nakhl*) in three installments, each seedling (*buneh*) paid 1 *qran*; wheat paid 10% (*yek-deh*) as did straw at the harvest of pulses. People who went pearling had to pay 2 *tuman*s/p.p. and on their return, while sailing trading boats paid one *galateh*, i.e. 10%. Sheikh Mazkur in his turn paid Qavam al-Molk, the governor of Lar, who issued receipts for each payment.[139] The usual situation was that not half the revenue was paid by Sheikh Mazkur and because the cost of getting it by force was higher, generally nothing was done.[140] In 1943, Gavbandi paid 6,000 *riyal*s in taxes.[141] In 1922, Mazkur Khan said there were no government buildings at all in his district, but he considered his property as if it were the government's, showing that he knew to say the right things at the right moment when it suited him, although nobody was fooled by these expressions of patriotism.[142]

To maintain law and order and security in his jurisdiction, Sheikh Mazkur Khan's governorate had 2,000 armed men, while for use outside the governorate he could raise 600 armed men. For the protection of his own person and family and his residence he employed 150 *tofangchi*s, whom he paid 7-10 *tuman*s/month. The presence of all those armed men was not superfluous, as is clear from the violent history of Gavbandi and its neighbors. Moreover, in 1922, Sheikh Mazkur complained that the Al Haram and Hamadis each year encroached on his revenues. In 1921, Sheikh Mohammad Ahmad Khalfan seized control over Kharreh in Gavbandi and looted and set fire to it, while in 1922 Sheikh Ebrahim Hammadi took Hashaniz, one of Sheikh Mazkur's villages and took its tower and killed 4-5 people in it. In his discussion with the *kargozar* in that year

---

137 *Administration* 1918, p. 12.
138 Vothuqi, *Tahavolat*, p. 76.
139 Vothuqi, *Tahavvolat*, pp. 76-77.
140 Adamec, *Historical Gazetteer*, vol. 3, p. 707. In 1922, the Customs agent at Asalu declared: The Al Haram and Al Nasur chiefs collected taxes but they didn't pay the government, and he added that it was everywhere like that along the coast. Vothuqi, *Tahavvolat*, p. 65.
141 Bastaki, *Tarikh-e Jahangiriyeh*, p. 328.
142 Vothuqi, *Tahavvolat*, p. 79. This statement is not entirely true as Hamidi and Taheri, for some reason, consider Sheikh Mazkur a patriot. However, as is clear from the discussion of his career, he, like the other Arab chiefs, was anything but. For photos and a description of the he Qal`eh-ye Gavbandi, which was constructed by Sheikh Jabbara b. Mohammad Hatem, see Gholamzadeh, *Me`mari*, pp. 418-20.

Sheikh Mazkur said that if the government would not take remedial action, he had no choice but to take protective measures.[143]

Shivu or Shiyu

Gavbandi's port was Shivu, also called Shiyu, as well as Tibin, and from there people traded with Oman and Persian Gulf ports. The anchorage of Shivu Bay or Bandar Kalat (called so by the locals due to the remains of fortifications on the west promontory) was tolerably well sheltered against northwesters, but quite exposed to south-easters. The best anchorage was about 8 fathoms offshore at 800 m distance. "A large flat black rock projecting in front of the village forms a small boat harbour, and the best landing place."[144] In 1835, according to Capt. Brucks, it was but a small village with about 100 men of the Abualank Tribe and it had but a few fishing boats. The inhabitants originated from different parts of the coast. In 1837, according to Kazeruni, some 30 families, who were all Shafe`i Sunnis, were living there in houses built from mud, stone, and palm tree wood. By 1900, its inhabitants were partly Arabs, partly Persians from Lar, and other locations, and mostly were Sunnis. Although Arabic was their mother tongue, they also spoke Persian. However, their dress and manners suggested a Persian origin.[145]

The village, which had three large Banyan trees, was situated at the foot of a small hill, where around its slope there was a small fort of mud and stone, with four bastions, on the summit of which there was an oblong tower, from where they defended their village against the frequent attacks of their hostile neighbors. In particular attacks by those of Asalu were feared. In 1865, the fort was in a very dilapidated state. In that same year there were 50-60 small square houses of mud and stone, with 300 inhabitants and 70 able men who were capable of carrying arms to defend the fort, in which people from the neighboring villages sought safety in time of attack.[146]

There was a moderate amount of good water from wells close to the beach, but vessels requiring water had to fetch it with their own boats and casks (because the local craft were of a very small size and the villagers did not have proper storage bins). Shivu's inhabitants were very poor; they did not even have large vessels of their own. This situation changed for the better in the decades thereafter. Around 1900, Shivu had 150 stone houses and huts and its people owned 15 trading-vessels, 9 sailing boats for pearl fishing on the west side of the Persian Gulf, and 24 small *baqarah*s for fishing and pearling on the coast. In 1904, migrants from Kangan and Taheri, sympathizers of Soleyman Khan Nasuri increased its population.[147] In 1922, Shivu had a population of 100 families numbering 400-500 persons.[148]

Probably until the early 1840 Shivu was part of the jurisdiction of the governor of Lar, who built a caravanserai there, after which it was under the Al Nasur Sheikh.[149] In

---

143 Vothuqi, *Tahavvolat*, pp. 76, 81-82.
144 Lorimer, Gazetteer, vol. 2, p. 182; US Government, *Persian Gulf Pilot*, p. 246.
145 Brucks, "Memoir," p. 594; Kazeruni, *Tarikh*, p. 102; Lorimer, *Gazetteer*, vol. 2, p. 182.
146 MacGregor, A contribution, p. 552; US Government, *Persian Gulf Pilot*, p. 246.
147 Lorimer, *Gazetteer*, vol. 2, p. 1813.
148 Vothuqi, *Tahavvolat*, p. 76. In 1918 or so, its population was estimated to be 1,000 people. US Government, *Persian Gulf Pilot*, p. 246.
149 Kazeruni, *Tarikh*, p. 102.

1865 it was reported that "The Sheikh is chosen by the villagers. Abdella Ben Ali being the present one; he is a very old man and apparently as poor as the rest of them, and is accountable to Sheikh Hassan ben Jubbareh of Gabandy, to whom he pays a yearly tribute of 150 Krans." Throughout the decades thereafter, Shivu was still under Al Nasur Sheikh of Gavbandi to whom the village paid an annual revenue of 70,000 *qrans*. Initially this was payable to the governor Lar, but towards the end of the nineteenth century to the governor of Bastak.[150] According to the *modir* of the Customs Department, Mirza Ali from Dashti in Gavbandi, the customs revenues in 1922 varied per month from 100 to 700 *tumans*.[151]

> All the villagers were very poor. They mostly subsisted on the produce of their fisheries, which they transported to inland villages, a journey sometimes of from two to three days. The entire family was involved in this work; the men fishing and landing their catch, the women and children sorting, salting, and drying the fish ready for sale. Most of its 'trade' was with Gavbandi, some 18 km inland. During the summer months Shivu was deserted with the exception of four or five men left in charge of the fort; for the inhabitants went inland to cultivate their plots of land in the valleys adjacent to the barren hills bordering their coast, and returned before the cold season and began to store up their winter supplies, and carrying on their fishing trade.[152]

The people of Shivu were poor, because they had no boats of their own and thus were unable to trade with the different parts of the Persian Gulf. The little trade there was amounted to trading in wheat brought down from the interior and shipped on some friendly vessel that might be calling there. This situation changed after the 1860s for the better, when the population acquired some boats (see Table 4.12). They were engaged in trade, navigation, fishing, pearl diving, cultivation and looking after their date groves. By 1920 the trade of Shivu consisted of the following imports: rice, beans, sugar, and textiles, while exports were: sheep, onions, firewood for Bahrain, and sometimes Bushehr. It also had a gypsum mine, which only for local use. Fishing likewise was for local use and Bikheh. The only crafts in Shivu were matweaving (*hasir-bafi*) and *tak-bafi*. Change was also coming to Shivu, because in 1922 there were plans to open a modern school and Sheikh Mazkur was trying to get two teachers from Bushehr. Meanwhile, students had to satisfy their thirst for learning in the traditional *maktab*.[153]

Table 4.14: Ships owned by inhabitants of Shivu

Year/Vessel type	Coastal vessel	Fishing boats	Tons	Crew	All vessels
1875	12	11	265	167	23
1900	8	10-12	-	-	18-20
1922	-	-	-	-	12

Source: *Administration 1875-76*, p. 42; Lorimer, *Gazetteer*, vol. 2, p. 972; Vothuqi, *Tahavvolat*, p. 77.

---

150 Waver, "Report," p. 189; Brucks, "Memoir," p. 594; Adamec, *Historical Gazetteer*, vol. 3, pp. 677, 707; Vothuqi, *Tahavvolat*, p. 76.
151 Vothuqi, *Tahavvolat*, p. 77.
152 MacGregor, *A contribution*, pp. 552-53.
153 Vothuqi, *Tahavvolat*, p. 77.

BOSTANEH

This village, about 20 km N.W. from Shivu, was situated at a small bay, which offered one of the best anchorages in the Persian Gulf. It numbered 50 houses and had one conspicuous square tower 300 m south of the village. A small creek north to the village was fit to receive dhows.[154] In 1922, the *kadkhoda* of Bostaneh, Mohammad was also *kadkhoda* of Dashti-ye Gavbandi. It was a village of 60 families, or in total some 150 people, who were all Sunnis. It only had some firewood trade that was shipped to Bushehr, Qatar, Bahrain, and Lengeh, and from Bushehr and Bahrain it imported various things. The village had 25 armed unpaid *tofangchi*s, and 20 did actual guard duty. Fishing was done for their own use and Bikheh with 5-6 small fishing boats. There were no craftsmen or traders in the village, only cultivators; the yield was four seed for one seed sown. During the pearling season many villagers went to Bahrain and Qatar, to which end the village had two pearling vessels. Not more than 30 people paid taxes, each one 3 *tuman*s to Sheikh Mazkur; the rest were exempt or had reduced taxes. Tax collection was once per year, but no receipt was given for the money paid. Customs revenues were on average 50 *tuman*s per month. Whenever ships came, the *modir* of the Customs Department of Shivu came to collect the customs duties. In his absence there were two *tofangchi*s sent from Lengeh, who received 8 *tuman*s/month, which they felt was not enough.[155]

---

154 US Government, *Persian Gulf Pilot*, p. 247.
155 Vothuqi, *Tahavvolat*, pp. 73-75.

Afterword

The Shibkuh coast was one of the areas in Iran where Arabs and Arab culture dominated. The first Arab settlers came already from Oman to the Iranian littoral in the seventh century as part of the Islamic conquering military force. However, then as later, their number was and remained small, due to the limited size of the available land between the shore and the hills that enclosed the *sif* or the beach. Not much is known about the Arab communities that lived there prior to the sixteenth century. Apart from a few names and a reputation of being engaged in the use of violent behavior and plundering nothing is known about them.

More is known about the so-called Niquelus or inhabitants of Nakhilu, who may have been the first wave of the Hulas that came from Oman and elsewhere to Iran in the late sixteenth century. Driven away from their homeland due to strife and scarce resources they settled in on the Iranian littoral and were engaged in fishing, pearl diving, cultivation, trade and the use of maritime violence. In particular their enmity towards the Portuguese acquired them a reputation of pirates and worse. That they were good fighters the Portuguese found out the hard way. Already in the seventeenth century, we learn about the presence of other Hula groups, which settled in places where they would continue to live until to-day, be it that nowadays their communities have much changed. The reason that we learnt about them, as usual, was because of the fierce fights that had broken out between Arabs at the head and the mouth of the Gulf, between Hulas and other Arabs.

However, by that time we also learn that the coastal Arabs were very useful to the land-based state in that the only ports having vessels adequate to transport troops were Bushehr, Kangan, Asalu, Charak, and Lengeh.[1] Therefore, they were used and called upon by various shahs as well as by the Imam of Masqat. Not only were they used to transport troops, they also supplied fighters, and under Nader Shah were the backbone of his Persian Gulf fleet. When they mutinied in 1741, much of the royal fleet's power was reduced. Similarly, Iranian plans in the nineteenth century to invade Bahrain were only feasible by calling on the service of the coastal Arabs.

The Banu Hula received much attention during the eighteenth century when they tried to fill the power vacuum in the Persian Gulf, which had come into being due to the fall of the Safavid dynasty and the civil war in Oman. However, the Hulas were a disparate group that had no common cause or objective and dissipated their strength by fighting among themselves. Although they were a power to reckon with they had no

---

1 FO 248/85, Hennell to Willoughby, Bombay 19 January 1839. [2649-56]

staying power as their economic base as too slim and narrow. Therefore, we observe that their spasmodic efforts to establish themselves as a maritime power had no lasting effect.

As a result, the Hulas, also in the nineteenth century continued to try and carve out a living for themselves through their traditional pursuits of fishing, pearl diving, cultivation, navigation and trade. Within the Persian Gulf the Hulas represented a small but vociferous entity as is indicated not only by their limited numbers, but also by their economic strength. For example, by 1900 4,473 boats were engaged in pearl fishing, of which the Shibkuh coast only represented 605 boats or 13% of the total. Consequently, trade by the Hulas was also of minor important, mainly limited to the export of agricultural products. At the same time, they regularly engaged in maritime violence against mercantile shipping, while they also preyed on each other. In consequence, there was constant feuding between the various groups, with shifting alliances, wich only weakened everybody's position. A case in point is the history of the Al Nasur, who, because of their feud with Dashti and Asalu, were totally exhausted by the end of the nineteenth century.

Because of the high level of maritime violence at the beginning of the nineteenth century, first the Bombay Marine, and later the British Navy, came to the Persian Gulf to provide security to shipping. Because of British direct involvement and treaties with the various Sheikhdoms it was able to rather quickly bring about the reduction of maritime violence on the Arabian side of the Gulf. However, the situation was different on the Iranian side. Here Great Britain only could intervene by providing guidance and counsel. Whereas on the Arab coast the tribes "readily accept our adjudication; the Persian government usually did not, even though it was unable to exercise its authority. It was only on rare occasion that it used our cooperation for the general good."[2] Nevertheless, British presence had also an impact on the Hula Arabs, because in many cases of maritime violence they asked the British Resident in Bushehr (the *Sarkar*) to intervene. They almost invariably stated that they did not want to use violence, and, therefore, asked for permission to do so, if the *Sarkar* did not want to do so itself, or had abandoned this function. However, also invariably they wanted the *Sarkar* to intervene on their behalf and get their boats and cargo back, and their threats to use violence sometimes sound hollow, therefore. The British, of course, perceived the dilemma, because the people on the Arabian side saw that their kinsmen on the Iranian side were not stopped by the British.

There was also much fighting ashore, as is evident from the four times that Kangan was sacked as well as the sack of other ports and/or villages on the coast and the almost constant feuding between almost everybody. Furthermore, the presence of forts and towers in the ports and the villages in their hinterland as well as the constant presence of *tofangchi*s who were on their guard for sudden attacks attest to the general insecurity of the coastal area, an insecurity that was increased by the government of Iran's policy to weaken the coastal Sheikhs by fomenting armed conflict among them.

According to Curzon, whose judgment was adopted by scholars more than a century later, the execution of Sheikh Mazkur Nasuri in 1882 signified the end of Arab rule on the Iranian coast. At the time it was a logical conclusion to make, as the Al Mazkur of Bushehr in 1850 and the Qavasem of Lengeh in 1879 had been rendered impotent and were ousted, it seemed that with the fall of Sheikh Mazkur the government of Iran's policy, initiated in the 1850s, to impose its will on the coastal communities through intrigue

---

2 FO 248/189, Jones to Rawlinson, Tehran 4 March 1860 ; 756-59]

and use of force was having its desired effect. As was shown above, however, nothing was further from the truth and the Arab chiefs, especially the Nasuri Sheikhs, continued with their age-old feuds, violence, maritime and otherwise, as well as non-payment of taxes until Reza Shah arrested them in 1931. But even then there was no immediate break with the past, because the people who occupied official administrative positions, such as that of district chief (*bakhshdar*) of Kangan and Taheri, in the newly created administrative structure, also were from the Al Nasur family.

Although it is very popular among Iranian scholars to ascribe an anti-imperialist (i.e. anti-British) and even a patriotic attitude to the various Arab sheikhs on the Shibkuh coast nothing is further from the truth. Unless forced to, the Sheikhs did not acknowledge the authority of the government of Iran. The latter had to enforce payment of taxes, which were usually not paid in full, while the Sheikhs, when opportune, resisted government interference in their affairs. Although some, like Sheikh Mazkur Nasuri, once had his men fire 4 or 6 bullets at a British ship that at the request of the government of Iran pursued him to make him restitute loot that he had plundered from his neighbors, this did not make him into an anti-British actor. Sheikh Mazkur, like all other Arab chiefs, was anti-anybody who was not under his command, or who wanted to impose their will on him.

In short, the story of the Bani Hula is one that is representative for much of Iran, where local families or clans dominated political and socio-economic life for centuries, often spanning more than one, or even two dynasties. It were these local families that guaranteed stability, continuity, and permanence even when at the national level there was turmoil, upheaval and profound change.

Bibliography

Archives

Arquivo Histórico Ultramarino, Lisbon, India, Cx 19, 5;
Arquivo Nacional da Torre do Tombo, Lisbon (*ANTT*)

AHU - Arquivo Histórico Ultramarino, Lisbon
       C.I.: Caixas da India
ANNT -Arquivo Nacional da Torre do Tombo, Lisbon
HAG -Historical Archives, Panaji, Goa [see *BFUP*]
NA   -Nationaal Archief, The Hague
       Collectie Sweers/Manis 9, f. 122

VOC - Records of the Verenigde Oostindische Compagnie (VOC) (Dutch East Indies Company) 1106, 1135, 1406, 1928, 2009, 2034, 2152, 2168, 2254, 2426, 2417, 2448, 2476, 2510, 2511, 2546, 2610, 2766, 2805, 2885, 3027, 3064, 3159.

National Archives (London, Kew Gardens, United Kingdom)

FO 248/ 38, 52, 85, 99, 113, 129, 146, 176, 183, 189, 198, 206, 232, 249, 255, 271, 290, 484, 567, 1025, 1026.

Books and articles

Adamec, L. ed. 1981. *Historical Gazetteer of Iran*. 4 vols. Graz: Akademie Verlag.

Administration Report = *Administration Report on the Persian Gulf Political Residency for the year (1873 to 1940)* in Government of India. *The Persian Gulf Administration Reports 1873-1947*, 10 vols. Gerrards Cross, Archives Editions, 1986.

Archives Research Staff Ltd., *Political Diaries of the Persian Gulf 1905-1958*, 20 vols. n.p., 1990.

Albuquerque, Brás Afonso de. *Comentários do grande Afonso de Albuquerque, capitão geral que foi das Indias orientais em tempo do muito poderoso Rey D. Manuel, o primeiro deste nome* 4 vols., translated into English by Walter de Gray Birch as *The Commentaries of the Great Afonso DAlboquerque, second viceroy of India*. 4 vols. London, 1875.

Amin, A.A. *British Interests in the Persian Gulf 1747-1780*. Leiden: Brill, 1976.

Anonymous, "Brief Account of the Province of Fars," *The Transactions of the Bombay Geographical Society* 17/1865, pp. 175-85.

___, "Les Reformes Administratives," *RMM* 23/1913, pp. 1-109.

___, *A Chronicle of the Carmelites in Persia and the Papal mission of the seventeenth and eighteenth centuries*, 2 vols. London, 1939.

___, *Do safarnameh az jonub-e Iran dar salha-ye 1256 -1207 AH*. ed. Sayyed Ali Al Davud. Tehran: Amir Kabir, 1368.

___. "Estado da India e aonde tem o seu principio," *Documentação Ultramarina Portuguesa*, vol. 1, pp. 197-228.

Barbosa, Duarte. *The Book of Duarte Barbosa* translated by M. Longworth Dames, 2 vols. London, 1918-21.

Bastaki, Mohammad A`zam Bani Abbasiyan. *Tarikh-e Jahangiriyyeh*. Tehran, 1339 AH/1920-21.

Binning, R.B. M. *A Journal of Two Years' Travel in Persia, Ceylon, etc.* 2 vols. London, 1857.

Bocarro, António. *Década 13 da Historia da India*, ed. Rodrigo José de Lima Felner, 2 vols. Lisbon, Academia Real das Ciências, 1876.

___, *Livro das plantas de todas as fortalezas, cidades e povoações do estado da India Oriental*. 3 vols. Lisbon, 1992.

Boletim da Filmoteca Ultramarina Portuguesa 50 vols. Lisbon, Centro de Estudos Históricos Ultramarinos, 1955-1990.

Boxer, R. "Anglo-Portuguese rivalry in the Persian Gulf," in E. Prestage ed. *Chapters in Anglo-Portuguese Relations*. Watford, 1935.

Bruce, J. *Annals of the Honorable East India Company* 3 vols. London, 1810.

Brucks, Captain George Barnes. "Memoir descriptive of the Navigation of the Gulf of Persia," in Andre S. Cook, *Survey of the Shores and Islands of the Persian Gulf 1820-1829*. 5 vols. n.p.: Archive Editions, 1990, vol. 1, pp. 532-634.

Bulhão Pata, R.A. and da Silva Rego, A. eds., *Documentos Remetidos da India ou Livros das Monções* 12 vols. (Lisbon, 1880-1972), cited as *DRI*.

Carré, Abbé. *The travels of Abbé Carré in India and the Near East (1672-74)*, 3 vols. London: Hakluyt, 1947.

Colville, W. H. "Land Journey Along the Shores of the Persian Gulf, from Bushire to Lingah," *Proceedings of the Royal Geographic Society*, XI (1866-67), pp. 36-38.

Cordeiro, Luciano. *Questões Histórico-Colonais* 3 vols. Lisbon, 1936.

Correia, Gaspar. *Lendas da India* ed. Rodrigo José de Lima Felner 4. vols. in 8 parts. Coimbra, 1860-66.

Curzon, G. W.. *Persia and the Persian Question*. 2 vols. London, 1892.

Darya'i, Abdollah. *Goftarha va Revayatha az Sargozasht-e Al-e Nasuri va Al-e Haram*. Shiraz: Novid, 1379/2000

Davies, Charles H. *The Blood-Red Arab Flag*. Exeter, Exeter Press, 1997.

de Almeida Teles y Cunha, João Manuel. *Economia de um império. Economia política do Estado da Índia em torno do mar Arábico e golfo Pérsico. Elementos conjuncturais: 1595-1635*. Universidade Nova de Lisboa, 1995.

de Barros, João. *Da Ásia de João de Barros e de Diogo de Couto*. Nova ed. 24 vols. Lisboa, Na Regia Officina Typografica, 1777-1788 [reprint: Livraria S. Carlos, 1973-1975], [henceforth cited as] *Ásia*.

de Couto, Diogo. *Da Ásia de João de Barros e de Diogo de Couto*. Nova ed. 24 vols. Lisboa, Na Regia Officina Typografica, 1777-1788 [reprint: Livraria S. Carlos, 1973-1975].

de Coutre, J. *Aziatische omzwervingen. Het leven van Jacques de Coutre, een Brugs diamant handelaar 1591-1627*. Berchem, 1988.

de Linhares, Miguel de Noronha Conde. *Diario de Conde de Linhares*. Lisbon: National Library, 1937.

de Matos, Luís ed., *Imagens do Oriente no século XVI. Reprodução do códice português da Biblioteca Casanatense*. Lisbon, Imprensa Nacional Casa da Moeda, 1985.

Della Valle, Pietro. *Les Fameux Voyages* 4 vols. Paris: Gervais Clouzier, 1664.

De Silva y Figueroa, Don Garcia. *Comentarios de la embajada que de parte del rey de España Don Felipe III hizo al rey Xa Abas de Persia*. António Baião ed., 2 vols. Madrid, 1903.

Disney, Anthony. "Smugglers and Smuggling in the Western Half of the *Estado da Índia* in the late Sixteenth Century and early Seventeenth Centuries," *Indica*, 26 (Mar-Sept., 1989), pp. 57-75.

Dunlop, H. *Bronnen tot de geschiedenis der Oostindische Compagnie in Perzië*. The Hague, 1930.

Eqtedari, Ahmad. *Athar-e Shahrha-ye Bastani-ye Savahel va Jaza'er-e Khalij-e Fars va Darya-ye `Oman*. Tehran: Anjoman-e Athar-e Melli, 1348/1969.

Fasa'i, Mirza Hasan Hoseyni. *Farsnameh-ye Naseri*. 2 vols. ed. Mansur Rastgar Fasa'i. Tehran: Amir Kabir, 1378/1999.

Willem Floor, "Pearl fishing in the Persian Gulf in the 18th century," *Persica* 10 (1982), pp. 209-22.

___, *Afghan Occupation of Persia, 1722-1730*. Paris/Louvain: Cahiers Studia Iranica, 1998.

___, *The Persian Gulf. A Political and Economic History of Five Port Cities 1500-1730*. Washington DC: MAGE, 2006.

___, "The rise and fall of the Banu Ka`b. A borderer state in southern Khuzestan," *IRAN* XLIV (2006), pp. 277-315.

___, *The Rise of the Gulf Arabs*. Washington DC: MAGE, 2007.

___, "Who were the Niquelus?" in Dejanirah Couto and Rui Manuel Loureiro eds. *Revisiting Hormuz. Portuguese Interactions in the Persian Gulf Region in the Early Modern Period*. Wiesbaden, 2008, pp. 89-105.

___, *The Rise and Fall of Bandar-e Lengeh. The Distribution Center for the Arabian Coast, 1750-1930*. Washington DC: MAGE, 2010.

___, *Bandar Abbas, the natural gateway to southeast Iran*. Washington DC: Mage, 2011.

Foster, William. *Letters received by the East India Company from its servants in the East* 6 vols. London, 1896-1902.

Fraser, James Bailie, "Notes made in the course of a voyage from Bombay to Bushire in the Persian Gulf," *Transactions Geolog. Society of London*, vol. 1, (1824), pp. 409-12.

Gholamzadeh, Faraz. *Me`mari-ye Bushehr dar dowreh-ye Zand va Qajar*. Theran: Abadbum, 1392/2013.

Government of Great Britain. *Political Diaries of the Persian Gulf* 20 vols., Archive Edition 1990.

Government of India, *Military Report on Persia*. 4 vols. Simla, n.p., 1924.

___, *Persian Gulf Administration Reports 1873-1957* 11 vols. Gerrards Cross: Archive Editions, 1991.

Hamidi, Ja`far. *Ostan-e Ziba-ye Bushehr*. Bushehr: Shoru`, 1384.

___, "Al Nasur," in Ibid., *Farhangnameh-ye Bushehr*. Tehran, 1380/2001, pp. 55-62.

James Horsburgh, *India Directory or Directions for Sailing to and from the East Indies* 4th ed. London, 1836.

Hotz A. ed. "Cornelis Cornelisz Roobacker's Scheepsjournaal Gamron-Basra (1645); De eerste reis der Nederlanders door de Perzische Golf" *Koninklijk Nederlandsch Aardrijkskundig Genootschap* 1897, pp. 289-405.

Hussain, A. Aba. "A Study of the History of the Utoob," *Al-Watheeka* 1 (1982), pp. 24-42.

Ibn Balkhi, *Description of the Province of Fars in Persia, in the beginning of the fourteenth century*, London: RAS, 1912.

Ibn Majid, *Arab Navigation in the Indian Ocean before the coming of the Portuguese*. Translated by G.R. Tibbets. London, 1972.

Kazeruni, Mohammad Ebrahim. *Tarikh-e Banader dar Khalij-e Fars* ed. Manuchehr Setudeh. Tehran, 1367/1988.

Kazeruni, Sayyed Ahmad Hoseyni, "Joghrafiya-ye Tarikhi va Siyasi-ye Mantaqeh-ye Asaluyeh," *Farhangnameh-ye Bushehr*, pp. 173-77.

Ali Reza Khalifehzadeh, "Asnadi az pisihineh'i-ye tarikhi-ye Al Mazkur," *Pazhuheshnameh-ye Khalij-e Fars* 3/1390, pp. 319-41.

Kinneir, J. Mc. *A Geographical Memoir of the Persian Empire*. New York 1973 [reprint of London, 1813].

Khurmuji, Mirza Ja`far Khan Haqa'eq-Negar 1380/1960. *Nozhat al-Akhbar. Tarikh va Joghrafiya-ye Fars*. ed. Sayyed Ali Al Davud. Tehran: Ketabkhaneh, Muzeh va Markaz-e Asnad-e Majles.

Le Strange, Guy. *The Lands of the Eastern Caliphate*. London 1905 [1966].

Lindberg, K. *Voyage dans le Sud de l'Iran*. Lund: Gleerup, 1955.

Lorimer, J. G. *Gazetteer of the Persian Gulf*. Calcutta, 1915 [1970].

MacGregor, C.M. *A contribution towards the better knowldge of the topography, ethonology, resources & history of Persia*. Calcutta, 1871.

Ma`sumi, Gholamreza. *Siraf – Bandar-e Taheri*. Tehran: Anjoman-e Athar-e Melli, 1352/1973.

Mendes da Luz, Francisco Paulo. *Livro das cidades e fortalezas que a coroa de Portugal tem nas partes da India e das capitanias e mais cargos que nelas e da importancia delles*[1581] in *Studia* 6 (1960) and as separate off-print.

Morier, James 1812. *A Journey through Persia, Armenia and Asia Minor in the Years 1808 and 1809*. London: Longman, Hurst, Rees, Orme, and Brown.

Mostowfi-ye Yazdi, Mohammad Mofid. *Mokhtasar-e Mofid*. 2 vols. ed. Seyf al-Din Najmabadi. Wiesbaden: Reichert, 1989.

Mustawfi, Hamdallah. *The Geographical Part of the Nuzhat al-Qulub*. translated by G. Le Strange. Leiden: Brill, 1919.

Najmabadi, Shahnaz Razieh. "The Arab Presence on the Iranian Coast of the Persian Gulf," in: Lawrence G. Potter ed., *The Persian Gulf in History*, New York: Palgrave, 2009, pp. 130-45.

Nasiri, Mohammad Ebrahim b. Zeyn al-`Abedin, *Dastur-e Shahriyan*. ed. Mohammad Nader Nasiri Moqaddam. Tehran, 1373/1995.

Newberie, John. "Two Voyages of Master J.N., One into the Holy Land; The other to Balsara, Ormus, Persia, and backe thorow Turkie," in Purchas, Samuel. *Hakluytus Posthumus or Purchas His Pilgrimes*. 8 vols. Glasgow 1905, vol. 8, pp. 449-81.

Niebuhr, Carsten. *Beschreibung von Arabien, aus eigenen beobachtungen und in lande selbst gesammleten nachrichten abgefasset nachrichten*. Kopenhagen: N. Möller, 1772.

___, *Reisebeschreibung nach Arabien und andern umliegenden Ländern*. 3 vols. in one. Zürich, 1997.

Özbaran, Salih. *The Ottoman Response to European Expansion. Studies on Ottoman-Portuguese Relations in the Indian Ocean and Ottoman Administration in the Arab Lands During the Sixteenth Century*. Istanbul, 1994.

Pérotin-Dumon, Anne. "The pirate and the emperor; power and the law on the seas, 1450-1850," in James D. Tracy ed. *The Political Economy of Merchant Empires* Cambridge, 1997, pp. 196-227.

Pires, Tomé. *The Suma Oriental of Tomé Pires, an account of the East, from the Red Sea to Japan, written in Malacca and India in 1511-1515* translated and edited by Armando Cortesão 2 vols. London, 1944.

Pissurlencar, P. S .S. ed., *Assentos do Conselho do Estado 1618-1750*, 5 vols. Goa, 1953-57.

Plaisted, Bartholomew. *A Journal from Calcutta in Bengal, by Sea, to Busserah* London: J. Newbery, 1757.

Potter, Lawrence G. "The consolidation of Iran's frontier on the Persian Gulf in the nineteenth century," in: Roxane Farmanfarma, *War and Peace in Qajar Persia: Implications Past and Present*, London-New York: Routledge, 2008, pp. 125-48.

Qadusi, Mohammad Hoseyn. *Nadernameh*. Tehran, 1339/1960.

Report on the Trade of Bushire (various years) in *The Persian Gulf Trade Reports 1905-1940*. Gerrards Cross: Archive Editions, 1987.

Sadid al-Saltaneh, Mohammad Ali Khan. *Sarzaminha-ye shomali-ye peyramun-e khalij-e Fars va darya-ye `Oman dar sad sal-e pish 1324-1332 h.q.* ed. Ahmad Eqtedari. Tehran: Jahan-e Mo`aser, 1371/1992.

Saldanha, J.A. *The Persian Gulf Precis* 8 vols. Gerrards Cross: Archive Editions, 1986.

Schwarz, Paul 1993. *Iran im Mittelalter nach den Arabischen Geographen*. 9 parts in 4 vols. Frankfurt am Main: Institute for the History of Arabic-Islamic Science (reprint of the 1896-1936 edition).

Siddiq, Abdol-Razzaq Mohammad. *Sahwa al-faris: fi tarikh al-Arab al-Fars* an unpublished local history cited by Najmabadi.

Silveira, Francisco Rodrigues. *Reformação da milícia e governo do Estado da Índia Oriental*, transcripted, annotated and indexed by Benjamin N. Teensma, and with a historical introduction by Luís Filipe Barreto, George D. Winius and Benjamin N. Teensma. Lisbon, Fundação Oriente, 1996.

Sirjani, Sa`idi ed. *Vaqayi`-ye ettefaqiyeh. Gozareshha-ye khafiyeh-nevisan-e englisi*. Tehran, 1361/1982.

Slot, B. J. *Les Origines du Koweit*. Leiden: Brill, 1991.

___, *The Arabs of the Gulf 1602-1784*. Leidschendam, 1993.

Smith, Ronald Bishop, *The First Age of the Portuguese embassies, navigations and peregrinations to the ancient kingdoms of Cambay and Bengal (1500-1521)*. Bethesda, 1969, pp. 65-66.

Stiffe, A.W. "Ancient Trading Centres of the Persian Gulf," *Geographic Journal* 13 (1899), pp. 294-97

___, "Ancient Trading Centres of the Persian Gulf- VI. Bandar Abbas," *Geographical Journal* 16 (1900), pp. 211-15.

Tabakoğlu, Ahmet. "The Economic Importance of the Gulf in the Ottoman Era," *Studies of Turkish-Arab Relations* 3 (1988), pp. 159-68.

Taheri, Reza. *Az Morvarid ta Naft. Tarikh-e Khalij-e Fars (Az Bandar Siraf ta Kangan va Asaluyeh)*. Tehran: Nakhostin, 1390/2011.

Taylor, Captain Robert. "Extract from Brief Notes," [prepared in 1818] in Selections, pp. 3-60.

Teixera, Pedro. *The Travels*. tr. William F. Sinclair. London 1902 [1991].

United States Government, *Persian Gulf Pilot, comprising the Persian Gulf, the Gulf of Oman and the Makran Coast*. Washington DC, 1920.

Vadala, R. *Le Golfe Persique* translated into Persia by Shafi` Javadi as *Khalij-e Fars dar `asr-e este`mar*. Tehran, 2537.

van Linschoten, J.H. *The voyage of Jan Huygen van Linschoten to the East Indies* ed. and translated into English by A.C. Burnell and P.A. Tiele, 2 vols. London, 1885.

Vothuqi, Mohammad Baqer. *Tahavvolat-e siyasi-ye safahat-e jonub-e Iran*. Tehran, 1381.

Waver, H.W. "Report on the Bay and Fort of Shewoo on the Shore of the Persian Gulf," *The Transactions of the Bombay Geographical Society* 17/1865, p. 180.

Wilson, *A Political Officer's Diary 1907-1914*. Oxford, 1942.

Yeroushalmi, David. *The Jews of Iran in the Nineteenth Century: Aspects of History, Community*, Leiden: Brill, 2009.

Glossary

`Amilah (عميله), a small fishing *baqarah*. Lorimer, p. 2326.

Baghlah (بغله), a large vessel able to carry 80-300 tons of cargo; it was decked fore and aft and had a poop and usually had two masts, with a crew varying from 25 to 50. The crew of a *baghlah* usually consisted of a captain (*nakhoda*), a navigator (*mo`allem*), a clerk (*karrani*), boatswains (*sarhangs*), helmsmen (*sokkanis*), a butler (*fowli*), cooks (*tabbakhs*), boys (*walads*) and sailors (*jashus*). Lorimer, vol. 2, pp. 2321-22, 2327.

Baqarah (بقاره) is similar to the *batil*, with one or two masts. It is moved both by oars and sails, had a crew of 10 to 15 men, were 10 to 20 m long and carried a cargo of 10 to 30 tons. Lorimer, vol. 1, p. 2322-23

Batil (بتيل) is a vessel with a long bow; on the Iranian coast with one and on the Arabian coast with two masts. Depending on its size it is propelled by oars and sails; the larger ones only by oars when pearling. It was used both for trading and pearling and had a crew of 10 to 20 men, and carried 15 to 60 tons of cargo. Lorimer, vol. 1, p. 2322.

Bum (بوم), a vessel in varying sizes; usually somewhat bigger than the *ghonchah*. They were from 11 to 26 m long and completely decked. It had a crew of 15 to 40 men and was used to carry cargo, although the smaller ones were used for pearling; its capacity was 20 to 200 tons. Lorimer, vol. 1, p. 2323.

Dinghy (دنگي), originally a small rowing boat or skiff, sometimes even a warboat; later often as a utility boat attached to a large vessel. In the Persian Gulf and Mekran Coast it seems to have been a rowing boat of varying size, small and larger, often use for warlike purposes. The word has been derived from the Hindi, *dingi* or *dengi*.

Gallivat (جاليبوت) an armed vessel, with sails and oars and small draught of water. The term may be a bastardization of the Portuguese term *galeota*, i.e. galiot or galley in English, which in Arabic became *qaliyat*.

Ghonchah (غنچه), is a small *baghlah*, with a crew of 15 to 20 men and from 20 to 80 tons of cargo. Lorimer, vol. 1, pp. 2322.

Mashuwah (ماشوه) was 7 to 13 m long, broad-beamed and square-sterned, and (partly) decked. Uusally they had one mast; the biger ones carried cargo of 8-10 tons, the smaller ones were used for fishing, with a crew of 6 to 12 men. Lorimer, vol. 1, p. 2325.

Sambuk (سمبوك) is like a *ghonchah* or a small *baghlah*; it carried a crew of 15 to 20 men and carried 15 to 60 tons of cargo. Lorimer, vol. 1, p. 2323.

Shu`ey (شوعي) was a small sambuk propelled by oars and one sail, mostly used by fishermen; usually 3 to 7 m long, with a crew of 6 to 10 men; it was decked. Lorimer, vol. 1, p. 2324.

Varji (ورجي) or *varjeh*, which on the Arabian side of the Gulf was called *shashah*. This vessel is about 3 m long and constructed of date stalks; it is not water tight and relies on the buoyancy of the date stalks. It is propelled by two oars, sometimes a sail was used. It had a crew of 1 to 3 men and was only used close to the shore. Lorimer, vol. 1, p. 2326.

Appendix 1

A Tale About The Origin of the Hula or Huwala

When General John Malcolm entered the Persian Gulf he was told by his Arab servant Khodadad that the Jouassimee (Qavasem) and other Arabs were monsters, which was not their fault, "for they are descended from a Houl, or monster, and they act according to their nature." As he wanted to know more about their descent he asked to be told how that came about. Here is that story.

An Arab fisherman, who lived in a village on the Persian Gulf, not far from Gombroon, being one day busy at his usual occupation, found his net so heavy that he could hardly drag it on shore. Exulting in his good fortune, he exerted all his strength: but judge his astonishment, when, instead of a shoal of fish, he saw in his net an animal of the shape of a man, but covered with hair. He approached it with caution; but finding it harmless, carried it to his house, where it soon became a favourite; for, though it could speak no language, and utter no sound except 'houl, houl,' (from whence it took its name), it was extremely docile and intelligent; and the fisherman, who possessed some property, employed it to guard his flocks.

It happened one day, that a hundred Persian horsemen, clothed in complete armour, came from the interior, and began to drive away the sheep. The Houl, who was alone, and had no arms but a club, made signs for them to desist; but they only scoffed at his unnatural appearance, till he slew one or two who approached too near him. They now attacked him in a body; but his courage and strength were surpassed by his activity, and while all fell who came within reach, he eluded every blow of his enemies; and they fled after losing half their numbers.

The fisherman and his neighbours, when they heard of the battle, hastened to the aid of the faithful Houl, whom they found in possession of the horses, cloths, and arms of the vanquished Persians. An Arab of the village, struck with his valour, and casting an eye of cupidity at the wealth he had acquired, offered him the hand of his daughter, who was very beautiful, and she, preferring good qualities to outward appearance, showed no reluctance to become the bride of this kind and gallant monster. Their marriage was celebrated with more pomp than was ever before known in the village; and the Houl, who was dressed in one of the richest suits of the Persians he had slain, and mounted on one of their finest horses, looked surprisingly well. He was quite beside himself with joy, playing such antics, and exhibiting such good humour, strength and agility, that his bride, who had at first been pitied, became the envy of every fisherman's daughter. She would have been more so, could they have foreseen the fame to which she was destined. She had four sons, from whom are descended the four tribes of the Ben Jouassim, Ben Ahmed, Ben Nasir, and Ben Saboohil, who are to this day known by the general name of Ben Houl, or the children of Houl. They are all fishermen, boatmen, and pirates, and live chiefly at sea, inheriting, it is believed, the amphibious nature of their common ancestor.

Source: Anonymous, *Sketches of Persia*. 2 vols. London: Murray, 1828, vol. 1, pp. 28-30. For a variant of the Houl legend, see Sidney Shay, *By Order of the Shah*. London, 1937, pp. 115-116.

Appendix 2

Translation of a letter from Major Hennell Resident in the Persian Gulf to His Excellency the Governor of Shiraz, dated 12 May 1847.

A.C.   Adverting to the letter from Your Excellency received on the 5th of January last regarding the proceedings of the people of Aseeloo, I now do myself the honour to forward an authentic copy of the Iltizam Nama furnished by the Sheik of that place, agreeably to the requisition made by Your Excellency in the above communicaiton.

I beg at the same time to bring to bring to the notice of Your Excellency, that Sheikh Ahmed ben Khulfan has declared to me that last year in the pursuance of a Firman directing the punishment of the perpetrators of the Piracy on the Karrack vessel belonging to one of our dependents, Shaheen the Chief of the village of Khirah was seized by Rashid Khan Sarteep and confined in Iron for 40 days until he paid 200 Tomans on acount of his lawless proceedings, that of this sum 50 *Tuman*s were taken by the Mohussil, who carried the Firman, and an equal amount by the Sarteep, while the remaining 100 *Tuman*s were paid by the latter into the Shiraz Treasury.

I have troubled Your Excellency, upon this subject, because it appears to me, that if 200 Tomans have been made good by the Instigators of the piracy above referred to, it would no be according to justice, that they should be called upon to pay to pay that sum over again.

Signed: S. Hennell.

Source: FO 248/129.

A.C. = After Compliments.

سواد مراسله جناب صاحب البرت سمی صاحب بهادر رزیدنت بوشهر بجناب حکومت پناه شیخ عبدالرسول خان حاکم بوشهر

شیانی ملاقات حضرت علامت‌ما... مجموعه خلوص و دوستی ... که از نفوس خوانی گردیده

که در هنگام نهم محرم احکام شرف زور وارد و زیاد دوست مخلص رضا محبت عزیز ملی گردیده

در این وقت بواسطه الفراری حاجی ... بندر بوشهر ... ملاء بردران زحمت فهم از راج رفع موانع آرامش

ملفوف وارد می‌حمت زفع آن کرده و به خیر لازم آمد و بهلو دارد اطلاع و لهذا بنابر اسکان بارکه

شیخ احمد و شیخ ولی خلفان که مکاری حجت رسال‌کرده بعضی مفاصلی را خیوص ازرسیدن نفر این

خاذک والک بارکسیا چون فرقه بسی بنگار سی سی منصوب و مأمور به واگذاری

گرفته شیان بنابر ضابط فرصت خره را کیفر کرده منت جدید روی اختیار و تحمیل ما به

بسیع قوت فلان و زار از عهدی رایان بنانی ... رایان بافتن نام برکسی ازنه صفحه

محضر را رفع سم و تباه ... لال خو عزیز سوء الفه که متوسل بان ... و زدرار این کمانیه ...

برازه سبب دست جال بر مصرع آنان خلفه بابت مکلف خلف و اصدار زول

مراد بلکه به چنان است که بسمع منظور وزارت گرامی بابت کار بانان این وقت ...

انصاف برون بست که در حال از کمک در ... اذدار آنان برای بابت معلوم گرفته می‌داند

خواهد بود و سیاسی قرار

Translation
Resident in the Bussora Gulf
to the Governor of Bushire
Dated 12th June 1807

Appendix 3

Substance of an Iltizam Nama or Engagement entered into by Sheikh Ahmed b. Khulfan of Asseeloo dated 22 Rubee or Akhir or 8th April 1847.

Considering that from the kindness and exalted favor of H.E. the Sahib-i Ikhtiyar the payment of the sum of 402 Tomans (equivalent to 4020 Mahomed Shah rupees) on account of property belonging to the Inhabitants of the Province of Fars which the Inhabitants and dependent of Aseeloo have plundered (and which was to be received through the medium of Major Hennell the Resident in the Persian Gulf from me Ahmed ben Khulfan the Governor of Asseeloo) has been forgiven and excused on the conditions, that from and after this date, neither I, nor any one of my subjects or dependents, shall be guilty of any irregularity or commit any aggression or outrage on the Sea, either upon foreigners, or upon the sunjects of the province of Fars, whether inhabitants of Congoon, or others. Accordingly, I the aforesaid Ahmed, do hereby bind and engage myself, that neither I nor my people will in any way or manner act contrary to the above Conditions, and if, which God forbid, any infringement of the same should take place, I then become responsible and liable to the payment of the above mentioned 402 Tomans. Moreover whatever damage or injury shall accrue to the Vessels or prosperity of them who violate these conditions they deserve the same, I have not to say a word in their behalf. This document has been drawn out in the form of an Iltizam or written engagement.

Sealed Ahmed ben Khulfan.

Source: FO 248/129.

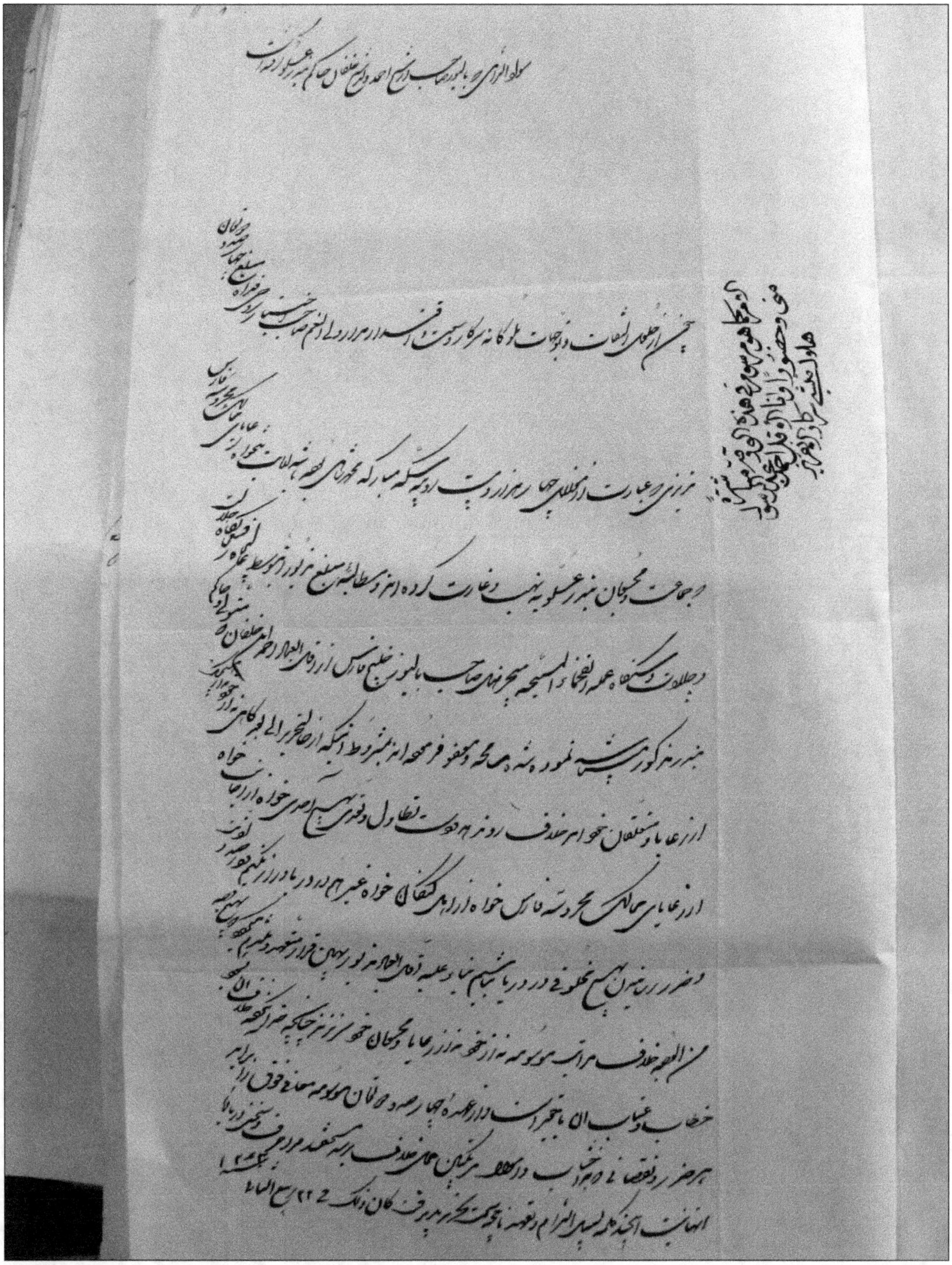

Appendix 4

FO 248/176.

Translated purport of a letter from Sheikh Hassan ben Jabbarah, Governor of Congoon

To Captain Felix Jones, I.A. Political Resident Persian Gulf.

Without date, recd. 24 January 1859.

A.C.   Your letter has been received. With regard to the vessel you had written about, I beg to acquaint you that on receiving your first letter on this subject, I released the vessel with all its gear etc. and restored it to its owner, a Charrack subject. I request therefore that you will direct the Charrack people to restore the property (belonging to my susbjects) and send peremptory orders to them to withhold it no longer, that they may know that your Government does see justice done, and hereafter reftain from acting contrary to its wishes, and that others may know that they will be called upon for retribution even if 100 years elapse.

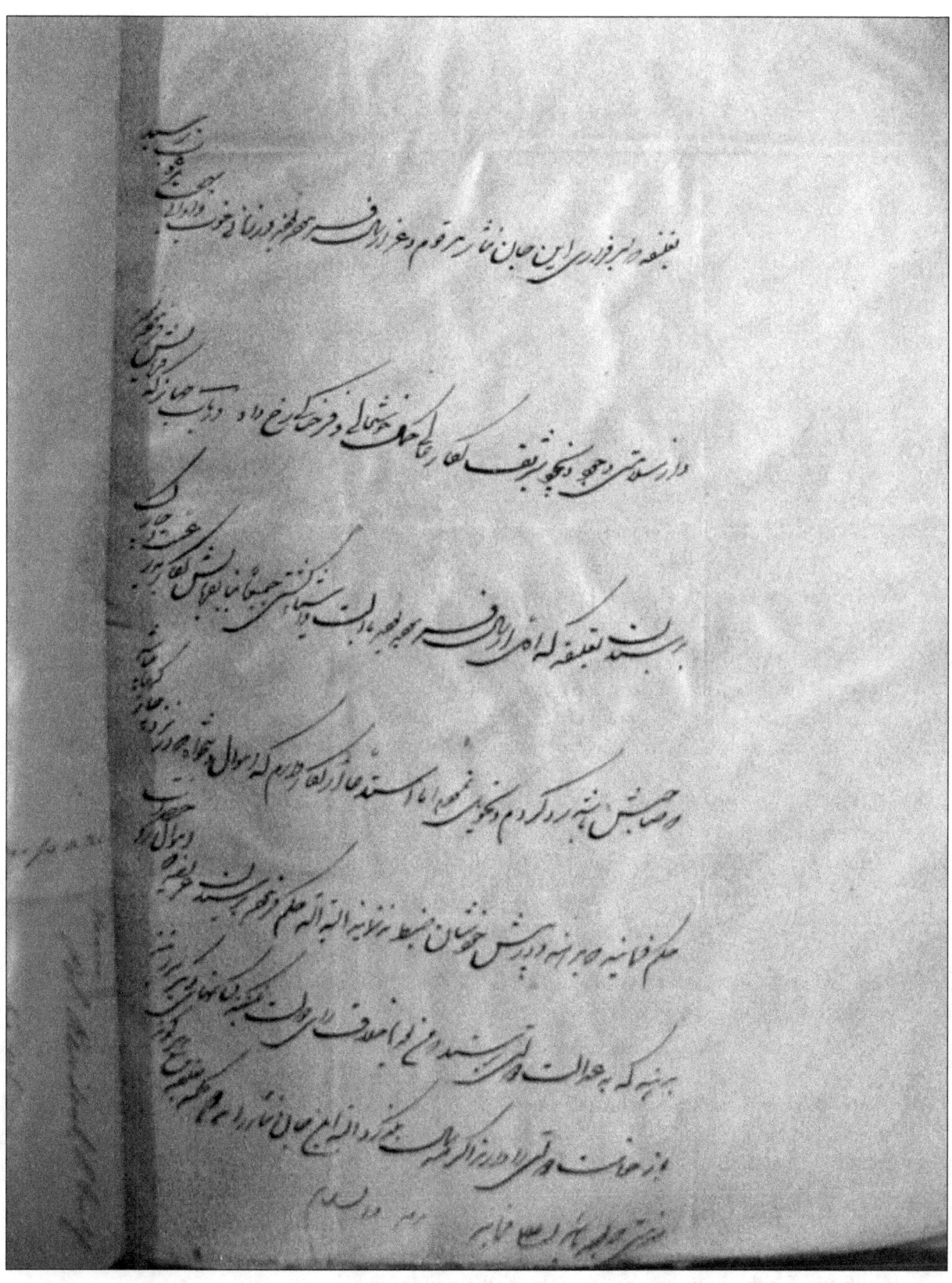

Appendix 5

FO 248/206, Disbrowe to Mirza Mehdi Khan, *kargozar* 25/8/1862 or 28 Safar 1279.

From: Captain H.F. Disbrowe, Off. Political Resident Persian Gulf
To: Mirza Mehdy Khan Persian Agent for Foreign Affairs Bushire
Dated: 28 Suffur 1279/25 August 1862

    C.A.   You must be equally aware with myself of the frightful deeds of bloodshed and devastation that have been recently perpetrated by by the inhabitants of Dashtee of the people of Congoon and its neighbourhood.

Children have been cruelly butchered. Defenceless women have been mercilessly massacred. In short, scenes of cruelty appear to have been enacted on the Persian shores within the past few days for which you will scarcely find a parallel in the annals of Persian events in these parts.

Much as I lament these painful occurrences, much too, as I pity the unfortunates, who have fallen victim to Dashtee inhumanity and violence, my object, however, in addressing you is not to interfere in the smallest degree with affairs that relate to the Persian Government on land. What I desire to do is to draw your particular attention to the fact that the deeds of violence and oppression on shore have unfortunately extended to the sea, and Her Majesty the Queen of England's Government, as you are well aware, is one with His Majesty the Shah of Persia's Government for the suppression of disorder at sea in the Gulf.

Natives of Congoon and its dependencies, situated as they were between two sets of enemies, having the Dashtees to their north, and the Asseelooites to their south, endeavoured to escape with their wives and families by sea. They put off from the shore in boats, were pursued, attacked, seized, and carried captives to the port of Asseeloo.

In consideration of the friendship existing between the kingdoms of Great Britain and Persia; in consideration of the desire I entertain as a well-wisher to His Majesty the Shah's Government, that, owing to the perpetrated disorders, so much Persian territory should not remain profitless, I do most earnestly request you will represent these heart rendering outrages to superior authority, and obtain the issue of the necessary commands to ensure the infliction of ounishment on the offenders.

I need hardly assure you that the Resident is ready now as heretofore to cooperate with Persian Government authorities for the preservation of maritime order in the Gulf, and for the punishment of pirates that frequent it.

I have the honour,
signed H.F. Disbrowe.

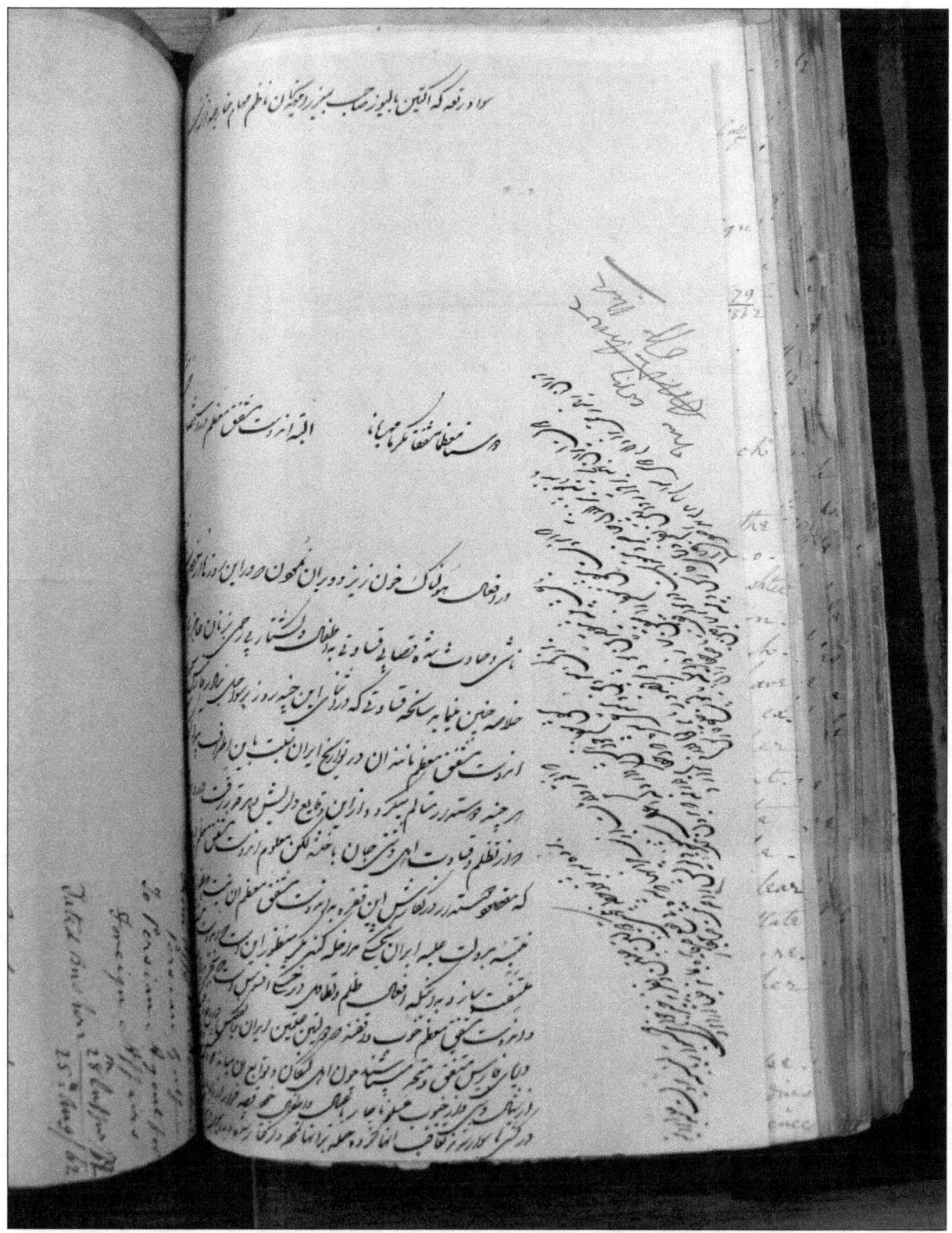

Appendix 6

FO 248/206, Mirza Mehdi, *kargozar* to Disbrowe.

To: Captain H. F. Disbrowe, Officiating Political Resident Persian Gulf
From: Mirza Mehdy Khan, Persian Agent for Foreign Affairs at Bushire
Dated: 29 Suffur 1279/26 August 1862
Received: 26 August 1862

After compliments and acknowledging letter;

You make known to me the grief and the pain that the proceedings of the people of Dashtee towards the population of Congoon, Taheree and the neighbourhood of those places have occasioned you. You also express yourself a well wisher to His Majesty's Government.

In consideration of the friendship and accord between the two States it is clear that the servants of either State will be as one in matters relating to the welfare of either State.

The grief you have experienced at these heart rendering occurrences, and the expression sof good-will communicated to me, I shall fully represent to the Persian Minister. Please God the requisite orders be speedily issued.

I have etc.

APPENDICES

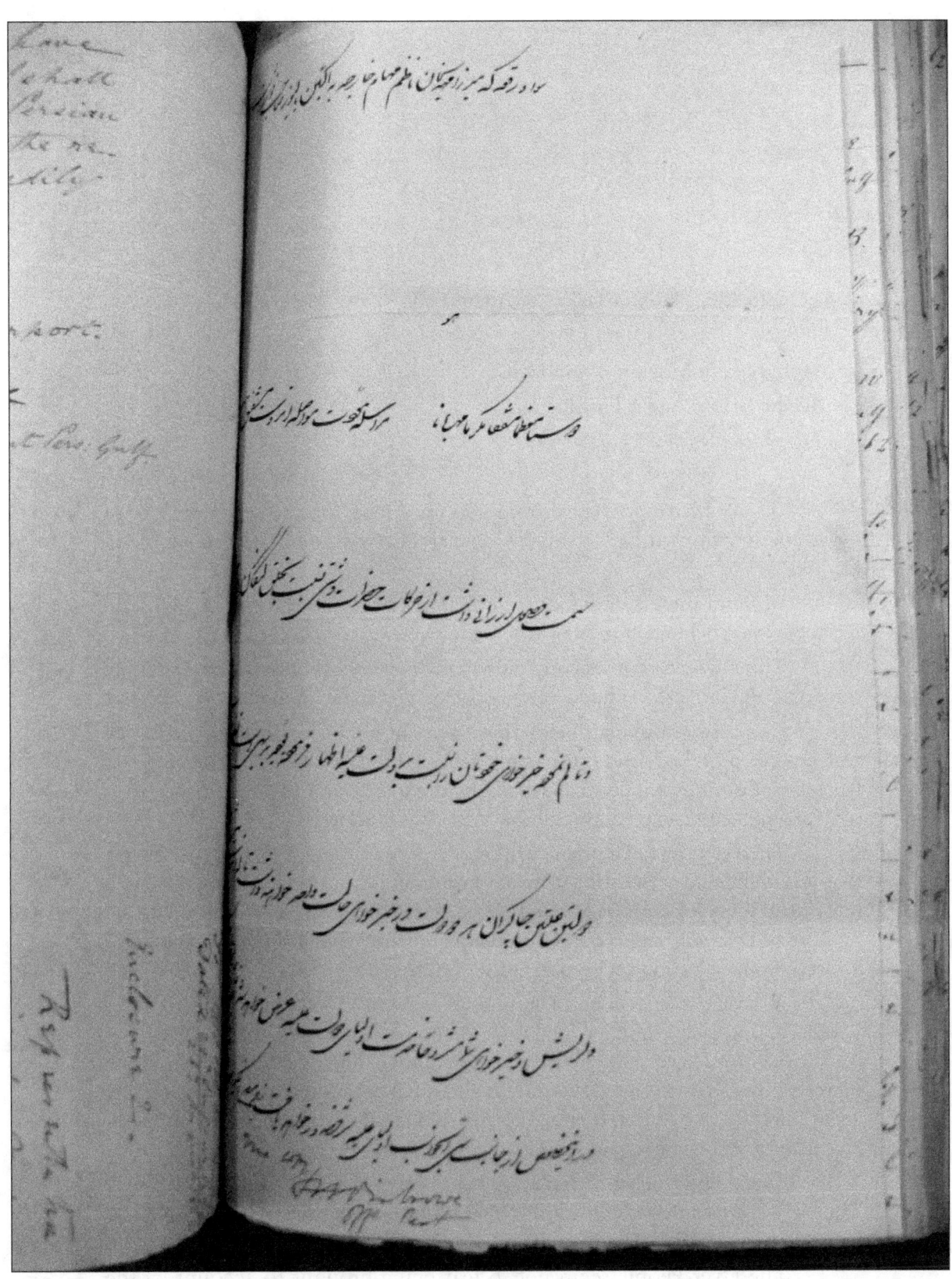

Appendix 7

FO 248/255, Sheikh Mazkur to Agent Lengeh, rec. 11 July 1867.

From Sheikh Muzkur of Naband
To the British Agent Lingah
No date/ received 11/7/1869

A.C. I have not heard from you for a long time, accordingly I must write and inform you concerning the quarrel between me and the people of Dashti.

I cannot understand about the Ghoncha belonging to Abdul Hossain Bahreinee that belongs at present to Dayyir.

This Ghoncha cruises constantly in my neighbourhood and oppresses my subjects. This Ghoncha captured a Buglah belonging to Ghaunum of Ras Nabend.

Also a large Bughlah belonging to me in which was a cargo of Barley that was taken of the Island (no name [probably the Long Island or Qeshm]) on her return from Lingah. This Buglah has by the intercesion of Abul Futtah Khan of Murbah been recovered. But all the cargo was plundered.

There also was a Ghoncha with property belonging to some of my people that was plundered at Sea. But it would from these occurrences seem as though the British Govt. did not as formerly keep the Peace at Sea. Is the liberty to act as those of Dyer do only accorded to them alone? or are all others permitted to act as they chose? - and each go in at the other at Sea?

If the Truce is at an end I am myself ready to try what I can do. If others have leave and I have not, let me know. Altho, as I said, I am able, yet I do not wish to begin as I have no desire for any misunderstanding with the English. Please represent this affair to the Government and quickly send me answer whether I am at liberty to act or not. If you wish me to furnish you with a list of property plundered I will write it, and send it to you.

Please don't delay in replay as I fear every day something worse may happen. If Government does not interfere with these peopole, poor people will be afraid to move out.

The Dyer People seem not to fear being brought to account by the English. But I am afraid of getting myself into any difficulty with the English.

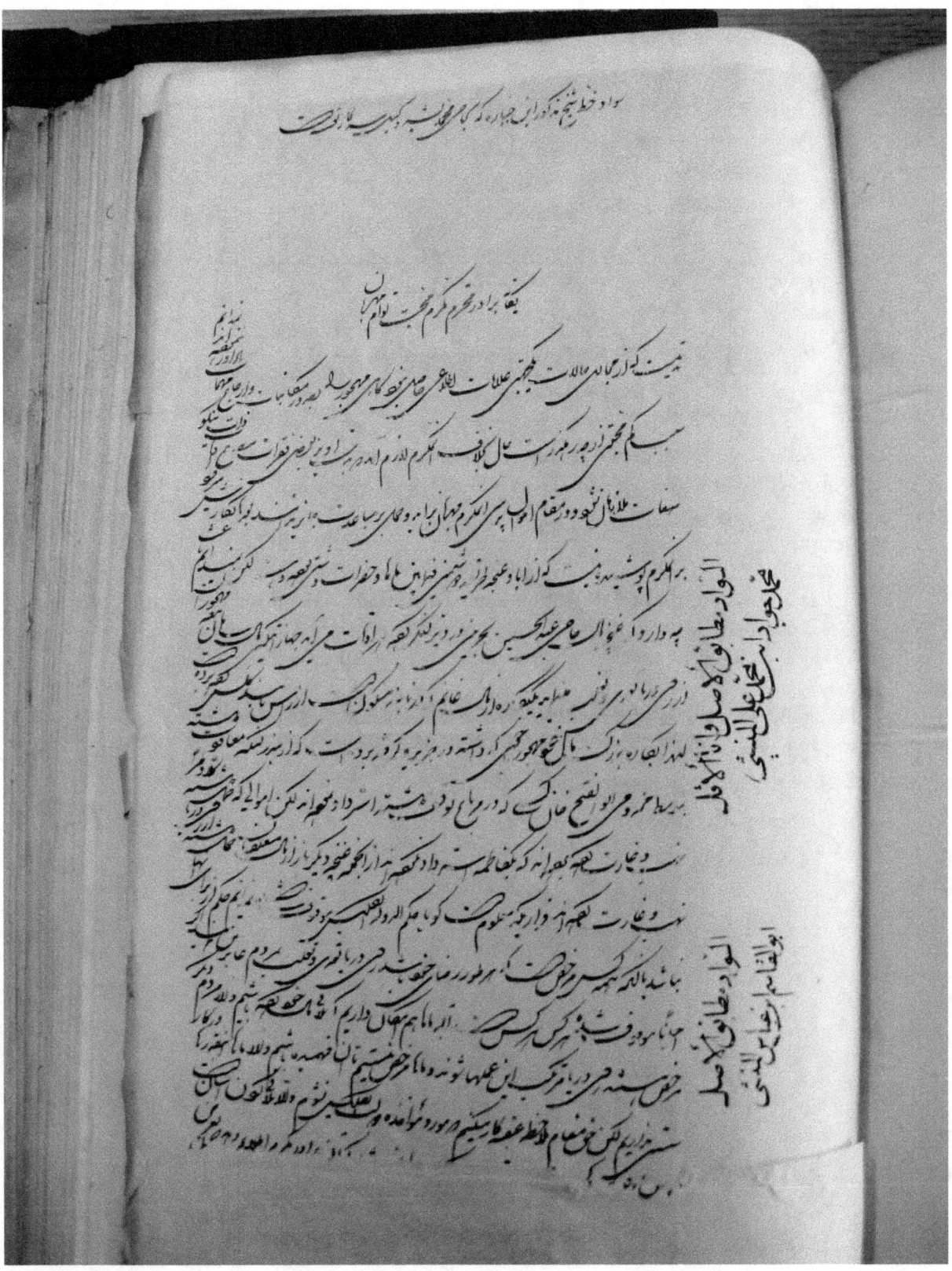

Appendix 8

FO 248/290, Sheikh Abdollah Musebbeh to Agent Lengeh, 23 Moharram 1290.

Purport of a letter from Abdollah Musebbeh to Agent Lingah 23 Moharram (1290)

A.C. I went to Morbagh and returned by sea to Tawenneh and thence embarked with 10 men on my way to Husseeneh. Mahomed Hassan oreoared a Buteel and Buggareh and pursued me with 70 men till near Husseeneh but did not reach me. I do not know whether the Sea is under control or not for when I was Chief of Charrack Sheikh Mahomed Hassan came out to Sea and arrived at Laz and God did not will that an encounter should take place between us at Ges. I complained to you but no one prevented him from moving by Sea. If the Sirkar is willing that that disturbance should take place at Sea let me know that I may take precautions. You know that I am not without power to act as Mahomed Hassan has done. If you permit I will write Abdollah Musebbeh to Agent Lengeh to [the] Resident.

الجناب المكرم الاحترم الوالد الحاج محمد بن الحسن

سلمه الله تعالى ثم السلام عليكم ورحمة الله وبركاته ومغفرته ورضوانه وأذكركم وأشرفكم

وبالمذاكرة طياب عما صار الذي ثم انشاء الله كذا المعنى لا يخفى على جنابك حضر اخي

الى ثاء ومن طاودكب في تجاره وبعض عشر ترا صار اخو حبيبه ومحمد حسن حرينا

وفيها اسبعين نفر طلعوا وداي الى عمال حبيبه يكلا يصغوا في كلامه فله حكمي است

ايام الذى كب ذاكر في جاد ت الشيخ محمد حسن طلع في الجو وصلى الى تيرنا اذ

بينا على الجو وشكيها عند جناب كلا احد يخدمن تطليع الجواد كان حاد

بان يصير وسادنا الجو حى يخلا نصرف وكان يا خذ بعض عشر يخلا صاد الله نصرف

مثلما محمد حسن يطلع في الجو وكلا احد يمنعه نفما كذا المراد كان جنابك مايركنه

الى ثاني يوم يعر ضوا السلام حوا دس ثاني يضع نعم

من عبد الله صالح

١٢٩٠

Appendix 9

FO 248/290, Rahma b. Saleh, chief of Tavuneh to Agent Lengeh, 22 Moharram 1290/11 March 1873.

From Ramah ben Saleh, chief of Tawenneh to Lingah Agent, 22 Moharram 1290/11 March 1873.

A.C. I beg to inform you that Sheikh Abdollah Mussubbeh came from Kalat in a Boat and wished to proceed to Husseeneh. I launched a Buggareh with 10 men to take him to Husseeneh while halfway Sheikh Mahomed Hassan launched a Buteel and a Buggareh put therein 80 men and followed in pursuit. I do not know whether the Sea is under Control or not and whether the order of the Sirkar extend to the Sheikh of Charrack. If there is permission at Sea all should have it. I await your reply and if the Sheikh of Charrack wish to proceed to Geis or any other place I will go after him. Do not be unmindful of us you know we are at enmity with the Chief of Charrack.

ومعفرته ورضاه وأنكي واشرف تحياته وجب الكتاب بالخ جنابك مناجبال الـ...

حالك على الدوام اهو ان سلم عنا فاناه الحمد لله بن بركاه وحول كيم و صلاه و من ...

ما جانا منك علم ولا خبر على الجانب خير يكون و ثم لا نجغا على جبابك وصلنا الشيخ ...

جاء من كلف في عبره وداد به إلى حميد وارقبا هاو مع عشرة النفار خي وصلـ ...

وساد فلما وصل إلى بضفاطر في الشيخ محمد حسن وقا بيلاه بقار وعين بهاد ...

وطلع وراهم وكلا ندري الوز حكوم ام طلق وحكم الركاب ما هو على شيخ جارك داره ...

الخ طلق يكون الجمي وخنا نظر الجواب من جبابك وكلا اذا استج جارك داد بـ ...

والعكان اخو نضا بانطلع ودامان كان في حكم الركاب ما هو على الجمي ما هو على واحدكـ ...

ناسب بان مالنا احد ابه ثم جبابك وخنا اخصامي هل جارك ولا يعرف المخـ ...

وسلم الناس على الجميع عبد العزيز وكامل من يحب ومن عندنا الوالد احمد بن خصال ...

الجميع يكم جميعكم الاثنان عباده وبارخ مخرم سنه ۹۰ ۲۲ من رجبان صالح

Calligraphed lintel headpiece from the gate of the Taheri residence

Index

A

Abadaly 84
Abbas I 8, 9, 10
Abbasi dynasty 19
Abdol-Baqi Mirza 74
Abdol-Fath Khan
    chief of Morbagh 78
Abdol-Hasan Khan
    beglerbegi of Fars 38
Abdol-Hasan Khan Shirazi
    beglerbegi of Fars 35
Abdollah b. Mohammad `Abdol-Rasul
    Obeydli Sheikh 90
Abdollah b. Mohammad Abdol-Rasul Obeydli 89
Abdollah Musabbeh
    chief of Charak 80
Abdol-Rahman
    chief of Naband 23
Abdol-Rahman b. Abdollah
    chief of Charak 70
Abdol-Rasul Nasuri 104
ab-e gavchah 113
Abu'l-Fath Khan 78
Abu Sho`eyb 11, 22
Agha Mir Abu⊠l-Hasan Fali 98
Ahmadah tribe 85
Ahmad b. Rashed
    chief of Moghu 90
Ahmad Khan Dashti 90
Ahmad Shah 55
Ahram 103
Ajman 85
Akhtar 51, 77, 87, 88, 97, 107, 108, 116, 117, 123
Al Abu Moheyr 24, 25
Alagiha 95
Al Ahneeyat tribe 75
Al Ali 19, 22, 34, 35, 39, 42, 43, 44, 48, 49, 50, 51, 52, 53, 68, 69, 79, 84, 85, 88, 89, 90, 91, 99
Alamarvdasht 74
Ala Marvdasht 81
Alanat 116

Al Bakalif 54
Albin Beshi 79
Albubalal tribe 51
Al Bu Moheyr 1
Albuquerque, Mathias 6, 7
Albusnarif 84
Albuya 84
Albuyareh 84
Al Hamad 49, 85
Al Haram 20, 23, 27, 33, 42, 43, 45, 49, 51, 53, 54, 56, 66, 75, 77, 85, 87, 91, 92, 93, 94, 96, 99, 101, 102, 108, 119, 127, 131
Al Harami 33
Ali Akbar Khan Gallehdari 86, 93, 101
Ali Beyg 33
Ali Kamal 10
Ali Khan Shahsevan 41, 42
Ali Morad Khan Zand 47
Ali Pasha
    governor of Basra 25
Ali Saudan 80
Allahverdi Khan 10
Al Mazkur 1, 24, 47, 56, 84, 136
al-Na`imah 27, 119
Al Nasur xi, xiv, 21, 23, 25, 26, 27, 28, 29, 35, 46, 47, 48, 49, 53, 54, 55, 56, 57, 58, 61, 62, 64, 65, 67, 71, 77, 79, 85, 86, 87, 90, 91, 92, 93, 96, 101, 107, 108, 110, 119, 127, 131, 132, 136, 137
Al Nasur family tree 57
Al Nasurin 27
Al Soleyman 85
Alyia 84
Al Zo`ab 25
a`mal-e sif xiii
Amariyeh 52, 88, 89
Amniyeh 103
Anak 30
Angali 102
aquaduct 50
Armaki 97
Armenian 45

Asalu 5, 23, 24, 25, 26, 29, 30, 33, 38, 39, 47, 51, 54, 55, 62, 65, 66, 67, 68, 71, 73, 74, 76, 77, 78, 85, 87, 88, 89, 90, 91, 93, 95, 100, 101, 102, 107, 109, 120, 131, 132, 135, 136
Asaluyeh 54, 62, 77, 87
Ashkenan 78
Ashkenanis 100
Asir 74, 81
Ayanat 51, 88
Ayenat 77, 107

B

Baghdad 6, 14, 31
Bagh-e Shah 87
Bagh-e Sheikh 51, 88, 124
Baharlu 86
Bahrain xiv, 2, 5, 6, 8, 12, 23, 24, 27, 28, 29, 30, 32, 33, 35, 37, 38, 39, 46, 47, 50, 52, 55, 58, 68, 74, 76, 86, 94, 103, 109, 114, 115, 119, 120, 124, 126, 130, 133, 134, 135
Baikheh Armaki 89
bakhsdar 61
Baluchis 3, 39, 123
Bambariyeh 27, 45
Banak xii, 19, 51, 64, 77, 79, 88, 97, 107, 108, 116, 118, 124
Bandar Abbas xi, xiii, 10, 11, 12, 26, 30, 31, 32, 33, 34, 35, 36, 37, 39, 40, 41, 42, 43, 45, 97, 100, 104
Bandar-e Deylam 25
Bandar Taheri 31, 32
Bani Hamad 79
Bani Hula xiv, 19, 137
Bani Khaled 27
Bani Malah tribe 119
Bani Malek 87, 119
Bani Tamim 20, 27, 65, 119, 127
Banu Khalid Khawl b. Mansur
    a.k.a. Yaser
    chief of Al Nasur 27

Banu Ma`in 34, 35, 36, 42, 43, 44, 47
Banyans 28, 45, 115
baqarahs 50
Baqer Khan
  chief of Tangesir 47, 99
Baqer Khan Gallehdari 82
Barak 51, 87, 88, 107, 118
Barand pass 78
Bardestan xiv, 20, 26, 47, 65, 72, 112
Barku 51, 87, 88, 89
Barley 50, 158
Barnhill 109
Basatin 79, 100, 108, 131
Bashiri Sheikhs 19
Basidu 30, 32
Basra xii, 2, 5, 6, 9, 11, 12, 14, 15, 16, 17, 23, 24, 25, 26, 29, 34, 35, 44, 47, 50, 65, 69, 113, 124, 126
Bassein 25
Bastak 19, 20, 21, 40, 56, 65, 66, 71, 78, 80, 87, 88, 89, 95, 96, 97, 99, 100, 101, 102, 116, 127, 130, 133
Batal Zavar Prased 100
Baverdun 88
Bavirdyun 89
bayaz 116, 126
bazzazi 115
Bedeh 53
Bed Khan 107
Ben Ahmed 84
Beng 108
Bengal 44
Ben Houl 84
Beni Ahmood 84
Beni Baphar 50
Beni Husan 84
Beni Khalid 84
Ben Jouassim 84
Ben Nasir 84
Ben Saboohil 84
berkeh 98
Beyram 96, 99
Beyzeh Khan 51, 107
Biddah 68
Bidhakhan 101
Bidkhun xiv, 54, 87, 93, 95
Bikheh 133, 134
Bikhehha 96
Bin Khalid Bin Mohammad
  chief of Al Nasur 27
boluk-e Maleki 54
Bombay 33, 39, 40, 45, 55, 114, 139
Boraghleh 88

Borghaleh 52
Borudel 95
Bostaneh 19, 50, 53, 79, 85, 88, 99, 134
Bostanu 52, 88, 129, 131
Botella ketch 47
Britannia Galley 30
Britto, Mateo de 11
Bulaskar 97
Buraghleh 127
Bushehr xi, 1, 17, 23, 24, 26, 27, 28, 29, 32, 33, 35, 36, 37, 38, 39, 46, 47, 48, 55, 56, 58, 63, 67, 68, 69, 71, 74, 76, 80, 81, 83, 84, 87, 90, 92, 93, 101, 102, 103, 104, 110, 112, 116, 120, 124, 125, 126, 133, 134, 135, 136
Bushire 23, 96, 99
Bu Sho`eyb 68, 73, 75, 80
Bushri section
  of the Al Ali 85
Bustanu 127
Bu Sumeyt xiv, 51, 54, 69, 87

C

Camara, Ruy Consalves da 2, 5, 6
camels 51, 113, 117
Cape Bardistan 107, 109
Captain David Wilson
  British Resident 56
Captain Disbrowe
  British Resident pro-tem 76
Captain Eyken 43
Captain Felix Jones
  British Resident 69
Captain Hennell
  British Resident 66
Captain Henry Willock
  British charge d'affaires 55
Captain Kemball
  British Resident 69
Captain Plaisted 47
Captain Sutherland 44
Captain William Bruce
  British Resident 55
cattle 51, 113, 117
Chah-e Varzang 53
Chah-Kur 108
Chah Mobarak 90, 101, 129, 130, 131
Charak 19, 22, 23, 24, 34, 35, 36, 37, 42, 43, 44, 49, 50, 53, 55, 65, 66, 68, 69, 70, 72, 78, 79, 80, 81, 84, 85, 87, 88, 89, 90, 96, 97, 98, 99, 100, 104, 135

charcoal 22, 51, 53, 113, 115, 119, 124, 126
Chiru xiii, 22, 23, 24, 51, 52, 53, 74, 75, 78, 79, 81, 85, 88, 89, 90, 98, 99, 100, 101, 108
Chiruyeh 19
Colonel Pelly
  British Resident 77
Congoon 26, 45, 57, 58, 76, 109, 150, 152, 154, 156
copper coin 83
cucumber 50

D

Dabestan-e Onsuri 110
da Gama, Luís 9
Darveh Asuh 87, 88, 127, 130
Daryabegi 97, 100
  governor of the Gulf Ports 32, 91, 92, 93, 94, 95, 100, 101
Dashtestan 33, 42, 66, 73, 74, 102
Dashti 56, 62, 64, 67, 72, 73, 75, 76, 77, 78, 87, 88, 89, 90, 91, 93, 95, 96, 98, 102, 103, 108, 109, 110, 113, 114, 116, 118, 124, 128, 131, 133, 134, 136, 158
Dastestan 56
Dastur 52, 88, 127
dates xiii, 14, 17, 19, 50, 52, 54, 75, 76, 94, 113, 114, 115, 116, 117, 118, 119, 124, 126
Dayyir 55, 67, 72, 74, 75, 76, 77, 103, 109, 110, 112, 114, 124
Dehestan-e Badawi 19
Dehestan-e Harami 19, 127
Dehestan-e Marzuqi 19
de Slot van Capelle 43
Deylam 24
dinar-e rayej-e soltani 116
dinghy 37
Djrd 50
donkeys 113, 117
Dovvan 51, 85, 88, 99
Dowraq 23
Drake 45
dulab 117
Dutch 12, 34

E

earthenware vessels 26, 114, 115
Ehtesham al-Dowleh
  governor-general of Fars 74
  governor of Behbahan 80
eltezamnameh 66

INDEX

Emamqoli Khan 24
Emily Schooner 66
English 10
Eshniz 98
Essin 37
Evaz 30

F

Fal xiii
Farhad Mirza Mo`tamad al-Dowleh 61
   governor-general of Fars 64, 80
Farur xii, 19, 22, 80, 88
Fath Ali Khan
   chief of Garash 81
Fath Ali Khan Garrashi 86
Fath Ali Shah 55, 63
Fath Rabbani 42, 45
Fath Rahmaniyeh 44
Fatta Soltanie 39
firewood 22, 113, 115, 119, 124, 126, 133, 134
Firuzabad 115
Firuz Mirza
   governor-general of Fars 71
fishing xi, 1, 5, 11, 12, 14, 17, 21, 43, 49, 50, 51, 52, 53, 54, 99, 113, 114, 116, 118, 119, 124, 126, 132, 133, 134, 135, 136, 145
Fox, HMS 97
Freire, Rui 10, 11, 12
Fumestan 19, 65, 66, 87, 127

G

gach-bari 120
galateh 131
galeotas 5
Gallehdar 41, 61, 62, 64, 74, 77, 80, 81, 82, 83, 86, 93, 94, 95, 98, 99, 102, 104, 108, 124
galliots 12, 16
gallivat 28, 32, 37, 38
Ganaveh 34, 38, 46, 47
Gaobandi 96, 100, 108, 127
gardens 46
Gavbandi 27, 28, 45, 49, 51, 52, 53, 54, 58, 61, 64, 65, 66, 70, 72, 77, 80, 81, 82, 83, 85, 86, 87, 88, 90, 92, 93, 95, 96, 98, 99, 101, 102, 104, 107, 116, 127, 128, 129, 130, 131, 132, 133, 134
Ghaf 51, 88
Ghamareh 87
Gholam Hoseyn Khan 96

Goa 2, 6, 7, 14, 16, 139
goats 51, 113, 117
goldsmiths 115
Golshan 19, 53, 87, 88, 90
grain 33
Gudeh 108
Guinea worms 109
gurab 32
Gurzeh 50, 52, 79, 85, 88
gypsum mine 114, 133

H

Hajj Abdol-Nabi 81
Hajji Gholam Hoseyn Warawi 96
Hajji Mohammad Amin Asiri 40
Hajji Mohammad kadkhoda 94
Hajji Salem
   chief of Dashti 87
Hajji Yusef Mohammadi 96
Hajj Mohammad Hasan Tajer-e Shirvani 86
Halat Naband 51, 89
Hamad Esma`il
   chief of Chiru 78
Hamadi
   district 19
Hamiran 53
Haonah 107
Harami 129
Hasa 2, 103
Hashniz 101
Hasineh 49, 53, 85, 88
hasir-bafi 133
Henderabi xii, 19, 22, 51, 52, 53, 79, 85, 88, 89, 100, 108
Heydar Khan of Dashti 72
Hindu 17
Hindus 50
Hofuf 103
Hormuz xiii, 1, 2, 3, 4, 5, 6, 8, 9, 10, 11, 12, 13, 14, 15, 16, 35, 36, 40, 41, 42, 44, 47
horses 113
Hoseyn Ali Mirza
   governor-general of Fars 55, 62
Hoseyni 80
Hoseyniyeh 19
Hoseyn Khan Dashti 64
Hoseyn Khan Moqaddam Maraghe'i
   governor-general of Fars 66
Hoseyn Khan of Galledar 64
Hoseyn Khan, son of Hajji Khan
   chief of Dashti 64

Hoseyn Qoli Khan Sa`d al-Molk 80
Houl 84
Hula 16, 22, 23, 24, 25, 32, 33, 35, 37, 38, 44
Hulas xi, xii, xiv, 5, 16, 17, 19, 20, 21, 22, 23, 24, 25, 26, 27, 28, 29, 32, 33, 34, 35, 36, 37, 38, 39, 40, 43, 44, 46, 48, 49, 54, 79, 84, 135, 136
Humeiran 98
Hunt, Capt. 97
Huwala xiv, 31, 35, 147
Huzu xiii

I

Imam of Masqat 25, 39, 55, 57
imports 21, 52, 115, 133
Irahestan xii, xiii, 113
Iraq xii
iron 33
irrigation 50
Ishkanu 96, 99
Islamabad 44

J

Jabbara Nasuri 27
Ja`far Khan
   deputy governor of Bandar Abbas 43
Jask 11, 99
Jazeh 52, 75, 79, 88
Jazza 97
Jebel Serai 109
Jebel Turunjah 97
Jews 17, 28, 45, 110, 115, 120, 126, 129
jihad 98
Jirzah 79
Jolfar 35, 37, 47, 65

K

Ka`b 35, 39, 44, 47
Kaharjan xiii
Kaki 72
Kal 96
kalantar 78, 89
Kalat 19, 50, 52, 79, 83, 85, 88, 98, 104, 108, 132, 162
Kalatu 27, 30, 52, 69, 70, 88, 95, 127
Kamalu, chief of the Jat tribe 98

Kangan xi, xii, xiv, 20, 23, 25, 26, 27, 28, 29, 35, 44, 45, 46, 47, 49, 51, 54, 55, 56, 57, 58, 61, 62, 63, 64, 65, 67, 68, 69, 71, 72, 73, 74, 75, 76, 77, 78, 80, 81, 83, 84, 86, 87, 88, 90, 97, 100, 101, 102, 103, 104, 107, 108, 109, 110, 111, 112, 113, 114, 115, 116, 117, 118, 119, 120, 126, 127, 132, 135, 136, 137
Kangun 23, 24, 26, 111, 120
kargozar 76, 92, 100, 131, 154, 156
Karim Khan Zand 34, 41
Kasheanaria 84
Kash Konar 129
Kashkuli Qashqa'is 101
Kazerun 41, 83
Kenn
  a.k.a Kish, Ges or Ghes 50
kerayeh-kesh 114
Khalafani 19, 78
Khalifah b. Abdollah Ebrahim b. Yusuf al-Monsharee 74
Khalifat 24, 25
Khan Bahador Aqa Badr 99
Kharabeh 52, 88, 127
Kharjai tribe 100
Khark 23, 35, 43, 46, 65, 73
Khasab 34
Khirreh 66, 67, 96
Khiyar 93
Khoda Karam Khan
  chief of the Boyer Ahmadi 82
Khodavan 88
Khonj xiii
Khormuj 72, 103
Khovadan 52
Khurmlu 104
Khuzestan xii, 25, 35
Kish xii, xiii, 7, 8, 19, 22, 31, 33, 45, 50, 55, 66, 68, 69, 70, 79, 80, 87, 88, 89, 119
Koenad, Karel 33
  chief of VOC trade in Bandar Abbas 33
Kondarun 49, 53, 85, 88
Kong 32
Kuhan 96
Kushkenar 96, 101
Kuwait 35, 38, 65

L

Laft 34, 39, 42, 44
Lahsa 2, 115
Lar 4, 5, 7, 16, 28, 30, 31, 34, 36, 37, 39, 40, 41, 42, 43, 64, 66, 72, 81, 86, 98, 127, 131, 132
Lara 6, 7
Lard-e Amir 9
Larestan 30, 31, 36, 40, 41, 65, 89, 100, 107
Laz 6, 7, 80, 160
Lengeh xi, xii, 19, 21, 22, 35, 42, 43, 53, 55, 61, 68, 70, 71, 72, 74, 75, 77, 78, 80, 84, 96, 97, 98, 99, 100, 104, 112, 134, 135, 136, 158, 160, 162
lime 110, 111, 124
Liravi 20

M

Mahalleh-ye Kangani 72
Mahi 68
Mahomad Hassan Khan Brasgoon 62
Mahurramath 74
Makahil 52, 88
Makran 33
maktab 133
Maleki 20, 65, 77, 90, 127, 128, 129, 130, 131
Malgaram 114
Mallabar 46
Manama 33
Mangalore 56
Maqam 19
Maraziq 42, 49, 53, 85
Marbakh 85
marsh melons 50
Marzuqis 21, 22, 49, 89
Mascarenhas, Jeronimo 5
Masheh 50
Masih Soltan
  deputy governor of Bandar Abbas 39, 41
Masqat 12, 16, 25, 33, 43, 44, 47
Masqat Arabs 32
Mayalu 75, 76, 87, 118
Mekran 2, 3, 37, 145
Menezes, Gonsalvo de 5
Meydan-e Tavileh 83
Mir Hoseyn 38
Mir Mehr-e Ali 30
Mir Mohanna 38, 44
Mir Naser 38
  chief of Rig 37, 38

Mirza Esma`il Zamindavari 31
Mirza Houma Behaban 62
Mirza Nabi Khan Qazvini
  governor-general of Fars 62
Mirza Na`im, vizier of Fars 72
Mirza Reza 33
Mirza Taqi 33
Miyalu 51, 88, 114
Mobarak Ra'isi 104
Mogam xii, 50, 52, 88, 90, 97, 98, 108
Moghu xii, 22, 34, 44, 49, 51, 53, 79, 85, 88, 90, 97, 98, 99
Moghuyeh 19
Mohammad Ali Khan
  beglerbegi of Fars 30
Mohammad Amin Khan
  vakil of Bahrain 33
Mohammad b. Ahmad
  Harami Sheikh 92
Mohammad b. Hasan
  chief of Charak 80
Mohammad b. Jaber 33
Mohammad b. Majid
  chief of Naband 23
Mohammad b. Rahman Bushri 100
Mohammad b. Sand?
  chief of Nakhilu 22
Mohammad Ebrahim Beg
  farrash-bashi 81
Mohammad Hajji 63
Mohammad Hasan Khan
  chief of Borazjan 80
Mohammad Hasan Khan Mafi 80
Mohammad Khan
  army commander 55
Mohammad Khan Baluch 31
Mohammad Latif Khan 31, 32
Mohammad Reza Khan 97
Mohammad Saleh Ra'isi 65, 127
Mohammad Shah 63
Mohammad Taher Khan
  brother of Sheikh Mazkur Kangani 82
  chief of Gallehdar 80
Mohammad Taqi 31
Mohammad Taqi Khan 32, 96
Mohammad Vali Khan 96
Molla ⊠Abdol-Karim Gallehdari 40
Molla Ali Shah 34, 35, 36, 37, 38, 39, 40, 41, 42, 44
Molla Hadi Gallehdari 63
Mollah Ali Shah 44
Molla Mohammad Ali 86

Molla Mohammad Taqi Khan 63
  chief of Jam and of the Modgo-
  maris 62
Montafeq 25
Mooamie 65
Moqam 93, 98, 100, 101
moqarrariyeh 4, 5, 8
Morbagh 19, 31, 50, 78, 80, 81, 160
Morbakh 97
Mostafa Khan of Bastak 78
Mostafa Qoli Khan of Bastak 71
Movaqqar al- Dowleh 116
  governor of the Gulf Ports 90
Mozaffar xiii, 90, 116
Mugam 96, 97, 98
Muqam 85
Musa Khan 92

N

Naband xiii, 23, 30, 37, 51, 54, 70, 71, 73, 75, 77, 78, 85, 87, 88, 89, 93, 127, 158
Nabiyu or Nabi Island
  or Little Tonb 22
Nader Shah 35
Na'eb Ebrahim Khan 86
Nakhilu xiv, 4, 5, 6, 7, 8, 9, 10, 11, 12, 13, 14, 16, 17, 19, 22, 23, 24, 31, 33, 51, 52, 53, 66, 68, 75, 79, 88, 97, 108, 135
Nakhl-e Ghanem 108, 119
Nakhl-e Hashel 107
Nakhl-e Hashem 51, 87
Nakhl-e Khalafan 78
Nakhl-e Mir 19, 88, 90
Nakhl-e Taqi 51, 80, 84, 89, 91, 92, 93, 94, 101, 107, 108, 119
Naser Khan
  governor of Lar 34, 35, 36, 37, 39, 40, 41, 42, 43, 44
Nasir Khan Thani
  beglerbegi of Lar 64
Nautaques 2, 4, 10, 11
Nik 107
Niquelus 1
Nistan 96
nitrate of potash 53
Nosrat al-Dowleh 99
Noutaques 9
Nowzar Mirza 86
Nussoor Tribes 84

O

Obeydli 19, 49, 53, 81, 85, 88, 91, 98, 101
Odin, HMS 97
Oman xii, xiv, 1, 4, 5, 10, 15, 19, 22, 23, 24, 27, 28, 29, 32, 33, 42, 44, 48, 49, 50, 53, 54, 56, 66, 84, 85, 126, 132, 135
Omm al-Hogum 78
Omm al-Hokum 78
onions 50, 113, 117, 118, 119, 124, 126, 133
Otub 24, 25, 35, 38

P

pakar 126
palms 51
Parak 84, 108, 118
pearl boats 50
pearl grounds 1, 24, 37
pearling 33, 50, 51, 52, 53, 54, 89, 118, 124, 129, 131, 132, 134, 145
pearls 38, 45
pedlers 115
Pereira, Pedro Homem 7
Persepolis 90, 92, 93, 101, 116
pishkesh 41, 63, 71, 81, 116
Pumestan 19
purslain 113

Q

Qa⊠ed Heydar 38
Qalat-e Sorkh 82, 83
Qal`eh Behdeh 66
Qal`eh-ye Bariku 63
Qal`eh-ye Derak 113
Qal'eh-ye Gharvizeh 101
Qal`eh-ye Kushkenar 101
Qal'eh-ye Sarvbash 101
qaliyat 28, 35, 145
Qasem Beg
  chief of Minab 36
Qashqa'is 101, 123, 124
Qasr-e Kenar 93
Qatar 114, 134
Qatif 2, 27, 33, 114, 115
Qavam al-Molk 78, 81, 89, 99, 100, 101, 131
Qavasem 21, 35, 37, 42, 43, 44, 48, 49, 50, 55, 61, 65, 84, 99, 118, 136, 147
Qayem 108, 119

Qeshm 8, 10, 11, 16, 22, 29, 30, 32, 33, 34, 35, 37, 39, 41, 42, 43, 44, 55, 75, 158

R

Rahmah b. Shahin
  chief of Nakhilu 22
Rahmanie 39, 42
Ra`is Ahmad
  chief of Tangestan 42
Ra`is Ali 96
  chief of Ashkenan 79
Ra`is Ali Fumestani 86
Ra`is Mohammad Saleh
  chief of Fumestan 19
Ra`is Soltan 96
Ras al-Khaimah 35, 42, 55, 65
Ras al-Shahr 87
Ras al-Shajar 51, 88, 107, 124
Ras Asfan 108
Ras Ghorab 51
Rashid Khan Sartip 67
Ras Zalee 108
Raziyeh tribe 85
Reza Shah 102, 104, 137
Rig 23, 24, 26, 35, 37, 38, 42, 46, 47, 58, 103, 120
Rishahr 9, 23, 24
Rishar 26
Riyad 103
roadstead 97
Rostaq shib 50
Rustami 97

S

Sabakheh 108
Sadeq Khan Qajar Develu 56
Saifal Shaikh 127
sailors 72
Saleh b. Mohammad Saleh
  chief of Charak 89
Saleh Khan Bayat
  governor-general of Fars 36
Saleh Sharif 98
  member Jat tribe 98
salt 17
saltpeter 53
sambuks 50
Sanjeh 126
Saqr b. Mobarak
  Tamimi Sheikh 130
sarkar
  British Residency 68
Sarvbash 92, 96, 101, 128
Satwat al-Mamalek 97

Saviyah xiii
Sayyed Abdol-Hoseyn 96, 99
Sayyed Hajji Baba Beyrami 96
Sayyed Mansur
   Tangestani 42
school 125, 133
Schoonderwoerd, Jacob 33
sculptures 120
Seyf al-Sheikh 52, 88
Seyf II Imam of Muscat 27
Shabankareh 102
Shah Ashraf 30
Shahin
   chief of Khirrah 66
Shahin Kuh 83
Shahnameh 120
Shahrokh 103
Shah Soltan Hoseyn 29
Shah Tahmasp II 30
shal-e longi 115
Shamal 54
Shatvar xii, 22, 79, 88
sheep 51, 113, 117
Sheikh Abdollah 79, 80, 96, 101
   chief of Hormuz 43, 44, 55, 67, 79, 98, 162
Sheikh Abdollah b. Ebrahim
   Sunni mojtahed of Bushehr 73
Sheikh Abdollah b. Sheikh Hasan
   Nasuri 101
Sheikh Abdollah Khan
   chief of Asalu 54
Sheikh Abdollah Obeydali 97
Sheikh Abdol-Rahman
   chief of Nakhilu 19
Sheikh Abdol-Rahman b. Abdol-lah b. Abdol-Rahman
   chief of Charak 69
Sheikh `Abdol-Rahman Sheikh
   `Allaq
   chief of Nakhilu 31
Sheikh Abdol-Sheikh
   chief of the Banu Ma`in 34, 39
Sheikh Ahmad 97
   chief of Asalu 66
   chief of Henderabi 22
Sheikh Ahmad b. Seyf
   chief of Asalu 89
   Harami Sheikh 92
Sheikh Ahmad Dashti 110
Sheikh Ahmad Khan
   chief of Asalu 54
Sheikh Ahmad Khan Asaluyeh Al
   Haram
   chief of Asalu 77
Sheikh Ahmad Madani 30, 31, 107

Madani Sheikh 19
Sheikh Ali Akbar Khan Jami 92
Sheikh Ali b. Khalfan 40
   chief of Charak 34, 36, 39
Sheikh `Allaq
   chief of Nakhilu 19
Sheikh `Allaq Hammadi
   chief of Moqam 101
Sheikh `Allaq (Ullag) Nasuri
   chief of Taheri 55
Sheikh Amir Mahin 24
   chief of the Al Abu Moheyr 25
Sheikh Chaueed of Jolfar 36, 37
Sheikh Ebrahim Hammadi 101
Sheikh Ebrahim Khan Al Haram 77
Sheikh Ebrahim Khan Asaluyeh
   Al Haram
   chief of Asalu 54
Sheikh Ebrahim Nasuri 92
Sheikh Hajar 29, 45, 46
Sheikh Hajji
   chief of Dashti 64
Sheikh Hareb Nasuri 104
Sheikh Hasan b. Abdollah
   chief of Charak 68
Sheikh Hatem 28, 35, 37, 38
Sheikh Hatem Jamavi 95
Sheikh Hatem Khan Al Nasur 90
Sheikh Hatem Nasuri 41, 93, 94
Sheikh Hoseyn of Chahkutah 103
Sheikh Jabbara 30, 31, 32, 33
   chief of the Al Nasur 28
Sheikh Jabbara b. Mohammad
   Hatem 56
Sheikh Jabbarah Congoon 62
Sheikh Jabbar Hula'i 32
Sheikh Jabbar Taheri 29
Sheikh Jaber 103
Sheikh Jamal
   Bushehri official 56, 57
Sheikh Khalfan Asseloo 62
Sheikh Khalfan b. Mosabbah Al
   Ali 99
Sheikh Khalfan Khan Al Haram
   chief of Asalu 54
Sheikh Khamis
   chief of the Al Zo`ab 25
Sheikh Madhkur 32, 34, 97, 100
Sheikh Mazkur 61, 75, 95
Sheikh Mazkur Khan Kangani 80
Sheikh Mohammad
   deputy-chief of Kangan 68
   Madani Sheikh 19
Sheikh Mohammad Ahmad
   Khalfan

Harami chief 96
Sheikh Mohammad b. Ahmad b.
   Khalifeh Harami 92
Sheikh Mohammad Bastaki 40
Sheikh Mohammad b. Hasan
   chief of Charak 79
Sheikh Mohammad b. Salem
   chief of Charak 36
Sheikh Mohammad b. Yusef
   chief of Nakhilu 66
Sheikh Mohammad Khan
   Al Haram 77
   chief of Moghu 19
Sheikh Mohammad Khan Bastaki 19, 21
Sheikh Mohammad Khan Kan-gani 77
Sheikh Mohammad Rahma
   Bashiri 97
Sheikh Mohammad Sayyed 36
Sheikh Mohammad Sheikh
   Abdol-Rasul 79
Sheikh Mohammad Sheikh
   Abdol-Rasul Obeydli 78
Sheikh Mohammed b. Ahmad
   Khalfan
   chief of Teben 103
Sheikh Musa
   chief of the Niquelus 5
Sheikh Musa Abu Moheyr 24
Sheikh Naser 38, 47
   chief of Bushehr 37
Sheikh Nasr Bakir Khan Tanges-tani 62
Sheikh Qaḍed
   chief of Jolfar 35, 36
Sheikh Qasem b. Jaber 33
Sheikh Rahma
   chief of Jolfar 35, 36, 42, 43, 45, 80, 97, 162
Sheikh Rashed 47
Sheikh Rashed b. Mostafa
   Madani Sheikh 19
Sheikh Rashid 31
Sheikh Saḍid 22
Sheikh Saleh Charaki 96, 97
Sheikh Sanct ?
   chief of Asalu 30
Sheikh Saqr 75
   Tamimi chief 93
Sheikh Saqr b. Mobarak
   Tamimi Sheikh 90
Sheikh Sayyir 101
Sheikh Seyf b. Abdollah
   chief of Asalu 73
Sheikh Seyf Khan
   Al Haram 77

Sheikh Seyf Nasuri 99
Sheikh Seyf of Naband 75
Sheikh Shamra 22
Sheikh Sho'eyb xii, 6, 19, 52, 72, 108
Sheikh Soleyman b. Sheikh Hasan b. Sheikh Jabbara 87
Sheikh Soleyman Marzuqi Al Ajman 19
Sheikh Soltan Hammadi 97
Sheikh Soltan Marzuqi 96
Sheikh Soltan Obeydali 78
Sheikh Taher
 chief of Gallehdar 61
Sheikh Yusef Nasuri 99
Sheikh Zaid
 chief of Nakhilu 17
Sherrif Khan Bawie 62
Shibkuh xii, 96, 97, 100
Shibkuh Coast xi, 20, 21, 31
Shibkuh-e Larestan 78
Shilu xiv, 23, 26, 29, 54, 107
Shiraz 24, 34, 46, 47
Shiru 97
Shitvar 11
Shivu xii, 52, 64, 70, 87, 88, 95, 97, 100, 127, 130, 131, 132, 133, 134
Shiyu 108, 132
siege 10, 11, 31, 38, 41, 46, 47, 55, 78, 96
Sif Bani Saffaq xii
Sif Bani Zoheyr xii
Sif Banu 'Umarah xii
Sif Muzaffar xii
Sif 'Umarah xii
Sif Zuhayr xii
Siraf xii, xiii, 107, 119
slaves 50, 74
Soleyman Mirza 116
Soltan b. Hasan
 chief of Moghu 80
Soltan Mohammad Amin 41
Sowlat al-Molk 96
sugar 33
Sugarloaf 109
sulfur 53

T

Tabin 89
Taheri xii, xiv, 20, 23, 25, 27, 28, 29, 30, 35, 36, 37, 38, 42, 44, 45, 47, 49, 51, 54, 58, 61, 62, 67, 68, 71, 72, 73, 75, 76, 77, 80, 81, 84, 86, 87, 88, 91, 92, 94, 95, 97, 98, 99, 100, 101, 104, 107, 108, 109, 117, 118, 119, 120, 123, 124, 125, 127, 131, 132, 137
Tahmasp Khan 30, 31
Tahmasp Mirza Mo'ed al-Dowleh governor-general of Fars 73
Tahuneh 19
tak-bafi 133
Tamil, HMS 98
Tamimi 54, 88, 90, 91, 92, 93, 101, 127, 129, 130, 131
Tang-e Ahlan 78
Tangesir 47
Tangestan 56, 102, 103
Tangestani 97
Tarakameh 96
Tavunah xiii
Tavuneh 52, 79, 80, 85, 88, 89, 90, 100, 162
taxes 21, 56, 62, 63, 76, 81, 90, 91, 116, 126
Teben 87, 103
terradas 1, 6, 7, 8, 9, 10
Thalitha 120
thani athneyn Muhanna 46
the Ali Rooka 45
the Britannia Galley 47
the Pastorena 45
the Swallow 45
the Tartar 45
Tibin 52, 74, 88, 132
tobacco 51, 52, 54, 115, 124, 129
tofangchis 78, 83, 96, 99, 101, 111, 117, 118, 123, 126, 127, 131, 134, 136
Tombak 51, 77, 97, 107, 109, 123, 126, 127
Tonbak 108
Tonb Island 22
trankis 31, 35, 36, 37, 38
Trucial Oman xiv, 19

U

Umm al-Quwain 50, 65

V

vegetables 50, 113

W

Warawi 96, 97, 98
water melons 50, 117

Y

Yaser b. Mansur 27
Yusof b. Mohammad Yusof 61
Yusuf b. Mobarak
 chief of Naband 70

Z

zabet 31, 57, 76, 77, 78, 86, 95, 99, 127, 131
Za'er Abdollah Khan 92, 93
Zaki Khan 46
Zanganeh 96
Ziyarat 52, 88, 127, 131
zowraq
 vessel 24

ABOUT THE AUTHOR

WILLEM FLOOR studied development economics and non-western sociology, as well as Persian, Arabic and Islamology from 1963-67 at the University of Utrecht (the Netherlands). He received his doctoral degree from the University of Leiden in 1971. From 1983 until his retirement, Dr. Floor was employed by the World Bank as an energy specialist. Throughout this time, he published extensively on the socio-economic history of Iran. His books include: *Public Health in Qajar Iran, Agriculture in Qajar Iran,* and *The History of Theater in Iran,* as well as, *The Persian Gulf: A Political and Economic History of 5 Port Cities, 1500-1730,* its second volume, *Persian Gulf: The Rise of the Gulf Arabs, 1747-1792,* third volume, *The Rise and Fall of Bandar-e Lengeh,* the fourth volume, *Bandar Abbas: The Natural Gateway of Southeast Iran,* and the fifth volume, *The Persian Gulf: Links with the Hinterland Bushehr, Borazjan, Kazerun, Banu Ka'b, & Bandar Abbas.* He has also published, *Travels Through Northern Persia, 1770-1774, Titles and Emoluments in Safavid Iran,* and *A Social History of Sexual Relations in Iran; Labor and Industry in Iran, 1850-1941; Guilds, Merchants and Ulama in 19th Century Iran; The Rise and Fall of Nader Shah; Games Persians Play.* His translations include: Samuel Gottlieb Gmelin's *Travels Through Northern Persia 1770–1774,* and *Astrakhan Anno 1770,* as well as *A Man of Two Worlds: Pedros Bedik in Iran, 1670–1675* translated from the Latin with Colette Ouahes. He has also translated together with with Hasan Javadi, Abbas Qoli Aqa Bakikhanov's *The Heavenly Rose-Garden: A History of Shirvan & Daghestan;* and Evliya Chelebi's *Travels in Iran and the Caucasus, 1647 and 1654.*

SOME OTHER MAGE TITLES

Discovering Cyrus:
The Persian Conqueror Astride the Ancient World
Reza Zarghamee

Shahnameh: the Persian Book of Kings
Abolqasem Ferdowsi / Translated by Dick Davis

Vis and Ramin
Fakhraddin Gorgani / Translated by Dick Davis
also available as an audio book

Borrowed Ware: Medieval Persian Epigrams
Introduced and Translated by Dick Davis

My Uncle Napoleon
Iraj Pezeshkzad / Translated by Dick Davis
also available as an audio book

At Home and Far from Home
Poems on Iran and Persian Culture
Dick Davis

Stories from Iran: A Chicago Anthology 1921-1991
Edited by Heshmat Moayyad

Garden of the Brave in War
Terence O'Donnell

Crowning Anguish: Taj al-Saltana
Memoirs of a Persian Princess
Introduction by Abbas Amanat
Translated by Anna Vanzan

Inside Iran: Women's Lives
Jane Howard

*Food of Life: Ancient Persian and
Modern Iranian Cooking and Ceremonies*
Najmieh Batmanglij

Silk Road Cooking: A Vegetarian Journey
Najmieh Batmanglij

From Persia to Napa: Wine at the Persian Table
Najmieh Batmanglij, Dick Davis, Burke Owens

Savushun: A Novel about Modern Iran
Simin Daneshvar / Translated by M.R. Ghanoonparvar /
Introduction by Brian Spooner
also available as an audio book

The Persian Garden: Echoes of Paradise
Mehdi Khansari / M. R. Moghtader / Minouch Yavari

Masters and Masterpieces of Iranian Cinema
Hamid Dabashi

Tales of Two Cities: A Persian Memoir
Abbas Milani

*The Persian Sphinx:
Amir Abbas Hoveyda and the Iranian Revolution*
Abbas Milani

French Hats in Iran
Heydar Radjavi
available soon as an audio book

A Man of Many Worlds
The Diaries and Memoirs of Dr. Ghasem Ghani
Cyrus Ghani / Paul Sprachman

www.ingramcontent.com/pod-product-compliance
Lightning Source LLC
Chambersburg PA
CBHW051149290426
44108CB00019B/2659